AF380870

VALIE EXPORT—In her own words

Edited by
Yilmaz Dziewior and Katrin Sauerländer

Verlag der Buchhandlung
Walther und Franz König

YILMAZ DZIEWIOR AND
KATRIN SAUERLÄNDER

This volume is the first in the series "In Their Own Words." The series is dedicated to contemporary artists who, in addition to their visual oeuvre, have produced texts that take an independent approach to the concerns of their times. Not infrequently, they comment on their own artistic and social situations. This new series presents, above all, approaches that have proved influential and continue to inform current debates.

From the outset, VALIE EXPORT has written not only detailed concepts for her projects but also theoretical essays, poems, notes, and lectures. A large number of her published texts have been made accessible here in one book, along with a selection of printed interviews and unpublished notes and lectures. All the pieces in this volume were created between 1967 and 2020.

VALIE EXPORT is regarded as one of the most important international pioneers of conceptual media art, performance, and experimental film. In the late 1960s, her often provocative installations, films, and actions caused an uproar. Works such as *Genitalpanik* (Genital Panic, 1969) shocked audiences with their boldness and, above all, with their forthright social critique. In her celebrated action *TAPP und TAST-KINO* (TAP and TOUCH CINEMA), 1968), the artist wore a cardboard box over her torso and let passersby touch her naked breasts through a curtain in order to draw attention to the sexualization and objectification of women in the media. Since then, EXPORT has created an extensive body of work that includes video, environments, digital photography, installations, performances, body art, feature films, experimental films, documentaries, expanded cinema, conceptual photography, body-material interactions, laser installations, objects, and sculptures.

VALIE EXPORT's comparatively late recognition as an artist has been hard-won. Although her work received attention early on, it was seldom positive. Not only did she venture into areas such as video and performance that had yet to find acceptance among a wider audience, she also frequently met with strong disapprobation on account of her themes and the way she realized them, causing scandals for which she was even taken to court. But as EXPORT has observed in a number of interviews, the main hurdle for her was the fact that she is a woman. Apart from the overall dominance of men in the art world, her own surroundings were particularly male-oriented and under the sway of the Vienna Actionists. The inequality between men and women has always been a major driving force in EXPORT's work. In an interview from 2017, she summarized:

> The female body is a construct—and this realization has always been central for me. I wanted to know: What does the body, not least my own, mean in society? What is the significance of the body as a sign carrier and symbol, what characteristics are loaded onto it from without? It is shaped according to a male image, and men define their power through access to the female body. I could never accept these rules, and had to controvert them in my art. I wanted to draw attention to these forms of repression and categorization and liberate myself from them. Radicality was an important way for me to respond to and challenge them. (p. 340)

The radicality of EXPORT's work is accompanied by a no less radical body of theoretical writings. Particularly succinct, and thus frequently quoted (also by herself), is her manifesto "Woman's Art," written in 1972 in preparation for the exhibition *MAGNA* (working title *Women's Art*) that she devised as an international show of work by women artists. In the first sentence, set in capitals, EXPORT distills the irresolvable entanglement of art and society into a few words: "THE

POSITION OF ART IN THE WOMEN'S MOVEMENT IS THE POSITION OF WOMEN IN THE ART'S MOVEMENT." (p. 55) She then goes on to outline how women can free themselves from a male-constructed image—a process of self-determination in which art can serve as a medium.

The *MAGNA* exhibition was not mounted until 1975 and was ultimately restricted to Austrian women artists. With her concept of an international exhibition featuring only women, EXPORT was in the wrong place at the wrong time: as she explains at length in the preface to the exhibition catalogue, the subject met with little interest (pp. 91ff). Meanwhile, her treatise on women's art and creativity had appeared in three parts under the joint title "Gertrude Stein & Virginia Woolf." Stein and Woolf are fundamental to EXPORT's blueprint for a feminist form of Actionism. It is clear from this text that her chosen female peers at the time were not Austrian: Meret Oppenheim, Lygia Clark, Niki de Saint Phalle, Yayoi Kusama, Anna Halprin, Carolee Schneemann, and Charlotte Moorman, among others, are the representatives of a feminist art who make up the pantheon in which EXPORT inscribes herself in later texts written in the third person. Since no one else in her circles was willing to do so, leaving her de facto on her own, EXPORT drew up a history and theory of feminist art of the 1960s and 1970s more or less by herself.

The woman's body as an object essentially oppressed by men remains the pivotal point in EXPORT's texts. In her wide-ranging essays "Woman and Creativity" and "The Real and Its Double: The Body," she demonstrates the subjugation of women by men historically, sociologically, and philosophically. EXPORT argues, with reference, for instance, to Margaret Mead's research on Indigenous peoples, resolutely against passive characteristics being designated as female and active ones as male, such that female creativity is simply

denied. In order to free themselves from the role
ascribed to them in a "phallocratic civilization," women
must "transform culture, transgress it even, because
in the real existing culture constructed by men they
really don't have a place. Only in the transgression of
culture can women gain consciousness and produce
art, produce their own image." (p. 217)

VALIE EXPORT has followed this path in her artistic
work since the mid-1960s, constantly accompanied
by her writing. Her archives contain countless hand-
written notes, typed-up texts, and collaged fragments;
in some cases several drafts exist for individual texts,
passages have been repeated, and parts rewritten.
Many of her notes are exposés for her artistic projects.
Her library contains books peppered with her own
marginalia and sticky notes, and her archive holds
collections of texts arranged by themes. Psychology,
anthropology, sociology, pedagogy, politics, and history
are all fields that EXPORT has studied in depth. Collectively, her texts form a cosmos that extends far beyond
what has been brought together here. The present
publication is aimed chiefly at providing a condensed
overview, performed in the certainty that other publications of EXPORT's writing will follow, especially as
she continues to be extremely active in producing new
works and further texts. The artist herself summed
up her unflagging productivity early on: "I was reading,
I was feeling, I was thinking, I was living"

# EDITORIAL NOTE

=========================================



The present volume brings together VALIE EXPORT's published theoretical texts, supplemented by a selection of printed interviews and partly unpublished notes, poems, and lectures. The material dates from the years 1967 to 2020.

A large number of these texts only ever appeared in German and are now published for the first time in English translation. A few were published exclusively or also in English, and both the artist's archive and the holdings of the VALIE EXPORT Center Linz contain several translations presumably created around the same time as the originals. Whether the English typescripts originate from the artist herself or a translator can no longer be established with certainty.

The translated poems at the beginning of this volume retain the lower case employed by VALIE EXPORT in part of her early German texts. The rigorous use of the lower case aimed at treating all parts of speech equally—an orthographical tool also employed by the Vienna Group and other Austrian authors in their early works that has no relevance in English. Therefore, all the other texts in this publication have been translated or transcribed using a standard style.

Misspelled names and work titles in the German texts have been emended without comment; others have been rectified in square brackets or commented on in the editorial notes (distinguished from the author's original notes by Roman numerals).

# POEMS, NOTES, SPEECHES

THEORETICAL TEXTS

- - - - - - - - - - - - - - - - - - - - - - - - - - - - - - - - - - - - - - - - - - -

## [I WAS BORN . . .]

- - - - - - - - - - - - - - - - - - - - - - - - - - - - - - - - - - - - - - - - - - -

### 1967

===========================================

i was born in the clinic that belongs to the city of linz
i drank at the breast that belongs to my mother
i hid from the bombs that belonged to the country
of england
i dressed in the clothes that belonged to my sister
i cried for my father whose death belongs to the
fatherland
i played with the balls that belonged to the
kindergarten
i've read the books that belong to the library
i rode in trains that belong to the state
i've sat in seats that belonged to others
i lived on the money that belonged to my friend
i've breathed the air that belongs to god
this is the life that belongs to me
i have screamed with the voice that belongs to me
i have bitten with the teeth that belong to me
i have scratched with the nails that belong to me
i have cried with the tears that belong to me
i have seen with the eyes that belong to me
i have thought with the thoughts that belong to me
i have laughed with the laugh that belongs to me
i have kissed with the mouth that belongs to me
i have slept with the dreams that belong to me
that is the life that belongs to me

---

# [BY A MASOCHISTIC FORCE . . .]

---

## 1973

===============================================

by a masochistic force i am thrust into this destructive attitude, all my thoughts are engaged in personal subjugation. i want to do that thing the outcome of which is certain in my thoughts, whose contents make me tingle, i don't want to submit as a woman, but i want to be the submitted one that shows my hate for humankind to which i belong, to see my hate upon me, daily feel it, forage in the muddy meadow of feelings or thoughts like a stubborn spitting of the spirit in a world having kitted me. i wish to officiate as gravedigger for my person and lustfully am i waiting for the rotting, the decay of my body, i want to feel within me the confluence of every current of hideousness, only then can i really suffer, a state that seems desirable to me, not born was i to suffer, to death i was brought to find myself, birth teaches me the path to becoming a cripple, i lick the water of the southern sea to feel lust in my vagina, my birth canal dried up to a clod of earth in clotted blood warmth, no object can penetrate this canal, only the thought of a consciously wrongly chosen existence brings it to weeping.

- - - - - - - - - - - - - - - - - - - - - - - - - - - - - - - - - - - -
## TIME RUN INTO ITSELF
- - - - - - - - - - - - - - - - - - - - - - - - - - - - - - - - - - - -

### 1973

==============================================

my hands are my identity, my face, and time is the time
that makes me is the time for me in the time in which
i make it is the time is my face
it happens in time if i lose time, i find it in my hands
again.

- - - - - - - - - - - - - - - - - - - - - - - - - - - - - - - - - - - - - - -

## [A TEARLESS HAND . . .]

- - - - - - - - - - - - - - - - - - - - - - - - - - - - - - - - - - - - - - -

1973

= = = = = = = = = = = = = = = = = = = = = = = = = = = = = = = = = = = = = =

a tearless hand i extend one day under stones
now the sea has become too large
for me
the black paving stones close up rolling the pores of the
cheeks
the eyeless air springs a step toward victory
takes place where it is absent
the gold
the sea here inside                              and
the sea here outside
covers the ice up with nails
a stone is not fear and fear
is no word
with a stone hand i shatter the tongue
and think withal:
won.

----------------------------------------------------

## METALLIC GESTURES

----------------------------------------------------

### 1973

====================================================

i drink the glass of water in the summer heat
i trickle the sweat between my feet and
i don't understand a word of your face
it is cold and a body stands beside me and
i pass your glass around and your heat cannot
be my heat
the glass of water i have never drunk
why should i drink a sea when life
i do not understand.

- - - - - - - - - - - - - - - - - - - - - - - - - - - - - - - - - - - -
## [TODAY IS SUNDAY . . .]
- - - - - - - - - - - - - - - - - - - - - - - - - - - - - - - - - - - -

### 1973
================================================

today is sunday, stayed a long time in bed, then did a
little something in the kitchen. just now i'm reading the
book by eve curie about her mother marie curie, a nice
book about a strong woman. reading this book i'm getting some ambition back, i'm also getting some courage
back: to advocate for my needs after all, my capabili-
ties, or if you will, my modest talents. because mostly
i'm hanging with myself in limbo.
it's a stolid state that none of my thoughts can wrest me
out of, and where my fancy fails to give me strength.
i whimper in a nothingness, my body bends in a stream
of spit-out saliva and stiffly i await the echo of courage.
am i weeping on my self because i can't connect the i
to the me?
i chop and bite at my fingernails as if they were ten
lovers for my ravenous teeth.
a bit more buffing and sculpting so that each clipped
nail, each flap of skin matches its pitiful state. how
often i have wanted to quit this habit, but then they
seem too smooth, my fingertips. it's a bit like arranging
flowers.
at once i am dead.

- - - - - - - - - - - - - - - - - - - - - - - - - - - - - - - - - - - -

## [I CONSIDER THE COMPUTER . . .]

- - - - - - - - - - - - - - - - - - - - - - - - - - - - - - - - - - - -

### UNDATED

========================================================

I consider the computer not just to be an artistic tool, but instead it also appears to me to be a symptom for the radical change occurring in our society because of the electronic revolution, namely the change in our sensory perceptions. That is accompanied by an altered relationship to the perception of reality, including artistic reality too or rather the artistic expression "reality."

I have worked in and with the mediums of film, video, and photography for years and for some time now I have involved the computer in my artistic expression as a partner in dialogue by working with computer-generated images. The computer allows me to expand my expression and begin a new/different engagement with the concept of representation and the concept of the real.

In my works with the computer, I confront analogue photography with DIGITAL PHOTOGRAPHY in order to disrupt photorealistic expression, simulation of the real, and to achieve a non-photorealistic environment that I would also like to see in cyberspace, not representing the real, but calling the real into question.

I also view my digital works as an expansion, a transformation of editing techniques, as this no longer involves cutting, gluing, and splicing together as was the case previously, with new mode arising from the material ITSELF instead.

I also refer to my works as media anagrams.

- - - - - - - - - - - - - - - - - - - - - - - - - - - - - - - - - - - -
### STANZAS IN REVOLUTION:
### FRAGMENTS
- - - - - - - - - - - - - - - - - - - - - - - - - - - - - - - - - - - -
### 1981
================================================



1.1 *Stone-tuning fork*

Move in an action
Necessary motion/sound
Motory acts                    keeping still
Feelings and place
Signs on the skin
Divisible sensory spots
Signs kinds of arousal             conductor a cable
Overhasty steps
Overhasty speech
Sound/less and less
Finally
Empty

2.1 In the hope of never again to lose anything, she
stands hour after hour at the open window, looking at
people's heads from above, from their forward striving
body movements shoved to and fro like billiard balls
on the playing field of the city. Sometimes she tries to
cast a net of lines over them, her finger slowly traces a
flame-colored streak, remains stuck on a child's head
and lets itself be carried along by it, until her fingertip
injures itself on a building wall. (She had once smashed
in a window.)

There's a mirror on the wall in the back room,
in which she had seen her eyes. She stared at the two
circles, a black disc with a white dot in the middle
and a red disc with a red dot in the middle, until she

realized he had already said "go away" for the fifth
time.

She kneels down with her face to the wall in the
corner.

The pain beds itself down tenderly in her welcoming
body.

Word bodies hang by tiny hooks from my lips, coated
blue by the sweat of sensitivity, and evanesce with a
hiss under the whirl of a turn of the tongue. The fate of
my ego gushes from urine-filled eyes, the fleshly pulse
drives time onwards with billions of cross-fades for a
dark agreement: repetition.

Fear shatters on the windshield in an echo of solitude, its petals falling in neon letters, the dragon whets
its eyes on the quivering tufts of grass, which thrust
their roots down into the mushy spume of the history
books. The awareness of time, the time of awareness
as a journey in yellowish-white trains along the newly
kindled fire tracks of knowledge:

My will splatters my blood into the leaden corner of
the room, the endless chains of symbols shatter in the
warm bed of imagination. Born on the outside of time,
carefully I draw the dried curtains of tacit memories
apart, the windows of my body tarnish me with the lead
vapors of perceptions, the tension wrinkles on the yel-
lowed gorge of perception. The ID card of my past is
divided into three chapters: nature, animal, desire.

She understands, and fetches her eyes back from the
silvered screen. By return she leaves her finger with its
bitten-off nails in the room.

2.2 *Beaten earth before the gutter* like a canal with a
blind goldfish pool the water that has to be in it without
clouds like a wilted leaf with the gold fish the mother
in the water gums together a grimy mucus from bread-
crumbs. Between menu prices illegible letters spat out
on white wooden tablets. A damp leaf on my shoe which

I shall love because it reminds of something I once knew.

Who will punish me and who should I fear. Pound the shit pound her face pound her cunt. Cells are empty, sea urchin.

Are you back?

Where and when did you alight a burnt-out vulture *stanzas in revolution.*

Lap the waters of the South Seas in my vagina feel deep pleasure, to a clod of earth in curdled blood warmth, picture colors caught in my breath, the thought of a deliberately wrong choice of existence makes him weep.

1.2 Tired and dead, lost and numb I feel the pain run quickly but fear casts its cowl over me the ant suffocates amid grains of sand my body is in a dark maw.

1.3 *Meal time:*
A bowl of love
A bowl of life
A bowl of lies

The secret of power cunning and sly the spirit world conjured up over many thousands of years a language, a thousand-year-old language, in many thousands of years a reign, a reign of a thousand years, a fairy tale— story that fails to convince when it shows the truth:

1.4 *The law of violence.*

1.5 Cuts grass
Cuts something
Cuts time
Cuts dress
Climbs ahead
Browses
Sketches out

Finds quickly
Knocks into shape
Stands before the gate
Leave me
Be.

1.6 *A spark* bursts on a fish
The scaly hordes wrench the breath from their gills.

3.1 *The futility of the searching repose:* live the light-
ness of the rain, shot the flight of the animal, killed the
poverty of the child, drawn the accuracy of the sym-
phony, see goodness without gazing, spilled a blaze of
tenderness with the body, wept the tiredness of stones,
murdered the forbearance of the eyes, smiled the
freedom of the parts, shed the autumnness of the wind's
gust, kicked the sadness of the plea, struck the accuracy of the word.

1.7 *Whimper* into a nothingness, body bends down
to spat out sputum and waits stiffly for the echo of
courage.

3.2 *Repetition* is the void in the cold
Shattered the endlessness of water, sung the plasticity
of the imagination, tiled the pressure of the heart,
fondled the nakedness of joy, buried the death of man,
assailed the blindness of compassion.

1.7 Metallic gestures
   i drink the glass of water in the summer heat i
trickle the sweat between my feet and i don't understand a word of your face it is cold and a body stands
beside me and i pass your glass around and your heat
cannot be my heat the glass of water i have never
drunk
   why should i drink a sea when life
   i do not understand.

In a hope in a credibility *of the words* that one speaks love, fear, and man, downcast like a dinosaur you lie down on top of me downtrodden like a monster, oh time, entangled petrified

postpartum whipped back to the coral reefs.

------------------------------------------------

# THE BIRTH OF THE PRISON: RESISTANCE OF ART AND THE ART OF RESISTANCE

------------------------------------------------

## 2000

================================================

We live in an age when the "power of surveillance" is revealing its hitherto invisible face. In thousands of words and deeds, we keep watch on the new forms of political power, hardly noticing the way this power is pushing us into a prison of our own making.

Rather than changing anything about the prevailing party-political situation, withdrawing from hard-won territory as an act of resistance leads precisely to this territory being occupied by others.

By acting this way, we play into the hands of those who would destroy and disavow decades of intensive emancipatory cultural engagement and years spent developing critical political processes. This would signal resignation in the face of a reactionary culture war of the kind conducted by the Freiheitliche Partei Österreichs [the right-wing Freedom Party Austria], as seen, for example, in this party's disparaging treatment of the internationally renowned Ingeborg Bachmann Prize.

## AGAINST THE RITUAL . . .

The long-standing trend toward the elimination of political territories in art and society—such as the abolition of the Ministry of the Arts by the previous government and the abolition of the Ministry of Women's Affairs by the current government—shows that party-political power strategies and a lack of interest in innovative

social processes seek to shape the image and contents
of culture and society. What will be abolished next?
The field of independent research and science?

Culture and society are shaped by the scenarios of
shifting party-political power struggles and ideologies.
Each field of action from which we withdraw of our own
volition will be occupied, in future serving the new government's vision of art and culture. The act of targeted
boycotting should not become an act of renunciation
that would be characterized by resignation and indirect
self-censorship.

With the name of the artist, the Oskar Kokoschka
Prize symbolizes the period of Austro-fascist and Nazi
art policy during which artists were persecuted and
artistic and cultural achievements were subject to
discrimination and elimination. The Oskar Kokoschka
Prize marks a symbolic field for art and society, for
criticism and analysis.

However highly I value the associated recognition
of my artistic work by an independent jury, it is impossible for me to accept this award from a member of the
current government.

For me, art has and always had the important task
of rendering us open and receptive to the Other and to
that which appears strange to us. Resistance to discrimination and ignorance is a powerful source of energy
for my work as an artist. Receiving an award for this
position and the works resulting from it from a member
of a government that discriminates against the Other in
the name of political power, and which thus represents
a position that is hostile to art, is something I cannot
bear to contemplate.


## . . . OF THE LIE


The Oskar Kokoschka Prize, which I can accept only
on the condition that it be presented to me by the jury
alone and not by a member of the government, has a

high symbolic value for me. The prize money is one building block in an initiative I see as my artistic project on the Oskar Kokoschka Prize and that will be devoted to a "media analysis of proto-fascist politics."* The work will focus not only on the written and spoken word, but also on images and the language of advertising and media. This will require cooperation with other people who work against the political manipulation and manipulative construction of falsehood and truth in image-making and information technologies: against the ritual practice of the lie with which we are confronted every day.

NOTE

The title of this piece is taken from Michel Foucault, *Discipline and Punish* (1975).

* I owe thanks to Sabine Breitwieser and Silvia Eiblmayr for their suggestions on this project.

- - - - - - - - - - - - - - - - - - - - - - - - - - - - - - - - - - - - - - - - -

## IDENTITY

- - - - - - - - - - - - - - - - - - - - - - - - - - - - - - - - - - - - - - - - -

### 2007

==============================================

It was always important for me in my work that I did not want to or could not tie myself down to just one identity, "my" identity. Especially not some social identity that society prescribes or grants me. Social history is a construct for creating identity, indeed, for constructing and arriving at identity, regardless of what kind, but above all a sexual identity. The "search" or the "rejection" of identity was my starting point, my point of entry, as I began to tackle feminism from a socio-political angle.

In my early diaries I come across entries from back then that focus strongly on the subject of "identity," and above all the concept of "non-identity." However, "non-identity" is totally impossible, because it presupposes identity. But my inquiries into "identity," into "gaining self-awareness" and an "awareness of the political, social, and artistic structures" in which I live were and are important for my artistic work. In today's society, cultural givens are shattered to give rise to umbrella symbols, configurations, patterns, etc.

Yet "identity" had for me a coercive character.

Identity and experience have an important connection. This is not a matter of designations, nor of the male-female dichotomy, which as we know does not even exist but is simply a construct. It's a matter of the force that is exercised to uphold a sexual identity, the force that informs speeches forging of the sexes so that the designation is made manifest.

I see another big step being taken here, accompanied by transformations in artistic expression, aimed at

avoiding and abandoning these unequivocal ascriptions
and taking them to the point of absurdity, whether in
terms of content or materials, or even in formal ways.
(Formula). This also has to do of course with changing,
with expanding symbols, conventional symbols, and
also with "signifiers," with the language of signification.
There are a lot of expansive new ideas and artworks
here, created by artists of different genders. I also call
such pieces social-psychological artworks, and they
can also be described as social psychological. They distinguish themselves by their greater complexity.

"If we assume that language is not the symbolic
means for interpreting a nonlinguistic world, but the
material location from which people 'speak' (V.E.),
it also becomes a matter of changing the meanings, of
arriving at other meanings."

This is the reason behind my piece *Stimmritze*
[*glottis*], in which I point to the "origin" or "source" of
the voice, the glottis. The "voice" is always there, it
forms itself into a beginning. The voice begins with the
anatomical structure of the body. The air, the breath
that is expelled from the chest—which also recalls the
first cry of the newborn child—is shaped by the additional instruments of the body architecture: buccal
cavity, lips, etc., as well as by the structure of the mind,
of thought and consciousness, the speaking of language.

For me this footage shot through a laryngoscope
as it is passed into the body, this artistic work is also
"real media work," because without the medium for
observing and recording it, without the visually repro-
ducing medium, without the reproduction of the obser-
vation, and its reality, the glottis would not be visible
to our eyes, to our minds, because perception as such
can only express itself via such media, even though
the architecture of speech is concretely real and in
operation—a media archive of the voice.

Could one say that the beginning of speech, of the
voice, requires reproduction through external media

in order to give visibility to the location, space that is invisible to us?

This immediately raises the question of how to assign speech a gender identity when the voice as such is invisible, and only becomes visible by means of "external devices," by acoustic imaging, by signs from the linguistic content, but which is generated by a socio-political cultural construct and employs manipulations and clichés. The voice as metaphor and reality.

All theories are full of meanings, with more meanings than interpretations are able to grasp.

Transformative artistic works can influence and change societies and cultures. Which is what art offers today worldwide—and here once again the concept "identity" is touched on. Identity is brought into the construction and context of the socio-cultural. The refusal to do so leads to transformations, and here perhaps to answers as regards "identity" that draw on philosophy, the social sciences, and psychoanalysis. Which is why I consider it important, still important if not especially important, to turn one's mind to gender issues in art, although the term "feminism" can no longer have or imply the same unequivocal meaning it had in the 1970s.

In the 1990s, the identity discourse revolved around the idea that identity can only be formed through difference to Other. I also felt that way, but it was not enough because what is also at stake here is gender dominion, the battle of the sexes that we still have because it fills our personal and collective identities. It was also simply a process of retaining and not of transforming. What is needed is new approaches, a personal image of self. It is a matter of existing as a self which, despite contrary experiences, differences, etc., can call attention to these "images" of contradictoriness.

For me the concept of identity is central. Yet not only "my" identity, personal identity, but also media-identity, the identity of the artistic means of expression, how far do these convey the artistic content, how far do they create a space for artistic work.

The artist has to be a "juggler" with his or her artworks, and create a space for transformation, for varying contexts. And also convey the "repression" imposed by the prevailing power relations, as well as recognizing how "subjects" are constructed by experience. Art, literature are also political expressions.

A specifically female identity can exist as self-identity, as narcissistic identity, but not for me, because that would be a rigid formulation of identity involving strict binary classifications, either—or

Standardization is repression.

Breaking out from society's binary code.

"Shifting" gender identity

"Shifting" the gender ideologies

Subject—individual

Speaking out against the rules

The rule of differentiation is a threat

Judith Butler: "Gender identity is an identity for which there is no original"[1]

Transgender

EDITOR'S NOTE

[1]   Probably VALIE EXPORT refers to Butler's sentence "Gender is a kind of imitation for which there is no original." Judith Butler,"Imitation and Gender Insubordination" (1991).

-------------------------------------------------
## VALIE EXPORT: ARTIST
-------------------------------------------------
### 2013
=================================================

I think my staying power comes from there having been so many obstacles and so little that might have satisfied me. Which certainly had something to do with growing up in a provincial town during and after the Second World War. I wanted to make these obstacles work positively for me. Once one limitation has been identified and overcome, the next comes along. It always takes an effort, of course, but it's also empowering because these aggressions make you stronger.

As a son, my status would have been better. But I also think that as a girl I had more freedom to be against something, because being a girl is akin to non-existence if you don't obey the rules. And my mother didn't drill a typical girl's identity into me, although I did go to a convent school. But convent school is a provocation in its own right. As a woman, being an artist was something I had to fight hard to achieve, it was not socially acceptable. As a man, I might certainly have been successful sooner.

- - - - - - - - - - - - - - - - - - - - - - - - - - - - - - - - - - -

## CHILDHOOD IN LINZ

- - - - - - - - - - - - - - - - - - - - - - - - - - - - - - - - - - -

### 2015

=========================================

My childhood up until the age of five was strongly marked by anxiety, by the terrors of the bombing of Linz, by frequent panic-stricken runs to the air raid bunkers in the Bauernberg, by bombed out, burning buildings, by the wounded lying on the streets and anxious waits in the shelters. I am also still affected by another trauma: whenever a passenger plane flies low overhead it awakens fears that were instilled in me by the low altitude bombers that flew over Linz and the Salzkammergut. At the same time, I also have quite beautiful memories from that time: the trees in flower on the Bauernberg, on the Freinberg, the blossoming magnolias on Herrenstrasse, the lovely outings to St Barbara's Chapel, which looks out onto Linz and the Danube. We, my mother and my two older sisters, often went for walks, when mother would take us to beautiful places in and around town. Everything grew calmer once the war was over: the end of the war became quite exciting for us as the American tanks advanced through Unterach am Attersee.

Everything was calmer after the war. Redevelopment began in Linz during the 1950s, which proved a difficult time for my mother because she was now a penniless war widow, and always had to economize. I attended the kindergarten and primary school run by the Sisters of the Holy Cross, and often went to their children's vacation homes in the summer, such as in Rindbach near the Ebensee in 1949. My mother ensured that we could spend time each summer in the countryside. Later she was able to buy a little wooden cabin in Grünau by the Almsee, where we spent some lovely

summers. Back home we had a small library which I
remember well, and which contained captivating books.
At times I was allowed to draw on the empty pages in the
front or back of them. My youth in Linz subsequently
became much freer, my oldest sister went to Germany
and I got an idea of what it was like to live away from
Linz, and Austria. When I was ten I traveled with my
other sister to visit her in Munich, where I was able to
get to know the museums and churches.

My loveliest memories, though, are of walking past
the tobacco factory (we went foraging on the other
side of the railway bridge to the Mühlviertel). I was
always fascinated by the building, the peace it radi-
ated, its façade—not that I could express such things
back then—but I loved walking past it, the color of the
"house" really impressed me. Today I think I learned
the meaning of "architecture" from that building. And
I also think one of my most incisive experiences was
my first encounter with Alfred Kubin's drawings at the
age of seven in the Kubin room at the Neue Galerie.
I visited them time and time again. Kubin definitely
had the same "feeling" I have for drawing, for stories
conveyed through drawings. By which I mean, if I say
so now, it awakened my artistic sensibility, my "love"
for or of a particular form of artistic expression; it
summoned that up in me. Which of course is why I felt
especially honored and delighted when the state of
Upper Austria awarded me the Alfred Kubin Prize
in 2002. Another, very different visual representation
at a museum also left a strong impression on me as a
child: the figural frieze at the Oberösterreichisches
Landesmuseum, which narrates the history of Upper
Austria. It impressed me, although it also reminded
me back then of "stone carvings," of the representations in cemeteries on graves and war memorials, but
perhaps that was just my imagination. I think, as I
would now say, these "stone pictures" influenced my
ideas about sculptural images, about stories. Memories

are something quite wonderful, because they bring so many wishes and fantasies, so many other images with them—and memories are identities. Another event also impressed me: my mother had a subscription to the theater, so sometimes my sister or I could go and watch a performance. When my mother came to collect me after one such performance she found me in a state of utter perplexity; I had no idea what I had watched, although it was supposed to be a straightforward play. My mother was likewise perplexed that I hadn't understood it at all, but then she looked at the playbill and saw that the program had been changed and that I had watched Torquato Tasso. The play had fascinated me, made me stop to think about words and sentences, I wanted to understand it. That has also remained one of my cherished memories, to this day.

I was very glad when I left Linz in 1960, because the city had nothing more to offer me, it had no art scene. So it was all the more surprising for me to see how the picture had changed in Linz as I returned after my stays in the US. I noticed the vital, expressive force in the city, the changes, the readiness to innovate, and the desire to give new shape to the city of Linz. The energy this requires has created the image of Linz. I felt that I could slip directly into Linz, the city was there for me.

I have been very happy to accept the challenge of serving as a member of the university council at the Kunstuniversität Linz, above all in the position of chairperson from the foundation of the council in 2003 to the year 2008. The period as a member of the council up until 2011 was an extremely productive one, in which I could draw on my experience at universities in the US and as vice president of the Universität der Künste in Berlin. In 2009 I was awarded an honorary doctorate by the Kunstuniversität Linz, and in 2011 the Kunstuniversität Linz inaugurated a biannual VALIE EXPORT stipend. For all these many reasons, Linz, the city of my birth, has a strong presence in my life story.

- - - - - - - - - - - - - - - - - - - - - - - - - - - - - - - - - - - - - - - - - - -

# A FEW REMARKS ON THE AESTHETICS
# OF MY TAPESTRY DESIGNS

- - - - - - - - - - - - - - - - - - - - - - - - - - - - - - - - - - - - - - - - - - -

## 1969

= = = = = = = = = = = = = = = = = = = = = = = = = = = = = = = = = = = = = = =

The repression the state metes out on art by dint of
the institutions and their directors, the press and the
critics, and the general public, is particularly evident
in design, not least in Austrian tapestry making. Here,
in the shadow of state subsidies, over the last two
decades a guild has gone to waste that had been happy
as a lark in the paddling pool of souvenir abstraction-
ism. The following proposals are my attempts to raise
tapestry to the level of contemporary art in its material
immanence—attempts to employ specific features of
tapestry for personal expression about the environment
and reality.

My works are meditations on wool and weaving,
which is to say: on what tapestries can tell us about
reality through figuration or abstraction. A first possibility is defamiliarizing the materials by deliberately
substituting other materials for those in the objects.
That is to say, using subjects that are either highly dependent on their material, the way for instance a mirror is
on glass, or a wall on solid bricks, and whose depiction
in alien materials breaks with convention. If such structures are woven solely in wool, the structure of the tapestry is also reflected. A mirror woven in wool, a textile
mirror, reflects in a defamiliarized way the structure
of both the mirror and above all the tapestry.

But not only mere substitution defamiliarizes: this
can also be achieved by the weaving technique. The
depiction of ice cream, which suggests an extremely
smooth and fluid character, by using a very coarse

weaving technique, modifies the *ice cream* into an aesthetic figure (lends a new attribute to its "reality"), which is due solely to the weaving materials and technique.

Further possibilities for defamiliarizing the materials, which is to say for reflecting on the subject and tapestry, are the insistence from/on the natural environment and the natural dimensions.

The natural environment is to be reflected in aesthetic and social terms. One aesthetically defamiliarized setting is for instance "a piano in the Alps"—(Arthur Rimbaud). But not only Surrealist juxtapositions work here; simply withdrawing from the concrete surroundings suffices, too. Normally a *sofa* stands on the floor, and does not hang on the wall above another sofa. (Design for a tapestry: Depiction of a rather old-fashioned sofa on a scale of 1 : 1. To be hung above a modern sofa. Or one could hang the tapestry, at the appropriate height, in place of a sofa as part of a suite of chairs.)

A *one thousand shilling note* lies inside a bag, it does not hang (greatly enlarged) on the wall. No more than the ice cream. Alternatively, instead of dragging objects on to the wall, which in this context thwarts the normal associations, another method consists in taking the wall itself as an aesthetic subject. Not depicted flat, but rather as woven material with a structure with the aim of appropriating its non-wall properties for the wall: its softness, stitchedness, and porosity. (Design for a tapestry: Depiction of a *knife* stuck into the wall, on an enlarged scale. Modeled on "hard edge" painting. Illusion of reality.) Or one takes objects one in any case sees every day on the wall, and that are not surprising when seen hanging there, yet are all the more surprising due to their defamiliarized material structure. (Design for a tapestry: Depiction of an *oval mirror* on normal scale. Using shadow effects for the frame and silvered threads for the mirror surface, a defamiliarization effect is created once again by the substituted materials, which clash with the classic notion of reality: enticed by the faithful depiction, the viewers think they are looking at a mirror, but discover they are facing a dull, blank textile mirror.)

(Design for a tapestry: Working title *Manifesto*, an important document, a product of human reason, such as the *Magna Carta*, the UN Universal Declaration, or the fundamental rights enshrined in the Austrian constitution, or according to the client's particular wishes or specifications, woven in handwriting. Designed for public buildings, judiciary buildings such as parliament, church halls, places of commemoration and culture of every political stripe, just as long as they breathe the spirit of democracy. The artistic import lies in the defamiliarization of the material, because one is accustomed to read handwriting on paper, or at least in print, especially as regards important public declarations. The medial character of this proclamation, which in turn removes it from the sphere of the individual and individuality, is to be brought back to the realm of private significance through the intimate character of the handwriting and the weaving.)

"Tapestry" comes from *tapis*, the French for carpet—a carpet that is hung on the wall. But how much longer must language dictate our reality and the way we deal with it: how much longer is a tapestry only to have the wall as its location and hanging as its means of presentation. Why not outdoors, suitably wrapped (in PVC, say), why not in motion (motor driven), why (if it has to hang) straight, why not crooked, twisted . . . and why not attune all these new ways and means and locations for its presentation to the subject matter—such as subjects that are only capable of showing their shapes and forms when in a twisted state and in a swiveled presentation . . .

Given that the labor costs for such a tapestry are so high that the price is beyond the reach of anyone on an average income (and selling to rich patrons cannot be the aim of a progressive artist), the subjects should chiefly be suited to hanging in public buildings or those belonging to public companies.

- - - - - - - - - - - - - - - - - - - - - - - - - - - - - - - - - - - -

## WOMEN'S ART: A MANIFESTO

- - - - - - - - - - - - - - - - - - - - - - - - - - - - - - - - - - - -

### 1972

= = = = = = = = = = = = = = = = = = = = = = = = = = = = = = = = = = =

THE POSITION OF ART IN THE WOMEN'S LIBERA-
TION MOVEMENT IS THE POSITION OF WOMAN
IN THE ART'S MOVEMENT.

THE HISTORY OF WOMAN IS THE HISTORY OF
MAN.

because man has defined the image of woman for
both man and woman, men create and control the social
and communication media such as science and art,
word and image, fashion and architecture, social trans-
portation and division of labor. men have projected their
image of woman onto these media, and in accordance
with these medial patterns they gave shape to woman.
if reality is a social construction and men its engineers,
we are dealing with a male reality. women have not yet
come to themselves, because they have not had a chance
to speak insofar as they had no access to the media.

let women speak so that they can find themselves,
this is what I ask for in order to achieve a self-defined
image of ourselves and thus a different view of the
social function of women. we women must participate
in the construction of reality via the building stones
of mediacommunication.

this will not happen spontaneously or without resistance, therefore we must fight! if we shall carry through
our goals such as social equal rights, self-determination,
a new female consciousness, we must try to express
them within the whole realm of life. this fight will bring
about far reaching consequences and changes in the
whole range of life not only for ourselves but for men,
children, family, church . . . in short for the state.

women must make use of all media as a means of
social struggle and social progress in order to free culture of male values. in the same fashion she will do this
in the arts knowing that men for thousands of years
were able to express herein their ideas of eroticism,
sex, beauty including their mythology of vigor, energy
and austerity in sculpture, paintings, novels, films,
drama, drawings etc., and thereby influencing our consciousness. it will be time.
AND IT IS THE RIGHT TIME
that women use art as a means of expression so as to
influence the consciousness of all of us, let our ideas
flow into the social construction of reality to create
a human reality. so far the arts have been created to
a large extent solely by men. they deal with the subjects of life, with the problems of emotional life adding
only their own accounts, answers and solutions. now
we must make our own assertions. we must destroy
all these notions of love, faith, family, motherhood,
companionship, which were not created by us and thus
replace them with new ones in accordance with our
sensibility, with our wishes.

to change the arts that man forced upon us means to
destroy the features of woman created by man. the new
values that we add to the arts will bring about new values for women in the course of the civilizing process.
the arts can be of importance to the women's liberation
insofar as we derive significance—our significance—
from it: this spark can ignite the process of our self-
determination. the question, what women can give to
the arts and what the arts can give to the women, can
be answered as follows: the transference of the specific
situation of woman to the artistic context sets up signs
and signals which provide new artistic expressions and
messages on one hand, and change retrospectively the
situation of women on the other.

the arts can be understood as a medium of our self-
definition adding new values to the arts. these values,

transmitted via the cultural sign-process, will alter reality towards an accommodation of female needs.

THE FUTURE OF WOMEN WILL BE THE HISTORY OF WOMAN.

- - - - - - - - - - - - - - - - - - - - - - - - - - - - - - - - - - - - - - - - -

## GERTRUDE STEIN/VIRGINIA WOOLF:
## FEMINISM AND ART

- - - - - - - - - - - - - - - - - - - - - - - - - - - - - - - - - - - - - - - - -

### 1973

= = = = = = = = = = = = = = = = = = = = = = = = = = = = = = = = = =

## 1. FROM MASCULINE TO HUMAN

"Religion," Hegel wrote, "is the place wherein a people gives itself the definition of what it holds to be true."[I] We may therefore visit this place in order to discover the grounds of our day-to-day politics, the "truth" of our culture.

Early religions and cultures, priestocracies and sun cults, saw the origin of life in woman. In the texts of their myths, "the male element is essentially mortal; the female essentially indestructible;"[II] heredity is presented as the highest creative principle, the female principle achieves everything on its own; the male takes second place, the son is the lover or the husband of the woman.

The immaculate conception in Roman Catholicism is the decisive cut-off point. Like it or not, the church must acknowledge birth, the maternal right—it thus shares with early religions the notion that the creation of life is not linked to a physical sexual act (a notion that still prevails, for example, among the Aborigines in Australia)—but the female principle now depends on the male principle to generate life, it becomes passive, receptive, receiving not a mortal man but God via the Holy Spirit in the form of a dove. The concept and value of the "virgin" comes into being, synonymous not with innocence but with waiting for a man, with being of secondary importance. Christianity ushered in woman's downfall and established the rule of man. The contempt for sexuality and women inherent in the concept of immaculate conception continues to this day, as the Holy Father endeavors to prove with his daily pronouncements. From God the Father, the highest universal principle, on downward there is a whole hierarchy of principles, at the end of which stands the female: woman as patient, passive, weak, cowardly, subservient, uncreative, beaten, stupid, enslaved. As its secret foundation, the mythology of our Christian civilization includes the infamous equating of the male and the creative principle. From abortion laws, via naming, to inheritance, from cultural to fiscal policy, we see the tips of this reigning principle's iceberg: man is the father of all things, and the male brings forth the female. This claim is false. It is a threat to the whole of civilization.

Mother Earth became Spaceship Earth. "War is the father of all things." This is the "true" face: destruction, enslavement, lust for power, blind dominance, death. These, too, or these in particular, are the attributes of the male. From housewife to mate, from femme fatale to pin-up girl: this is the gallery of diminished sexuality and male-deformed femininity.

In art, the market of creation, the man had a monopoly on creativity. The same applied in science: a woman was only admitted as a muse, a lover, a servant to the man's work. In creative terms, the woman was admitted, if at all, to the handmaids of art, to fashion and dance, the remnants of feudal rituals at courts and temples. For the past hundred years or so, however, women have begun to fight back. In politics, science, and art they have been trying to "man up," meaning not imitating men, but demonstrating their creativity. In the following I will cite examples of creative contributions by women to the development of art. There are so many creative women in art and science that I must limit myself to a very specific selection.

I write this article in the firm belief that reuniting the creative and the female must be the origin of the emancipation of women. Women's liberation is "causally" connected with their creativity (that need not express itself in artistic products only). Fostering the one serves to improve the other.

## 2. WOMEN ARE MORE CREATIVE

In a magnificent creative uproar, Gertrude Stein (1874–1946) embodies the resurrection of the female principle as a creative principle. She created artistic models that influenced generations of artists over decades, from Hemingway via John Cage to the Wiener Gruppe (Vienna Group)—compare, for example, her work on automatic writing (1896) and [Gerhard] Rühm's current works.

For pedagogical reasons, I will ignore the chronology that would have me deal with Stein first and begin with Virginia Woolf. She is a brilliant example of the link between female sensibility and creative impulse that leads to commonly applicable art models. Stein and Woolf are connected not only by the message of their works: Stein's play *Yes Is for a Very Young Man*, in which the man always says yes, the woman almost always no, portraying man and woman as an antagonistic principle with woman as the negative, pessimistic, repressed, passive, resisting element—and Woolf's magnum opus *The Waves* (1931) that ends with the words "O Death!", a novel between resignation and revolt, a novel of societal reification ("veil of being"), of linguistic rebellion ("I have done with phrases"), and of loss of identity ("nor do I always know if I am man or woman"). Stein's style is lyrical and constructive, Woolf's metaphorical style is embedded in audacious constructions that encompass units greater than sentences, entire chapters and paragraphs. The story of a day is told, described at the seaside with its waves, intercut with the story of a person's life. Herbert Marder has noted the implications of Woolf's feminism for her art, rightly bringing together the outstanding pamphleteer and the experimental novelist, the propagandist and the artist.

According to Woolf, the subjugation of women and the suppression of feminine ways of thinking are the source of most of our social and psychological disorders. In her view, feminism is a way of perceiving reality (*things as they are*, G. S.), just as art is a way of changing it (*the business of art*, G. S.).

In her view, this involves allowing female influences free rein within society and within the individual. Her ideal is the androgynous mind, a mind in which male and female elements achieve perfect equilibrium. Women's task is to "bring the feminine principle into an entirely masculine world and thereby make the world human instead of only masculine."[III] This social doctrine is the driving force behind Woolf's oeuvre, what Marder describes as "a quest for the androgynous mind."[IV] Bringing together feminism and art was the most important struggle in her development as a writer, a struggle she portrayed symbolically in her novels. Who's afraid of Virginia Woolf?

In Gertrude Stein it is also clearly evident how female problematics, subjective sensibility, can lead to a common artistic model, an objective technique. Her works, held in the tension between her phrases "well feudal days were the days of fathers" and "once upon a time I met myself and ran," between acquired Puritanism and innate passions, searching a new form of self-definition, of identity, that is independent from society and culture.

I want to speak here not so much about her style— "to reawaken the sound and sight of a word and their relation to its meaning, to gloriously destroy the context, adjectival, and syntactical inhibitions that make all poetry verbiage"[V]—but about how Stein managed to liberate herself from her American environment, why this was necessary, and what it led to. The technique and the product of this liberation is her style.

Her first three works are primarily about the fate of women, dealing with Stein's own true reality and identity. Once this had been achieved, she wrote *The Making of Americans* (1911)—personal emancipation followed by societal emancipation. *The Making* tells the story of an American family and was written at a time when Stein herself had broken free of her family. On one level, the novel describes the struggle of a woman, Martha Hersland, to emancipate herself from her family, from the relationships and interdependencies of the family members, and to attain a consciousness of her own. Stein's style, developed on the basis of her experiences and personal needs, was only constructed as a theory after the fact. Her semantic relativism aimed to reframe differences and sever false associations, namely the differences between the sexes (Hodder episode) and between peoples—not "As A Wife Has A Cow A Love Story" but "He was the one who was the one who was the one."[VI]

Her first novel bears the telling title *Things As They Are (Q.E.D.)* (1903) and deals with three women who endure a love triangle, probably the fruit of her romance with May Bookstaver when they were students in Baltimore which led, among others, to Stein abandoning her medical studies. After this, she wrote the so-called Hodder episode that was later integrated into *The Making of Americans*. A male professor, a female colleague, and a female dean with a deep belief in sexual equality who devotes her life to the development of this doctrine. The female dean has as her girlfriend the female colleague for whom the professor leaves his wife.

Her next book, originally titled "The Making of an Author Being a History of One Woman and Many Others," was called *Three Lives* (1906) [1909]. The stories of three women, with lots of sex, set mainly in Baltimore's immigrant and Black milieu. In Baltimore, Stein had enjoyed her medical training and worked with a Black

midwife bringing babies into the world. The story's
main protagonist, Melanctha, "cannot remember right,"
she lives for the moment, because she "remember[s]
right just when it happens to you, so you have a right
kind of feeling." In Stein's early days, the events, when
they occurred, were mostly of a sexual nature. Her
Cubist style is a longing for the now, a resisting of the
past, of historicizing morals, a full feeling of satiety
in the moment.

Hence her later statement that "the business of art
is to live in the actual present, that is the complete
actual present, and to completely express that complete
actual present."[VII] Her logic of simultaneity derives
from her consciousness and her consciousness articulates itself here: she is against remembering and recognizing. In *The Geographical History of America or: The
Relation of Human Nature to the Human Mind* (1935),
probably the finest of her philosophical writings, she
asks herself who she is and how she knows who she is,
based on the dame who went to market (in the nursery
rhyme) her eggs for to sell, who fell asleep on the king's
highway (manly power), thieves came by and "cut
her petticoats away," and when she came back home,
her doggie barked at her and she knew "this couldn't be
I, because my little dog didn't know me." This turn
of phrase is often deployed aggressively, against people
who build their identity on the fact that their dogs recognize them. She was against such a superficial identity.
In *Melanctha* she justifies a life of spontaneous composition as a life in the present, in order to fully realize an
identity and to cut loose from the male, authoritarian
past, thus achieving full emotional liberation and intellectual clarity.

Her Baltimore experiences also find expression in
her appreciation of militant Black writing, but also
in the legendary feminist texts of *Matisse, Picasso and
Gertrude Stein* (also known as *G.M.P.*, another abbreviation as in *Q.E.D.*). One of the stories is a fantasy about

love between Picasso and Matisse where a series of symbols take the place of explicit sexual descriptions. Another is about how it feels to be a woman and have no children, although she loves children, because her sexuality does not speak for childbearing.

The third story, "Many Many Women," is exclusively about women, men figuring only obliquely, and the characters have no names, they are simply women. A piece of feminist erotica like the later poems of *Lifting Belly* (1917), *G.M.P.* (written between 1909 and 1912) is the least mentioned work in the Stein canon. In the light of the above-mentioned theory, it is clear that this book about homosexuality and lesbian love is also her most difficult work and that it is not valued by the (mostly) male critics. In this very human book, Stein attained the finest and profoundest formalization of her sensibility and worldview.

Stein's oeuvre, a phenomenology of her mind, attempted to portray her consciousness in words, pledging to smash the male construction of culture by smashing its syntactic canon. Living in a male society, threatened by non-existence, by sexual exploitation, her main themes were sexual ordeals, independence of mind, identity, the fear of death. The artistic models she created, on a level with Joyce, Proust, etc., have found many (mostly male) followers to this day— compare, for example, the massing of platitudes in *Lucy Church Amiably* (1927) with Beckett's "Texts for Nothing." Unsatisfied with all existing ethics, in the life she shared with her companion Alice B. Toklas she tried to clarify the ramifications of her consciousness and to obliterate the traces of the kind of western thinking that has led to today's ethics. This experience led to her style so extremely freed from constraints and conventions.

This search for a consciousness distinct from language also led her to the theater. Her plays are a kind of instant theater, resembling the picture-like

happenings. Correspondingly, her first play is called
*What Happened, A Five-Act Play* (1913). It premiered
in 1963 as a triumph of "total" theater, where the text
is treated in the same way as the elements of movement, sound, and music. Her claim that plays are "the
thing anybody can see by looking"[VIII] anticipates John
Cage's claim that there are "things to hear and things
to see, and that's what theater is."[IX] But she also asked:
"If it can be done, why do it?"[X] by which she means:
Things that happen are seen. But why do what can be
done? The real story lies outside the visible action. The
idea of *What Happened, A Play*, then, was "to express
this without telling what happened, to make a play the
essence of what happened." Within this insertion of
the text into the spatial and temporal elements of the
theater, the theatrical elements are used as solid objects[XI] (the piano as a mobile sculpture, a portable cho-
rus). The words have no meaning in relation to one
another, but extensions and alterations in the text create a shared context, straight lines of consciousness
through the world of thought. This search for one's own
consciousness leads her among others to happenings
as a technique for action not held together by the meaning of words.

(To be continued in the next issue)

EDITOR'S NOTES

I    G. W. F. Hegel, *Introduction to The Philosophy of History* (1837).
II   Bertha Eckstein-Diener, *Mothers and Amazons: The First Feminine History of Culture* (1932).
III  Herbert Marder, *Feminism and Art—A Study of Virginia Woolf* (1968). This is actually quoted by Marder from Alison Neilans, "Changes In Sex Morality" (1936).
IV   Quote from the inner front flap of Marder's book.
V    From a statement by Joe Byrd, quoted by John Cage in Richard Kostelanetz, ed., *John Cage* (1970).
VI   Here VALIE EXPORT is presumably referring to the following quotation from *Many Many Women* (1910): "She was the one who was the one that was that one."

VII  From her lecture "Plays" (1935).
VIII From *Everybody's Biography* (1937).
IX   From Kostelanetz, *John Cage*.
X    From "The Gradual Making of The Making of Americans" (1935).
XI   Presumably a tacit reference to Woolf's short story *Solid Objects* (1920).

---

## FEMINISM & ART: PART 2 OF THE ESSAY "GERTRUDE STEIN & VIRGINIA WOOLF"

---

### 1973

===============================================

While Gertrude Stein portrayed the essential using new sound structures, CLARENCE SCHMIDT took a visual approach.[1] Decisive for both is that the essential, the actual meaning, is not present as an object or in the words. Schmidt's untitled environment of 1930 looks like the stage set for a play by Stein, like her torrent of words frozen in place. The cultish, processional quality of Gertrude's work flares up brightly in Clarence's. Using banal objects, just as Gertrude used banal words, she [sic] dealt with rituals of socialization. Her [sic] sculptural environment, assembled over many years using chairs, beds, boxes, statues, mirrors, connected and held together by rods, has totem-like qualities. It is a rejection of feudal gods, idols, and fathers. In the elements of this dynamic sculpture, long before [Jean] Tinguely, she [sic] used the everyday objects deposited by our culture to stoke a fire in which the evil spirit of our civilization burns to death.

This fetishism of the object as a site of repressed and suppressed sexuality is also manifest in most works by MERET OPPENHEIM (born 1913). Her objects are imaginations of female sensibility and fantasy. Banal objects like shoes, teacups, and belts are repurposed as totems of our civilization that unmask taboos. She too faces the problem of identity, her drawing $X = Rabbit$ (1930), the struggle against time and against the erotic fetishes of the men's world, *Venus primitive*. In 1936, her fur-lined tea service unleashed a scandal.

A crisis of identity was probably also what stopped her from spending the rest of her life covering all kinds of objects with fur. *Animal-Headed Demon* (1961), a small wooden box combined with a leather-covered piece of furniture, reflects the familiar complaint.

The Surrealists' famous dinner party on the body of a naked woman (1959) was her idea. Max Ernst wrote: "Her coloration is full of plant and animal remains. Meret is a living example of the ancient theorem: woman is a sandwich spread with white marble."

Meret Oppenheim's oeuvre is substantive evidence of the way female creativity generates an original artistic universe that is still being copied by men today— in particular the Pop artists' use of her material illusions and reversals.

The object world of LYGIA CLARK (born 1920) pursues this line, the female hallmark that is autonomous artistic potential. She, too, treads a path from specific constructivism to magic object. Co-founder of the Brazilian neo-concrete group MAM, first abstract paintings, then (1959–64) aluminum sculptures that she calls "animals." Her spatial constructions are different because they examine movement and time in art in a distinctive way, from the standpoint of the viewer, who becomes a participant, using his/her own energy to develop self-awareness.

Clark is not interested in the hierarchy of forms. Her forms, she says, have "no wrong side." Just as Melanctha could only remember the present, here form comes into its own. Prompted by spatial relations, she began thinking in material terms. In 1964, Clark attached green rubber to a tree, folded like a caterpillar, and called it *Grub*. Space and viewer are joined by elasticity. Rubber bands are used to create mollusk-like objects with a tension between their presentation and manipulation. Clark referred to them as "going." From 1966, she used even simpler materials like air, stone, water, shells—water, the female element (see "waves"), symbol of the mother and of life—to evoke physical sensations, warmth—tenderness—sex. The process of interiorizing the object that began with Meret Oppenheim, to stop the old meanings and call forth stronger new ones, a process that does with objects what Gertrude Stein did with words, and that will return in performance art (e.g., the repetition of words and the repetition of gestures and actions, until they become first void of meaning before acquiring a new independent subjective meaning), becomes a kind of "kineticism" of the body. The objects now become bodies that make us aware of our own bodies.

NIKI DE SAINT PHALLE (an alias derived from the Holy Phallus)[II] became famous when she used a gun to shoot at bags of paint hanging against her canvas, creating tachiste reliefs. The sexual aggressiveness of this art shooting, the identification with male symbols—gun as phallus, hunting, the splashes of paint on the canvas as scalps, the harvest of war, the spurting—adds up to a war that needs no interpretation from me. Later, after a dynamic labyrinth environment in Amsterdam (1962), she derived artistic stimuli from her own identity. Working with others, she created her large-scale female sculpture at Stockholm's Moderna Museet that could be entered through the sex, with a bar under the breasts, etc. From then on, she made many plump female figures, painted in bright colors, with which she filled gardens and galleries and which she named "Nana."

In 1964, YAYOI KUSAMA created her *Driving Image Show*, an environment that emanates signals of pure female representation. Banal objects like chair, table, a plate on the floor, a make-up table, a dress hanging on a screen, a glove, a rowboat in the middle of the room (portraying movement in contrast to the static-looking objects, a flight from rigidity and the unreal), all of these items are covered with hand-sized white penis-like objects. Beside the rowboat stands a mannequin that is totally covered with a lace-like fabric, including its hair and face. The artist stands alongside, similarly dressed, but with her face and hair uncovered.

The face, the customary mask in the hierarchy of social class, remains free here, without adornment, an affirmation of personal identity. The mannequin and the artist are both brushing their hair. The bizarre, unreal, fantastic quality of these scenes is the real world of women, measured against the ideology of men.

ANNA HALPRIN's pieces are influenced by constructivist architecture (Bauhaus) and dance. Supported by composers like La Monte Young, Terry Riley, etc., they are above all kinetic communication, new ways of freeing the mind of preconceived ideas and the body of societal and habitual reflexes. With *Birds of America or Gardens Without Walls* (1960), *Rites of Women* (1961), and *Five Legged Stool* (1962), her activity has focused increasingly on pure happenings. Her material—space and time—develops in accordance with distinct organizing principles. Autonomy of the material.

In *Birds of America*, music, movement, and words become independent elements that enter into arbitrary relations. *Five Legged Stool* shows a method of juxtaposing everyday actions in illogical ways in order to break through conventional associations and expectations. As the audience entered the hall, its sounds were recorded and when everyone was seated this material was played back in its entirety, slightly distorted. During this time, a man and woman stood on stage, stared at the audience, and pulled faces corresponding to the audience sounds. Later, two actors repeatedly crashed into one another (repetition). A large window on the stage that looked out directly onto the street was opened, letting in noise and light from outside. In *Apartment 6* (1965), the actors sat on the stage eating and drinking. Echoes of a psychodrama where real elements were integrated into the art process, making it hard to distinguish between life (spontaneity) and art (planning). Halprin sought to produce "a collective statement based on the need for audience and performers to be assembled; so that what occurs is a process that evolves out of both the moment and all the people there."

This interest in audience participation prompted her to carry out experiments, for example with audience members writing responses to what was happening on stage on pieces of paper that were collected and read aloud. At the next performance, a man was selected from the audience, "The Mouth," who read a selection of the sentences, to which the actors were then to react. Ritualized portrayals, repetitive process, mirrors in theater.

Sensual sensations, body kinetics, total theater, psychodrama—all this culminates in CAROLEE SCHNEEMANN's "kinetic theater" in which sensual art is used in an attempt to achieve the kind of direct altering of reality in accordance with female experience that Woolf spoke about. Her texts and performances are full of sexuality, but she combines the obsession of the flesh with cheerfulness; with her candid affirmation of female sensuality, the sexual ordeal of earlier artists becomes joyous aggression. Her theatrical inspiration has its roots in action painting. She takes the idea of abstract expressionism—that with a sufficiently active and gestural painting style, any material can serve as content (an idea shared by the early happenings)—and applies it to the body. In 1962 she made an environment out of glass, mirrors, glass sounds, light reflections: *Glass Environment for Sound and Motion*. Her personal experience of how random scraps of memory enter the present via sensory orientation before and after waking led her to make *Eye Body*, a series of photographs about her naked body as a collage environment with furs, lamps, water, and plastic. A visual and tactile expansion of this was her famous *Meat Joy* (1964).

Painting the unclothed body reduces it to an ordinary object, to the point where there are correspondences

between human body and animal body. *Meat Joy*, as
the title suggests, is an entreaty against the evil of
non-sensuality, elaborating a female dream of a warm,
sensual, meaningful, fulfilled life. The struggle for
the sexual liberation of women. Schneemann's non-
literary, non-verbal theater of physical movement in
space (within the formal unity of kinetic theater), is
an exploration and elucidation of the female realm, of
the veiled signs to which she is clearly committed. A
theater of feeling that is based on tactile/kinetic experiences and that involves group experience. A meaty
celebration of all kinds of materials, an extension of
the flesh (fish, chickens, sausages, brushes, ropes . . .),
between ecstasy and tenderness, banality and wildness,
precision and abandonment. Wilhelm Reich inspired
her work, gave her the courage to realize her visions.

Schneemann staged many more kinetic theater
events (*Snow*, 1967, etc.) and films about lovemaking.
She fought a societal, artistic battle for the rights of
women, wrote for magazines as a pamphleteer, made
montages of quotations and sayings that showed how
much women were absent everywhere, how far male
culture has already flowed into our civilization. She
took daily random samples from written culture showing that men automatically raise their voices only
for other men. "A man's word is his bond, the man of
the moment, mankind . . . etc." Woman—the missing
gender (!) in the grammar of everyday civilization.
"You are in the kitchen because you do not have a penis"
is the slogan for her liberated "cock book" for women.
She deals directly with the emotional and intellectual
constraints of gender, directly opposing control over
feelings as an effort of the will because one is always
thinking of self-image, of family, of school, of one's
team, one's country, one's president. She created a
"Sexual Parameters Chart" that was an anti-Kinsey, and
in 1972 she published a major work, *Parts of a Body
House Book*.

RUTH KRAUSS's first poem-play is called *A Beautiful Day* (1961). It consists of two sentences and two words: "Girl: *What a beautiful day! The sun falls down onto the stage. End.*" *Pineapple Play*: "Narrator: *In a poem you make your point with pineapples. Pineapples fly onto stage from all directions. Spy: And it would be nice to have a spy going in and out. End.*" In Krauss's plays, fairytale techniques and childish fantasy are presented in a sophist manner to become clear structures.

The same sophistry, which turns factual restrictions into triumphs of creativity, also characterizes the work of YOKO ONO. Elements of the male mythology about women (e.g., the child-woman) are seemingly reinforced, but actually rendered ineffective. "It is nice to keep oneself small," is a sentence that bears its opposite meaning within it. "See little, hear little, think little"[III]—with this call, she repeats the restriction imposed on women. But only on the surface, because within this universe of clarity she creates for herself a reality of mental richness that turns the restriction into its opposite and soon outwardly overcomes it.

In her early phases, she developed the poetics of this clarity; later, she demonstrated its overcoming. *Voice Piece for Soprano* (1961): "Scream 1) against the wind 2) against the wall 3) against the sky." *Painting for the Wind* (1961): "Cut a hole in a bag filled with seeds of any kind and place the bag where there is wind." *Cut Piece* (1966) [first performed 1964]: Yoko sits on the stage, beside her a pair of scissors, asks the audience to come on stage one at a time and cut away part of her clothing. "People went on cutting the parts they do not like of me. Finally there was only the stone remained of me that was in me, but they were still not satisfied and wanted to know what it's like in the stone."[IV] *Stone* (1966), mixed media: during the performance, the audience sat in bags. During the screening of *Film No. 4* in Knokke, Ono lay outside the entrance to the festival venue, wrapped in a black bag. *Film No. 4* is "a film of many happy endings" and, indeed, over seventy-six minutes, it shows three hundred bottoms.

Bag, stone, smallness, seeds, cutting, comb are the marks of an existence that scatters the mirror of its problems across the world. "There is a wind that never dies,"[V] this is both longing and imagination. Liberation from forms of objectified life, from life as a thing, starts with the experience referred to in one of her latest pop songs: "Woman is the n***** of the world."

CHARLOTTE MOORMAN bases her work on similar musical structures. In 1966, Yoko asked: "When a violinist plays, which is incidental: the arm movement or the bow sound?"[VI] Charlotte, too, answers: the bow sound. She broke out of the rigid framework of conventional concerts by making one small change, to her clothing: she played topless, or naked. By bringing her sexual characteristics into play, she revealed male culture to be an arm movement. The violin as a breast, as a female symbol, revealed what underlies the music, be it therapy or stultification, and she protested against stultification. Music as a male Eros: in her *Opera Sextronique* (1967)[VII] she had small TV sets attached to her naked breasts, a collage of media voyeurism, of the media exploitation of women.

ALISON KNOWLES began by collaging fragments of everyday life. She put a silent chair on stage as a piece of music. In *Nivea Cream Piece* (1962) an actor comes on stage and massages his hands with Nivea cream in front of the microphone. Other actors come and do the same. Then they join together at the front of the stage to form a mass of massaging hands. Then they leave the stage one by one. *Simultaneous Bean Reading* (1964): actors roll out the *Bean Rolls* over the audience and begin to read. Meanwhile, a performer goes round cutting holes in the paper scrolls. Later, she made a life-size book to live in. The familiar motifs of repetition, groups, audience, participation, cutting, banal objects, silence, etc. are combined to create a form of actions.

DOROTHY IANNONE resists male behaviors, demonstrates them, insists on her female independence. In 1971, she collected seventy-five complimentary cards in a box and seventy-five uncomplimentary ones in another. (I love you when you bend your neck to me and I can give you all my tenderness.—How like the conqueror you look as you labor over me—I love you because you can embrace me even after I scored a point. Uncomplimentary: Do you think it's significant that I do my best work when you are away?—I long to hurt you ultimately). These two boxes contain the complete reservoir of our forms of behavior, the repertoire of our hate and our love, the destructive logic of man and woman in our civilization. They are an attempt to make it possible to see through this logic and thus to overcome it, to arrive at direct spontaneous modes of behavior whose injuries are not predictable, whose testimonies of love are not known. In her book of *Lists*, Dorothy describes and makes drawings of her lover. A public declaration of her freedom to choose. All of her figures, even when fully clothed, are drawn with their sex, with a penis or vagina. She looks behind the scenes and knows what's at stake. And this attracts censorship! In her book *The Story of Bern*, she tells how an exhibition in Bern, put together by friends, fell through because her contribution was censored.

In her works, REBECCA HORN represents the relation between body and civilization. Men with added horns, wrapped in hoses (*Überströmer für Christoph* [Overflowing Blood Machine], 1969). A walk-in frame that traces the body's outlines with protruding metal rods. Adornments of civilization—symbols of civilization. Attempts to clarify the principles discussed above in simple elements and symbols.

(Conclusion to follow)

I    For unknown reasons, VALIE EXPORT assumed that Clarence Schmidt (1897–1978) was a woman, as becomes evident from the context and the use of the feminine pronoun in the following. It is also unclear which environment, dated 1930, she refers to; his earliest work is around 1940.

II    In fact, only the Niki part was an "alias," she was born Catherine Marie-Agnès Fal de Saint Phalle. The false notion that "Saint Phalle" was an artist's name was widely shared at the time though.

III  From Yoko Ono, "To the Wesleyan People" (1966) in *Grapefruit* (1970).

IV  Yoko Ono, "Statement" (1966).

V    From Ono, "To the Wesleyan People."

VI  Ibid.

VII *Opera Sextronique* is actually a work by Nam June Paik in which Charlotte Moorman performed.

- - - - - - - - - - - - - - - - - - - - - - - - - - - - - - - - - - - - - - - -

## TAP AND TOUCH CINEMA, ETC.:
## PART 3 OF THE ESSAY "GERTRUDE STEIN
## & VIRGINIA WOOLF"

- - - - - - - - - - - - - - - - - - - - - - - - - - - - - - - - - - - - - - - -

### 1973

= = = = = = = = = = = = = = = = = = = = = = = = = = = = = = = = = = = = =

Elucidation, the study of behavior—passive-active, object-subject—in the process of civilization is also a general characteristic of my own work (the artist as commodity: VALIE EXPORT). Stein deals with the relationship of the self to other individuals, to the family, to the nation; she seeks the identity of the self in a rejection of society. Her work was to recognize signs and their manipulability. Schneemann and others represent analytical processes via group therapy and games with the audience; they use signs to achieve liberation via direct portrayal of emotions. I and others destroy signs, clambering out of the catacombs of analysis, reinterpreting signs in the social process, bypassing analysis via direct processes for personal liberation, to change humankind. In February 1968 Peter Weibel and I did an action together: *Aus der Mappe der Hundigkeit* (From the Portfolio of Doggedness). I led him "on a leash, crawling on all fours, along Vienna's main street. The sexual message of the action triggered anxiety and irritation among spectators" (photograph in NF, February 1973, p. 47). This rendered visible the need of human beings to display animal behavior, as well as showing that humans often behave like animals. Repression within social structures, constraint, and the hope of an animal/human breakout lies hidden within us all. Via the man-woman relationship, transformed here into an animal-human relationship, with humans as its signifiers, sadomasochism is rendered clearly explicit. By means of direct signs, sexuality penetrates the social process and social communication, thus conveying a real message. History of identification. Where do the boundaries of gender run, the borders between animal and human as part of a cultural process? This admission of animal behavior on the part of humans is a symbolic representation of animal-like conditions within society. This would no longer apply if society were to overcome nature. Which underlines the need to do away with social orders of animal origin.

In 1968, I made *TAPP und TASTKINO* (TAP and TOUCH CINEMA) as the first genuine women's film. The female attributes, which in our culture are turned into an object for male sexuality, were abolished and put on the street in a form that broke society's rules. Tactile and visual experience in sexuality is permitted by the state only within the family, only in the private sphere. Visual experience through newspapers, books, and films encourages voyeurism and only seems to permit sexuality outside of the family. The state forbids tactile experience outside the private sphere because it has no meaning for the state. When the senses are liberated, this process cannot be integrated into the rules of the state in any way. As that would lead to a direct liberation of sexuality. This is the first step for woman from object to subject. Disposing freely of her breasts, she no longer obeys social regulations. Because everything takes place on the street, and the consumer can be anyone, man or woman, it represents an unveiled breach of the taboo of homosexuality. Since the breasts are no longer the property of a man, with the woman disposing freely of them instead, the morality of state regulations (state, family, property) is breached.

Text on "Cycle of Civilization," a portfolio of photographs that highlights aspects of my work to date:

The human being is a communications medium, a bearer of symbols and information for other humans. An important role is played here by the skin, which is at the origin of adornment and clothing. Even today, the skin as a value within civilization's hierarchy shows how much the characteristics of ritual cultures persist in social cultures. The skin is also used to display other values, which explains the way indigenous peoples and women are hung with jewelry and make-up ("woman is the n***** of the world," Y. Ono). In other cultures the body and the skin are used directly as arenas for the negotiation of social belonging. Just as in the course of the socialization of nature, animal bodies came to be branded as property, so humans are embedded in the social community via their bodies, to which social signals are attached, talismans and insignia of belonging to tribes and territories.

Civilization reveals itself as a veiled, abstract ritual. In ritual, the embedding takes place physically, while in civilization it is abstract, but in both cases on the basis of the human body. The more these concrete and abstract institutions are broken out of, the more we demolish the architecture and cut open our clothing, the closer we come to the human body as a site of the mind, the bearer of interpersonal communication. It is a coming-to-ourselves, an overcoming of socialization, a way into personal liberation, a way out of social ordeals, a rejection of signs, their meaning and their likeness. Social communication presses us into the institutions, burying the body-mind function that leads to a liberated consciousness, to a free meaning of the body. The social institutions as a tattooing of the mind. That deform consciousness and force it into a stone structure.

Tattooing the body demonstrates the link between ritual and civilization. In the tattoo, the garter appears as a sign of past enslavement, clothing as a repression of sexuality, the garter as an attribute of self-determined femininity.[1] A social ritual that conceals a physical need, our culture's opposition to the body, is revealed. The garter as a sign of belonging to a class that demands a conditioned behavior becomes a souvenir. The female body casts off and discards the stamp of a world that has to date not been a woman's world, to arrive at a human world in which she can determine her female existence herself.

Where society has demonstrated its dominion over the body via social signs, *Eros/ion* shows ways and means for people to escape this violence. The biological order that is still forcibly imposed in our society by making physical attributes determine how we live, can only be expunged once the force of the body over the mind has been overcome. Humans writhe in glass without bleeding to death. They prove stronger than the system that surrounds them by overcoming the arena where that system is implemented, the body.

The "ritual"-like action reveals the consciousness that has freed itself from the signs and signals of civilization, from the meaning of the material. The reconstruction of the ritual takes place from the standpoint of overcoming the ritual. The meaning of the material prescribed for us by society is overcome here in the body by the mind, it does not hurt what it is meant to hurt. The cuts to the skin are no longer deadly, they are openings onto the intima, onto the innermost skin of our vessels, onto ourselves. The state private sphere is cut up, the traces on the body are signs of social processes, pointers from ritual to action, from suppression to free determination, from order to chaos.

BIBLIOGRAPHY

Gertrude Stein, *Stanzas in Meditation and Other Poems (1929–1933)* (New Haven: Yale University Press, 1956).
Richard Bridgman, *Gertrude Stein in Pieces* (New York: Oxford University Press, 1970).
Michael Benedikt, ed., *Theatre Experiment: An Anthology of American Plays* (Garden City, NY: Doubleday, 1967).
Donald Sutherland, *Gertrude Stein: A Biography of Her Work* (New Haven: Yale University Press, 1951).

Virginia Woolf, *The Waves* (1931) (London: Penguin, 1964).
Richard Kostelanetz, *The Theatre of Mixed Means* (New York: Dial Press, 1968).
Jürgen Becker, Wolf Vostell, eds., *Happenings* (Reinbek: Rowohlt, 1965).
Hanns Sohm, ed., *Happening & Fluxus* (Cologne: Kölnischer Kunstverein, 1970).
Guy Brett, *Kinetic Art* (London: Studio Vista, 1968).
Allan Kaprow, *Assemblage, Environments & Happenings* (New York: Harry N. Abrams, 1966).
*Meret Oppenheim*, exhibition catalogue, Moderna Museet, Stockholm, 1967.
Carolee Schneemann, *Parts of a Body House Book* (Cullompton: Beau Geste Press, 1972).
Yoko Ono, *Grapefruit* (London: Peter Owen, 1970).
Dorothy Iannone, *The Story of Bern* (self-published artist's book, 1970).
Herbert Marder, *Feminism & Art: A Study of Virginia Woolf* (Chicago: University of Chicago Press, 1972).


EDITOR'S NOTE

I    VALIE EXPORT is referring to her work *Body Sign Action*, 1970.

- - - - - - - - - - - - - - - - - - - - - - - - - - - - - - - - - - - - - - -
## HE WHO IS NOT PAINTED IS STUPID
- - - - - - - - - - - - - - - - - - - - - - - - - - - - - - - - - - - - - - -
### 1973
====================================

"He who is not painted . . . is stupid," say the Kadiweu in Brazil, as I've just read in Claude Lévi-Strauss. As I read in the media, that is what men today still say to their women.

Which is why I want to create a "message for all" using a private kind of messages such as a diary. Every available channel must be used to reach the public and pave the way to a metanoia that will bring about a change in outlook on life and the arrival at a new world-view. Because that is where women's metanoia, which is the concern here, must be achieved.

## MONDAY

Lévi-Strauss writes, "Tattooings . . . are not only emblems of nobility and symbols of rank in the social hierarchy, they are also messages fraught with spiritual and moral significance." Their purpose "is not to imprint a drawing onto the flesh, but also to stamp onto the mind all the traditions and philosophy of the group." He who is not painted is stupid. This "expresses a . . . fundamental splitting . . . between the 'stupid' biological individual and the social person whom he must embody," and who is invested with society's emblems. Yet this split already amounts to a sociological theory, one that establishes a class division, not only of social classes—between stupid underlings condemned to physical labor, and those above with the stamp of spiritual nobility—but also a difference in social class based on the biological differences between man and woman.

Woman is assigned the emotions, man the power of reason, woman body, man mind, etc., with the ultimate aim being that power remains up there and oppression down here. Just as long as we continue to submit to the rituals of class division, we voluntarily bow to a repressive system, and perform our assigned roles.

## TUESDAY

The mind of woman has been imprinted with the tradition and philosophy and male race—which is to say: by gender fascism. She passively endures humiliations, torments, and physical blows because it is anything but an exception for men to be mean and cruel to their women. For the sake of social life, woman requires a man as partner so as to fulfill her customary duties in society, and even today is always ready to feel guilt and embarrassment and with that to undermine her self-confidence, which in most cases has already been put on shaky ground by her upbringing and surroundings. While the man acts as her punisher with the moderacy or harshness he deems fit, she is the willing victim of his despotism. Humble, unresisting, cowardly, she swallows his brutality where kicks, struggle, and insurrection would be more apt. Although clearly these are not the best of weapons, what do we want: repression, or the feeling of life lived freely? The millions of tears wept over the canvas of pain, curdled into fear and despair, are the Niagara Falls of female enslavement.

## WEDNESDAY

A strict division—child raising by mother, social provision by the father—already leads to a fundamentally wrong upbringing. Fixed, handed-down roles inject the child with false ideas about mothers and fathers, men and women, these key techniques for inducing social identification. Because women's weakness, her need to be protected etc. are acquired characteristics and not causes—a consequence of the division of labor in the male state. The best possibility for bringing up children to become different people would be to raise them in family groups or family kindergartens, because then one could free the terms "girl" and "boy" from their rigid chains of associations. With group families it is also easier to solve the problem of illegitimate children, and the same for the problems in failed marriages when children are involved. It seems perfectly obvious to us that the child stays with the mother and the father vanishes. Day after day we see the self-evident picture of the mother with her illegitimate child, which has destroyed thousands of lives. Good riddance I say to this hypocritical morality, invented by men and lapped up by servile women.

## THURSDAY

Woman must have the same social rights as man. Emmeline Pankhurst and her daughter Christabel first took up the struggle and fought for women's suffrage. The *Daily Mail* quickly named them "suffragettes" at the beginning of the twentieth century, which still sounds ridiculous to some ears. But it was they who climbed the barricades for us, who won women the right to vote, who had themselves imprisoned so that we could talk today about the pill and abortion. So that we could arrive at a human solution to our biological makeup and do away with the inhuman solutions we have had up to now.

## FRIDAY

I dreamt I was in a little artists' bar that resembled Kienholz's bar installation, which I had seen at the Stedelijk Museum in Amsterdam. There in the bar were my Viennese artist friends. Suddenly the police proceeded to raid the place, an art raid. Nobody but me showed any disquiet. I wanted to hide from the police, so I escaped to the toilet, was tracked down and brought back to the bar. I was scared, I felt sure the raid would end badly for me. I hid myself behind an artist, so that he would shield me in case there was a shootout. But a policeman dragged me out, then the police turned into civilians that I knew. The policeman pushed me up against the bar, put a pistol to my temple. Everyone watched as if nothing was happening, although I felt I was now about to be shot. I couldn't understand why I of all people should be the victim of this art raid, although it seemed obvious to everyone else. The pain gripped my head like an iron clamp, encircled it like a steel ring, the fear of death was so great it tore my feet from the ground and they started to swing around frantically. The fear increased to such a pitch that I woke up . . . I woke up completely liberated, leapt out of bed and put on a Janis Joplin album.

## SATURDAY

The androgynous spirit, the harmony of man and woman: if the wife of a Jambi man thinks she is pregnant, the man does not go fishing. The sea, the great amniotic waters, should not be disturbed by his oar strokes.

There are principles that bring man to life and those that spell his death. The present state of human relationships tends more to the latter. The relationship between man and woman is warped and contaminated. What could be a paradise becomes mortal agony. This state hinders us all from developing ourselves freely. Which means that men have to emancipate themselves every bit as much as women, emancipate themselves from the old ideas so that we can step out of the age of male communication into the age of human communication. Into the human age.

Idea for an action: "blood warmth." On a beach on the northern coast, Belgium or Holland: dig two parallel channels in the sand, down to the sea, fill one with blood, the other with gasoline, ignite (man and woman). In one channel flows blood, in the other fire. (Blood warmth, union, life.)

---

## MAGNA: REMARKS ON THE GENESIS
## OF THIS EXHIBITION

---

### 1975

========================================

In the winter of 1972, prompted by reports of the vigor of the women's movement in America, my years of experience, as an artist who happens to be a woman, in dealing with the press[1] and with colleagues in my immediate art milieu—experiences that were, with few exceptions, exasperating—culminated in the idea of organizing a European women's symposium on female creativity that would manifest the "new" women's consciousness via an exhibition, lectures, films, actions, etc., and strengthen it via the public impact of the event. Although less an artistic than a sociocultural development, that had gone unnoticed by the administrators of the public sphere or been perceived in a false light, calling for the participation of girls and women who would articulate and demonstrate the social issues, the "new" emotionality, and the "new" behavior, I nonetheless wanted to use the institution of art for this purpose, for reasons that can be found in my text "The Position of Art in the Women's Movement Is the Position of Women in the Art's Movement" (*Neues Forum*, Vienna, 1973) [Woman's Art: A Manifesto, 1972] and that can be summed up as follows:

Because art must be understood, among other things, as one component of the communications media with which social reality, a reality oriented toward the needs of men, is constructed; because women must use all media as means of social struggle and to promote societal progress; and because the political/economic conditions for a social revolution are obviously not (yet) given, art is a possible place to advance the liberation of reality from male ideologies. As well as cultural history (India, Syria, American Indians, etc.), it is important to address specific issues faced by women (career, housework, abortion, kindergarten, parenting, marriage), to explain the importance and objectives of women's work in the social process, and to make known our demands to male society. For this reason in 1972–73 I either wrote to or visited women's groups and artists in Germany, Holland, Denmark, England . . . to gather information about them and their work and to suggest that we collaborate.

On my travels I met many women who were dealing in specific works with problems both personal and general, who were aware of their disadvantage in the (mostly) male art world, and who were no longer willing to submit to male (social) demands. I watched videos and films, looked at artworks, met women's groups, action groups, street theater groups, etc. All of these endeavors strengthened my resolve, and I proposed the project of a women's symposium to Galerie nächst St. Stephan (1972), and the positive initial response gave me a naïve courage. I wrote letters to various museums, art associations, and galleries in Germany, Holland, and England requesting or suggesting for the planned exhibition to travel there. In most cases I received no answer, or the rejection was hedged about with phrases like "interesting project, etc., but we are currently unable . . . " It quickly became clear that there was no interest or, apparently, no need for a women's symposium. After the Münchener Kunstverein showed an interest, I spent more than four weeks in Munich, contacted women's groups, and developed specific proposals (local group work, target groups, demonstrations . . . ) etc. In spite of this commitment, which was also a financial commitment as my travel and accommodation costs all came out of my own pocket, the Kunstverein left the project hanging, again giving no final confirmation. On my return to Vienna, I had a large amount of material, information, and documents with which I went back to Galerie nächst St. Stephan, but those running the gallery had reservations due to the political and sexual content and due to the budget. During 1973–74, the exhibition was delayed again and again. Talks were held with other interested galleries in Austria, but positive responses were again withdrawn. A meeting with Dr. Schmeller, director of the Museum des 20. Jahrhunderts (Museum of the 20th Century), to discuss a joint project with Galerie nächst St. Stephan was unsuccessful. All this wore me down and at times I lost faith in the project. I even wrote to the Federal Ministry of Science and Research in Vienna (headed by Dr. Firnberg), as I had by now invested a large amount of my own money and a great deal of work in this exhibition, but I never received an answer.

By this time I had realized that the original European concept simply could not be realized in Austria. As a consequence, in the second half of 1974, when Prof. Oberhuber, the new director of Galerie nächst St. Stephan, suggested reducing the project to Austrian contributions, I accepted. A date was agreed for late '74, then postponed to March '75, and the Austrian exhibition was expanded, within the means of the available budget, to include international video, film, and music works. Prof. Oberhuber kindly brought forward to the spring the International Art Talks that usually take place in the fall, allowing speakers to be invited for lectures. In addition, for the catalogue, which posed a number of further challenges, I received sisterly greetings from two prominent American members of the women-in-art movement. With this structuring of the exhibition, the program, and the catalogue, I hope we have managed to reflect the broad international reach of the movement. Beyond this, what Lucy Lippard wrote me in a letter applies: ". . . getting it together under adverse circumstances, each time somebody has

the guts to do this the circumstances will be less lousy
for the next person."

I hope that this event will achieve its goal to some
extent, that goal being not only to manifest women's attempts at self-realization and self-exploration and their
claims to participate in and shape culture, but also to
make some small contribution to the free development
of women's buried strengths/talents and to altering the
consciousness of both women and men, as well as lend-
ing fresh impetus and added strength to the women's
movement.

In this spirit I would like to thank all of those who
helped make the exhibition possible: all of the partici-
pating artists and poets; Maria Lassnig, Lucy Lippard,
Meret Oppenheim, and Carolee Schneemann for their
contributions to the catalogue; all speakers; Peter
Weibel for his emotional and intellectual support; the
Federal Ministry of Education and Art and the Austrian
Trade Union Federation for their financial support
during the preparatory phase; Dr. Erika Patka, secre-
tary at Galerie nächst St. Stephan, for her organiza-
tional assistance; and, last but not least, Prof. Oswald
Oberhuber who put the gallery and its resources at
our disposal.

NOTE

1    Perhaps this exhibition will manage to "finally put an end to the
prehistoric atavism of the press on this topic" (Gislind Nabakowski, in
a letter).

- - - - - - - - - - - - - - - - - - - - - - - - - - - - - - - - - - - -

## MAGNA: ON THE HISTORY OF WOMEN IN THE HISTORY OF ART

- - - - - - - - - - - - - - - - - - - - - - - - - - - - - - - - - - - -

### 1975

= = = = = = = = = = = = = = = = = = = = = = = = = = = = = = = = = =

Most history books are marked by profound sexism: women do not figure. In the history of our culture, women are the missing sex. The word history itself reflects this: our history is HIS story, the story of men. In history books written by men, the development of civilization has always been dealt with from a male perspective: men were the main protagonists on the political scene, the great inventors, discoverers, artists, women mostly just mute figures on the historical stage. When women do appear in these books, then as a hidden root cause à la "cherchez la femme" or as the lovers of prominent men. The story of Aspasia, for example, tells that she won the favor of Pericles, but not that she wrote some of his best speeches. There are more stories about the men's crusades than about the millions of women, roughly nine million between the fifteenth and eighteenth centuries, who were burnt as witches in the so-called Christianized countries. Books about the Wild West describe adventures with warring Native American men, but they don't mention that it was women who, after a female revolt, ruled the great Five Nations regarded by colonialists as the most civilized Indian tribes on the East Coast. The history of women is either restricted to a few empresses and famous scientists of the modern period, or it is nonexistent. Like other minorities and repressed groups, women themselves were not able or not allowed to develop an awareness of their own history. The extent to which their history is mutilated is shown, for example, by our understanding of the witches of Europe and America, an understanding shaped by the projections of Christian colonization and the resulting sexual neuroses in men (in *Malleus Maleficarum*, published in 1486, a Papal Commission declared that "all witchcraft comes from carnal lust, which is in women insatiable," meaning in concrete terms that if a prison guard masturbated in front of a female prisoner, this was attributed to her power of witchcraft!). The history of witches as an alternative counterculture, as a hidden and suppressed history of women, has yet to be written. Another example is the history of feminism itself. Due to the lack of history books written by women, due to the isolation in time and space imposed by society, each generation believed it alone had discovered the women's question, for the first time, and had little knowledge of earlier protests and declarations. Only today's women's movement seems to have the power to understand itself in more total terms and to cut through the historical separations.

As early as 215 BC, women in Rome protested against sexist laws made by men, such as those prohibiting women from being represented in the Senate. We know of bloody harem revolts in tenth- and eleventh-century Turkey that ended in the killing of a caliph. In the twelfth century, Queen Eleanor of Aquitaine and her daughter Marie de Champagne actively fostered women's rights and created sanctuaries where women could get away from male control, so-called "courts of love," where customs and behavior congenial to women prevailed. In the fourteenth century, Christine de Pisan, a court writer and astronomer, wrote her utopian *Livre de la Cité des Dames* calling for political awareness among women. Marguerite de Navarre, a French queen of the sixteenth century, Madame de Lambert, Mme de Staël and many others demanded human rights for women without knowing of each other. A strong feminist movement with a broader basis existed during the

French Revolution, as documented by Marc de Villiers du Terrage in his *Histoire des clubs de femmes et des légions d'amazones* (1910). In numerous petitions to the National Assembly or the Commune, they sought to participate in political life and developments. But the "Declaration of the Rights of Man and the Citizen" spoke only of *l'homme* and *le citoyen*, not *la femme* and *la citoyenne*, prompting Olympe de Gouges (a former courtesan who at thirty-six began writing theater plays, including an anti-slavery drama, as well as calling for a second Comédie-Française to stage only works by women) to publish a "Declaration of the Rights of Woman and the Female Citizen" in 1791, reiterating the original declaration point by point for women. But the legislative assembly decided otherwise: "Nature created woman for the comfort of man. Women, do not interfere in public affairs!" The March on Versailles by women (denigrated by historians as fishwives), their participation in the storming of the Bastille, the formation of Amazon Battalions, and the administration of Lyon by its female citizens for three days in 1792 were all triumphs achieved against the male character of the Revolution in general. The Convent banned women's clubs, women were not allowed to call themselves revolutionaries, they were derided as hysterical and mad, and dismissed from the Convent. Olympe de Gouges, Manon Roland, and others were executed; Théroigne de Méricourt was declared insane; after the Revolution, the Code Napoléon openly required women to obey their husbands. Mary Wollstonecraft, who in 1792 published her famous *Vindication of the Rights of Women* (but who also wrote *Maria: or, The Wrongs of Woman*), was enthusiastic about the French Revolution, some of which she experienced in Paris, but finally had to admit that this uprising had made a detour around women. (Her daughter Mary, whose father was the anarchist utopian William Godwin, later married Shelley and wrote *Frankenstein*, the parable of a repressed creature that

turns against its creator—which can be interpreted
not only in Marxist but also in feminist terms.) Flora
Tristan (1803–1844), the grandmother of Paul Gauguin
(who never met her in person), returned to the "Décla-
ration des droits de l'homme" and pointed out that the
word *homme* mostly stands only for man rather than
human. In 1836, Herbinot and Madeleine de Mauchamps
founded the *Gazette des Femmes* where they constantly
published petitions campaigning for causes including
the reintroduction of divorce, the abolition of women's
duty of obedience, admission of women to universities
and all other institutions of education (after which the
*Gazette* was confiscated!). Mme Dudevant (George
Sand) was granted a divorce and care of her children
on the basis of an agreement with her husband that she
would pay him an annual pension of 500 francs. In 1825,
William Thompson published a book addressed to James
Mill, the father of John Stuart Mill, entitled *Appeal of
One Half of the Human Race, Women, Against the Pretensions of the Other Half, Men, to Retain Them in Political, and Hence in Civil and Domestic, Slavery.* James
Mill was of the opinion that women should be denied
political rights because their interest is "involved either
in that of their fathers or in that of their husbands."
The last chapter of Thompson's book was written by
Anna Wheeler, a zealous collaborator of the early socialists who, having read Godwin, Wollstonecraft, and
Jeremy Bentham, after twelve years of marriage left
her husband with her daughters Henrietta and Rosina
(who went on to marry the writer Bulwer-Lytton and
of whom Flora Tristan said: "This elite woman is one of
the numerous victims of the indissolubility of marriage
and so her first book is a long cry of anguish . . . Oh Lady
Bulwer, I pray that your husband's hatred may forever
be powerless.") and dedicated herself to the emancipation of women (Disraeli called her "very clever but
awfully revolutionary"). Wheeler introduced Tristan
to Robert Owen, to whom Tristan devoted a chapter

in her book *Promenades in London*. Some seven years before Karl Marx, in 1843, Tristan published *The Worker's Union*, her own call to all workers, both men and women, to found a union. In 1829, Scottish-born Frances Wright co-founded the Working Men's Party in New York.

The women's movement thus became more concrete, moving from general humanist demands to political ones; the struggle for human rights became the struggle for the right to vote. [Dorothy] Thompson was perhaps the first to recognize the issue of women's suffrage in all of its urgency, a question that had been more or less overlooked by Wollstonecraft, for example. The much-maligned suffragettes (from Denmark to Britain) must be credited, from the second half of the nineteenth century, with having identified suffrage as the means by which to achieve their other goals (such as the right to property). In 1867 [1869], Mill published *The Subjection of Women* in which he highlighted the legal disadvantages of women. In 1869, Léon Richer began publishing the weekly newspaper *Le droit des femmes*. In 1885, it was written into law that, just as in earlier times the king had only been "king of all Frenchmen," and not of Frenchwomen, in electoral terms, too, the word "Frenchman" did not include Frenchwomen. Incidentally, the attacks from opportunistic women writers (e.g., Marie Corelli: "one never sees any pretty women among those who clamor for their rights," 1907) and a sexist press were very much the same as what we see today. Rosa Mayreder (1858–1938), whose libretto *Der Corregidor* was set to music by Hugo Wolf, founded the General Austrian Women's Association. In her book *A Survey of the Woman Problem* (1905), she claimed, in a statement worthy of McLuhan, that the bicycle had done more for the emancipation of women than many other things because this sport broke through earlier notions of feminine gracefulness. In Austria and Germany the women's struggle was not as political as in Britain, for example. German women fought with the pen, while Emmeline Pankhurst's eldest daughter, Christabel, went to prison. In the second half of the nineteenth century, the rapid increase in the number of women beginning to write and the major role of women in Naturalism reflect an increased focus on women's issues: Bettina Brentano, *Goethe's Correspondence with a Child* (1835); Johanna Schopenhauer, the mother of the philosopher, who legally and personally fostered equality of the sexes in her salon; Luise Aston, *My Emancipation: Censure and Vindication* (1846); Ellen Key, *Misused Female Power* (1898 [1896]); Margarete Beutler praised free motherhood; Helene Lange, editor of *Die Frau*, founded the first high school for girls in 1885. These writing women were much influenced by Goethe, Schopenhauer, Nietzsche, and Romanticism—which explains their tame, reformist tendencies. In her essay "Ketzereien gegen die moderne Frau" (Heresies Against Modern Woman, 1899), Lou Andreas-Salomé opined that women should consider their literary talents as accessories. While such liberal trends prevailed in Germany, influenced by Romanticism, etc., and tailored to men, with women forbidden to belong to any political societies until 1907, the English Suffragettes were organizing militant actions and demonstrations, allegedly attended by up to 500,000 people. Emmeline Pankhurst introduced methods like hunger strikes, etc., to America where the "world's most dangerous woman," Emma Goldman, publisher of the journal *Mother Earth* and author of *Anarchy and Other Essays*, had long been combining the causes of anarchy and feminism (against the resistance of anarchist leaders like Peter Kropotkin). When, at a meeting of 600 people in 1915, she became the first person to publically explain the use of contraception in America, she was arrested and jailed for fifteen days. After her release, she gave this same lecture again and again, all over America, and was repeatedly arrested, turning courtrooms into tribunals where she publicized women's right to control their own bodies ("Women need not always keep their mouths shut and their wombs open!"). In the period 1907–23, women in various European countries were finally given the right to vote, which calmed the women's movement a bit, although it was just the beginning. In the 1930s, the feminist scene was somewhat revitalized, with the writing or publication of *Woman as Force in History* by Mary Beard, *Mothers and Amazons* by the Viennese writer Helen Diner, and *Sex and Temperament* by Margaret Mead. Individual calls to action published after World War II, like Ruth Herschberger's *Adam's Rib* and Simone de Beauvoir's *The Second Sex*, remained isolated protests. But the political movements and counterculture of the late 1960s gave rise to a very strong new women's movement with a very comprehensive consciousness.

So what does this rough, incomplete outline of the women's movement have to do with the title? It explains why the history of women in art is still so short and not as famous as that of men in art. For someone who is shut out of society, who is nonexistent in political life, can also not be existent in culture. Sexist questions like "Why is there no female Beethoven, no female Shakespeare, no female Michelangelo, no female Newton? No great artists and scientists, at least not so great, not so many?" are as repulsively cynical as if a Greek had asked "Why is there no great art and science by slaves?" or if an American were to ask "Why is there no great art by Black people? Why is there no Black Beethoven, no Black Shakespeare?" In any case, such remarks do not prove the "natural" inferiority of women, as the sexists claim. Until the appearance of Mahler, Schönberg, etc., Jews were often accused, as proof of their inferiority, of having produced no great musicians beside Mendelssohn. Seventy years ago, the Europeans were still telling the Americans they had produced no great artists, etc. Today there are great Jewish musicians, great American artists and scientists, just as tomorrow there will be "great" women in the arts and sciences.

Vera Pavlovna, the heroine of Nikolai Chernyshevsky's revolutionary novel *What Is to Be Done?* (1863), describes the situation of women in the last century precisely: "Almost all paths of civil life are closed to women. Many, almost all, are closed to us in practice, even those paths of social activity not barred by obstacles. Of all spheres of life we are crowded into only one, family life: to be a member of a family, and that's all." In 1953, Pope Pius XII was still declaring: "Every woman is called to be a mother . . . To this end the Creator has fashioned the whole of woman's nature: not only her organism, but also and still more her spirit, and most of all her exquisite sensibility." This is the formula that has been used for centuries to justify the exploitation of one human sex by the other as natural and God-given. Which is why, at the beginning of this century, "cultured women rebelled against the role of childbearing animal" ([Wilhelm] Stekel). And what kind of achievements can one expect from a creature whose existence has been reduced to biological reproduction, that has had no right to its body or its mind? In past centuries, when a woman sought to develop and use her mind, this was prevented as something unnatural and insane. Simone de Beauvoir: "Woman is shut up in a kitchen or in a boudoir, and astonishment is expressed that her horizon is limited." Virginia Woolf in *A Room of One's Own*: "any woman born with a great gift in the sixteenth century would certainly have gone crazed, shot herself, or ended her days in some lonely cottage outside the village, half witch, half wizard, feared and mocked at. For it needs little skill in psychology to be sure that a highly gifted girl who had tried to use her gift for poetry would have been so thwarted and hindered by other people, so tortured and pulled asunder by her own contrary instincts, that she must have lost her health and sanity to a certainty." When Sophie

Germain (1776–1831), one of the founders of mathematical physics, discovered her interest in mathematics, at a time when the École Polytechnique in Paris did not accept women as students, her family were so worried for her health that they denied her light and heating in her bedroom and confiscated her clothes to prevent her from studying. In her correspondence with Gauss she initially used the pseudonym Monsieur Le Blanc. At age fifteen, Mary Fairfax Somerville (1780–1872), author of *Mechanisms of the Heaven*, etc., happened upon the word algebra. When she began developing an interest in mathematics, her family and relatives tried to stop her and have her declared insane: "She wastes her time with reading, she sews as little as if she were a man, if she doesn't stop she will end up in a straight-jacket, etc." Only at age thirty-three, after the death of her first husband, was she able to study mathematics seriously. Sofya Kovalevskaya (1850–1891) had to enter into a marriage of convenience in order to be able study mathematics outside Russia as a private student of Weierstrass, etc., in Germany. Although one of her works was awarded a prize by the French Academy of Science, Weierstrass was unable to secure her a post in Germany. In Sweden, where she later became a private lecturer, she was vehemently attacked by Strindberg, who found it an intolerable act of mere gallantry that women be allowed to teach mathematics. And so on and so forth in the history of mutilation from which only extraordinary and extraordinarily few women managed to free themselves. The history of psychiatry offers many examples of stifled creativity pushing women into neurosis. After her husband's death, Dylan Thomas's wife, Caitlin, who was also a writer, published *Leftover Life to Kill*; the poet and revolutionary Louise Bryant, wife of the historian John Reed (*Ten Days that Shook the World*), died in obscurity of alcoholism; the poet Leonora Carrington, wife of Max Ernst, spent time in psychiatric hospitals; Zelda Fitzgerald, the wife of the author of *The Great Gatsby*, who also wanted to write, burned to death in an insane asylum; the poet Sylvia Plath, who was married to a poet, committed suicide; Elisabeth Packard; Ellen West; Marie Cardinal etc.— all bear witness to the torments of a creative woman in male society. Which is why only a male linguist would find it quirky that Zinaida Hippius, the uncrowned queen of literary life in St. Petersburg before World War I who wrote *The Eternal Woman* and tales of the temptations of bisexual attraction between both men and women, used masculine endings for Russian verbs and possessive pronouns. She used the masculine forms, as she explained to a friend, as a way of emphasizing, as a woman, her status as a human being. The fact that the artistic professions are known to us only as male nouns (author, writer, poet, sculptor, painter, musician, director, cameraman, etc.), that in French it is not even possible to make feminine forms of *auteur*, *écrivain*, *sculpteur*, *compositeur*, *peintre*, etc., the fact that we say *Forscher* and *Frau Professor*,[1] and that expressions like sculptress, camerawoman, painteress, poetess, etc., strike us as linguistic violations has everything to do with the fundamental violations in history, with the fact that still applies today: beginning in childhood, the creativity of women is misdirected and/or stifled.

Women's issues, then, are social issues. The causes of the position of women within society, defined in general terms by the division of labor in prehistory, by industrialization, etc., can certainly not be explained in biological terms. Having conquered elementary education, employment, financial independence, etc., by means of social struggles, some of which are now coming to an end, having reconquered their bodies, women will and must now conquer and reconquer their minds. For many women have unmistakably adopted men's idea of women, internalizing socially conditioned character traits (self-sacrificing, in need of protection, coquettish, etc.) as gender-specific and behaving as indoctrinated by the dictates of male civilization. Appeals to women's creativity are based on the assumption that it will not only change the image men have of women, but that it is also capable of bringing about fundamental social change (from the division of labor to motherhood, from social intercourse to politics).

If (as it is claimed) the oppression of women was historically necessary for the development of humanity, then the same now applies to their liberation.

EDITOR'S NOTE

I    *Forscher* is the German for scientist/researcher, in the masculine, while *Frau Professor* combines a feminine form of address with the job title in the masculine.

- - - - - - - - - - - - - - - - - - - - - - - - - - - - - - - - - - - - - - - - - - - - -

## MAGNA: POSSIBLE QUESTIONS

- - - - - - - - - - - - - - - - - - - - - - - - - - - - - - - - - - - - - - - - - - - - -

### 1975

= = = = = = = = = = = = = = = = = = = = = = = = = = = = = = = = = = = = = = = =

1.  What is the legitimation in your opinion, if any, for an exhibition of artworks by women shown collectively?

2.  Do you find an exhibition presenting works of female artists only, to be an isolation or a competition with men or something else?

3.  Is it possible through the presentation of such an exhibition to draw attention to the problems of women working in the realm of the arts and furthermore to the more general problem of the creative woman?

4.  The main part of culture and art brought forward to this day has been created by men. Is it possible to envisage that in the future women too will make an essential contribution?

5.  Will the conceptions, which men have created about women in his creations (novels, paintings, films etc.) as well as the characteristics of culture be changed by these cultural achievements of women?

6.  Could you envisage an exhibition to be arranged around the themes of religion, or sport, or mania, or the woman?

7.  Could you further envisage an exhibition in which the subject of mania will be presented to insane people only? Or the subject of women only to women?

8.     Is it possible to point out the problems of the woman in our society and her problems with herself through art?

9.     Provided that the experiences a human being goes through in the world and the perceptions which a human being undergoes in life are not only determined by his general being a human being, but also by more specific characteristics as for example that of sex, as for example to be a woman—will then the expressions of this human being not also express his specific experiences and perceptions?

10.   Are the rules and forms, expressed by his specific-personal perceptions objective? Or are they rules of the arts?

11.   Few women have up to now expressed themselves in the arts, can one therefore ascertain, that predominantly masculine contents have been formulated in the arts and female experiences have been neglected?

12.   Is it possible that there are no female rules of art (i.e. no male or female art), that there are however, male and female perceptions, experiences, visions, desires etc. as concepts of art.

13.   If one decides between good and bad art, between art and non-art, it is done according to criteria (rules), what are they?

14.   It is not a question of female art, but art produced by women, i.e. good and bad art produced by women.

15.   Is it possible that that which seems good or bad in the arts i.e. criteria and rules of the arts, are to be considered as male conceptions created by men?

16.   That art produced by women, may therefore change the conceptions about art, about the rules of art (that which is good or bad) etc.?

17.   Do competent people of the art world (i.e. critics, galleries etc.) recognize women artists working in an established art style (s.a. Op Art) more than a woman artist changing the conceptions of art?

18.   Has Gertrude Stein's literature, the literary model created by Stein been discovered independently of her feminine attitude?

19.   Do you believe that in order to be able to be an artist certain social and personal conditions are required and that society has so far denied them to women? (see Virginia Woolf "A woman must have money and a room of her own if she is to write fiction". I should like to remind of the many women writers whose careers have been destroyed because of their social condition (wife and mother etc. ) (s.a. Sylvia Plath, Zelda Fitzgerald, Elizabeth Packard, Ellen West)

20.   Does the society created by men not give more consideration to the requirements of men than those of women and accordingly to the cultural values, myths and moral systems etc. created by them?

21.   Does this society not restrict and stifle a woman's creativity (by the social roles forced on the woman)?

22.   Do you believe that the social function of the woman (home, children, mother, education of children etc.) restricts her creative forces? That she has to try and get away from these old conceptions? That she has to fight for a better social position? That art may help to bring these problems and perceptions to people's awareness?

23.   I believe that literature has produced great women writers who were completely aware of these feminine problems and who have also described them (f.e. Virginia Woolf, Katherine Mansfield, Gertrude Stein etc.). Why have there not been such artists in the field of fine arts of the past? How can they be imagined today—in theory?

24.   Do you believe that art is a class phenomenon, f.e. that of the bourgeois society and therefore there can be no art which intends to change the position of the woman in this bourgeois society?

25.   Do you believe, as some men do, that the development of art will continue without women or do you understand such an argument to be an outrageous defamation of the woman, a subjugation determining who will be or will not be qualified for the arts and who will be and will not be permitted to produce art?

26.   How come so many women are occupying themselves with the problems of this cultural condition, as we see in many exhibitions of women?

27.   Can we hereby detect an independence claiming its right?

28.   Should we try to be more open in our attempts to break out of the chaos of the compulsion of experiences levied on us by society and not to measure these representations according to methods which are patterned after art created by men?

----------------------------------------

## WOMEN AND CREATIVITY

----------------------------------------

### 1976

========================================

Before I attempt to offer some new ideas on the subject suggested by my title, some terminology needs clarifying. What do I mean by feminism?

I could view feminism quite simply as the women's movement dedicated to women's rights. But for radical feminists, the new feminism is not just the resurrection of a major political movement for social equality that brought us the vote around 1920, but a revolutionary movement that calls into question the most essential relations between the sexes, between parents and children, etc., the underlying pattern of power and subjugation, in order to implement egalitarian structures in a material way. For radical feminists, for example, a left-wing analysis is not radical enough because it fails to trace the structures of economic class society back to its roots. The new feminism is thus interested not in equality of the sexes as expressed in the term emancipation, but in overcoming all gender-specific roles and classifications. The goal of the feminist women's liberation movement—which like all movements has different camps that can be divided roughly into conservative feminism à la Betty Friedan, political feminism, and radical feminism—is thus to abolish the sex-specific class society that has consolidated itself over millennia and conferred unjustified legitimacy on the archetypal male and female roles.

In this light, men's fears are well founded, because it really is about taking power out of their hands. The fact that the emergence and success of feminism was positively influenced by changes in the material

environment (overpopulation, birth control, war fatigue,
industrialization, ecological crises, etc.) is beyond
doubt, as is the fact that professional organizations for
women have only been founded since the beginning
of the women's movement, that the entry of women into
so-called men's professions did not happen without a
fight, and that it is only recently that women have joined
together as feminists for intellectual, economic, emotional, political, and social purposes. For many women,
feminist groups, entirely new kinds of social experiment
with links to extended families and communes, were
a refuge in their wish to replace a mode of stylized self-
portrayal programmed by the consciousness industry
with a process of becoming someone who takes responsibility and learns from experience. These encounter
groups were an attempt to institutionalize the ideology
of sisterhood. In the press and in popular perception,
they earned feminists the reputation of being lesbians.
Using the term "militant lesbians," the male culture and
gossip industry sought to discriminate and invalidate a
fundamental change in society. Let me say in passing, to
rehabilitate one group of women, that the true essence
of female homosexuality is to be found not in a sexual
but an emotional fixation, so that the term "homoemo-
tional" would be more fitting for lesbians.

"And if nature is invoked," says Simone de Beauvoir,
"it can be said that every woman is naturally homo-
sexual."[1]

It must therefore be stressed that female homosexuality cannot be separated from the qualities reserved
for women in early history, when they founded the first
closed communities and cities in the era of matriarchy.
I will now repeat something I never tire of repeating:
that the so-called typical woman is a social construct
and that we do not know the nature of woman, meaning
that a lesbian woman may be more natural than a normal woman. We do not know the nature of woman, because there are hardly any places where civilization has

not established itself. And even where it has not done so, the woman as a bride is merely part of a system of barter, since marriages are negotiated between men. There, too, however, the cruelty and inhumanity of such bartering is perceived, so that mythology points to the rule of women, recalling a time when men had perhaps not yet sealed the antinomy, as Lévi-Strauss puts it, that always existed between their roles as takers of women and givers of sisters, making them both perpetrators and victims of their own barter. But here and now in the industrialized west, the external appearance and the behavior of women has been shaped by industrialization, by the division of labor, by private property, by the accumulation of capital, etc. If I may quote Charlotte Wolff:

> Men, too, are subject to and shaped by the constraints of civilization. But less so than women, because men have largely created this civilization according to their own needs, thus almost creating woman herself, as a product of this civilization, always required to become what men wanted. Lesbians have not been able to escape all these influences, but they have been far less touched and affected by the male dictates that have determined the character and emotional reactions of normal women. Does this make lesbians closer to the true nature of women? The female psyche has for centuries absorbed the idea that women are reactive and placid, and their emotional responses are tuned accordingly. This and similar demands have been accepted by women as inevitable necessities and as the leitmotif for their emotional repertoire. How, in this situation, can emotions caused by external constraints be distinguished from those that are truly natural? In behavioral terms, however, the following distinction can be made, for example: women do not call young men by animal names, but women and girls are often referred to as "hens" or, more tenderly, "chicks." Women are put into the same category as pets. And perhaps this is the source of the famous feminine mystique: you should not feel inferior as a person, but you must be feminine, i.e., inferior and object-like, in order to get a man.[II]

Yes, civilization and its mechanisms, especially the rules of language and thus the signifying chains of power, have, as Peter Weibel writes:

> made relations between the sexes into the complication where happiness appears as a crime and the partner as an accomplice in that crime. . . . Can you see the motley map of relations between

the sexes that announces things whose location is not only uncertain, but whose mere existence is nowhere to be found? The archetypes of animus and anima, assigned by C. G. Jung to man and woman respectively and postulated as psychological givens, were not something he actually found, derived instead from books in which the prevailing established networks of meaning were stored. The antagonism of animus and anima, man and woman, reason and nonsense, is an expression of imaginary lexical relations. Woman embodying the principle of the soul, as an elf, and the birds, belonging to the animus, as reason—can you hear the rusty old chains of word association rattling?[III]

On the subject of birds, attentive visitors to the exhibition I organized in Vienna will have noticed that birds figured as symbols in the work of several women artists, putting them in the field of anima/woman, and not in that of animus/man as Jung claims. Perhaps it has become clear, then, that the women's liberation movement wants more than just to liberate women, and that Herbert Marcuse is right when he says:

> I believe the Women's Liberation Movement today is perhaps the most important and potentially the most radical political movement that we have, even if the consciousness of this fact has not yet penetrated the Movement as a whole. . . . Secondly, the Movement operates within a class society—here is the first problem; women are not a class in the Marxian sense. The male-female relationship cuts across class lines but the immediate needs and potentialities of women are definitely class-conditioned to a high degree. Nevertheless there are good reasons why "woman" should be discussed as a general category versus "man." Namely the long historical process in which the social, mental and even physiological characteristics of women developed as different from and contrasting with those of men.

Here a word on the question whether the "feminine" or "female" characteristics are socially conditioned or in any sense "natural," biological. My answer is: over and above the obviously physiological differences between male and female, the feminine characteristics are socially conditioned. However, the long process of thousands of years of social conditioning means that they have become "second nature" which is not changed automatically by the establishment of new social institutions. There can be discrimination of women even under socialism.

In patriarchal civilization, women have been subjected to a specific kind of repression, and their mental and physical development has been channeled in a specific direction. On these grounds a separate Women's Liberation Movement is not only justified, but it is necessary. But the very goals of this Movement require changes of such enormity in the material as well as the intellectual culture, that they can be attained only by a change in the entire social system.[IV]

So much for the subject of women, the situation of women, and feminism.

Now for the second part of my title. A number of people think creativity is an umbrella term that covers art, that creativity already includes art just as the term "furniture" includes "armchair." This, too, is a misunderstanding on the level of words rather than concepts, since the relationship between art and creativity is far from clear in conceptual terms. But to respond to the schoolteachers on the level of their homework essays: I want to take a feminist look at the relationship between art and creativity, and not between mathematics and creativity, or anything else, in order to show, perhaps, that certain social preconditions are required for the creative process and that these preconditions come from an institutional power, so that an altered definition of creativity can alter the existing definition of art, etc. Rather than writing a lifeless tautology on the blackboard, my aim is to inscribe a dynamic process into the living brain, in the remote hope that feminist art—and that is not women's art, but art by conscious women—might change the social situation in favor of a more human society. Art is just one part of overall human coexistence. Art alone as the expression of an individual consciousness is certainly not able to change its surroundings (to overcome oppression, to implement wishes, etc.). Creativity operates not only on abstract levels like space and time, not only with the tensions between different materials etc., but also against social norms. And maybe that is the terrible thing male artists fear about feminist art, objective formalism, the prospect of art being embedded, via general forms of creativity (as they find expression in other disciplines, from mathematics to sport), in a social matrix, because then stimulation, doping the senses with drugs and alcohol in the service of the market, along with the cult of madness and genius that is all too often compatible with healthy business sense, will be unmasked as fake narrative.

One needs to recall the origin of the word creativity, namely creature, the living entity, the being that creates and can create (with all its biblical allusions), to recognize the importance of the notion of creativity for women. If the creature is denied creativity by the power of social conditions, then the living entity is denied an essential aspect of its life; because creativity is an inventive reshaping of one's surroundings by individual forms whose values are anchored in one's own field of experience. The content of creativity—those liberating steps out of what is prescribed, out of imposed experience, that reordering of the world according to one's own needs—will by definition not be shaped by general and universal rules of philosophy, science, and art. Creativity means experiencing and making for oneself, creativity means consciousness. Creativity does not necessarily contain art, then, especially not art governed by rules. So creativity—as an essential aspect of every creature—is of huge importance for women's consciousness.

Academic research, too, admits that the desire for creative expression is among the most elementary needs of all human beings and that it is present in all children and only disappears in the course of their development. How it is lost sheds light on the mechanisms by which a society's ruling class taps into the potential of the other classes, be it that of women or that of workers. In children, creativity is not a gender-specific trait. Two-year-old boys are not said to be more or less creative than two-year-old girls. But the mechanisms of socialization soon begin to take effect, and the non-gendered capacity for creativity becomes specific. In the opinion of many educators, children should behave like other children of the same sex and age, or in accordance with these people's ideas of gender-specific and age-specific behavior.

[Abraham H.] Maslow (1958), [E. Paul] Torrance (1964), and others have shown that this attitude impedes the development of creative potential. Boys with feminine interests (e.g., painting) are ridiculed and thus pushed into other fields of interest. And this although [Viktor] Löwenfeld (1962)[v] has shown that children who were able to fully exploit their creative abilities in painting mature into creative adults, even if they were later raised with strict regulations and discipline. In girls, on the other hand, taking pleasure in solving scientific problems etc. is viewed as masculine and undesirable. This means that girls often do less well than boys in tests that call for scientific-creative thinking, but that girls achieve the same results when the hostile attitude to scientific problems is altered by discussions with teachers and parents. That cultural norms present an unfavorable situation for women with scientific interests is not only shown by the lives of individual mathematicians like Sophie Germain, Mary Somerville, Sofya Kovalevskaya, etc., but has also been verified by [Lindsey R.] Harmon as generally valid in our own times.

In this phase, gender-specification can also impede men and their creativity, but as they develop further, women and their creativity are always more impeded during their passage through the institutions, while men and their creativity are granted sufficient possibilities, and it is especially important that it is specific institutional careers that foster creativity.

I won't subscribe to the false idealism that all humans come into the world equally gifted. But no psychologist would deny that every infant has the prerequisites for creative behavior. Since few people develop these gifts into adulthood, however, it has been suggested that creativity is lost in the course of the ageing process (through development per se, as [Lawrence S.] Kubie cynically claims). That a few people do retain it, that it is lost by a specific social class, that it is lost mainly by female infants—these facts must be attributed not to development per se, but to concrete social mechanisms— mechanisms that benefit those in power. Because if a worker were fully creative, would s/he be able to bear working on the assembly line?

As we can see, the gender-specification of creativity is not natural but institutional. Looking back at such gender specificity over the centuries, in the Gothic period linearity was considered male, whereas in the Rococo the male sexual type was depicted with female attributes, etc. This constant switching of traits into the male or female field reveals that these traits cannot be explained in biological terms but that they are instead implemented institutionally, socially. In this light, creative behavior appears as the expression of a position of power that can bring forth conditions allowing it to adapt the surroundings to its own needs. In this context it is also worth noting that modern creativity research came into being in 1950 in the United States in a situation of competition with the USSR, as the Soviet education system was producing more capable people than the American one. Since it had been found that parents of creative children are mostly not authoritarian, giving their offspring a large degree of freedom, and that typical creative traits also cause school pupils to have serious problems with discipline, finding it hard to obey rules and stick to routines, America's allegedly non-authoritarian school system was expected to be superior to the Soviet system. But it transpired that the Soviet education system is in fact very open at early ages, becoming stricter only later when creativity has already become established, whereas the American system is not democratic, instead applying a misunderstood notion of democracy with the aim of making people more similar than different. And precisely such striving for conformity and mediocrity, for the mental and emotional well-being of normality, are widely named as the greatest obstacles to the development of creative potential. Creative children try to work independently, on their own; rather than helping someone else, they would rather do something themselves; their behavior is therefore "unsocial"—something that is much at odds with the everyday pressure to conform within American society. This situation between the USA and the USSR is repeated metaphorically in the relation between men and women. Being raised as a woman, with all the female attributes the child is trained to acquire, impedes creativity, while being raised as a man is more likely to promote creativity, self-reliance, unsocial behavior, positive self-image, etc. What Flaubert called *l'éducation sentimentale* is conducted by power for power, serving to legitimize the securing of privileges and the fulfilment of needs. Worse still, the fallacy of gender specificity, that seeks, for example, to deny women abstract thought and to deny men empathy, also locates creativity within the horizon of the man, doing so as an instrument in the dialectic of the battle of the sexes.

To substantiate our assertion, the theory of this essay, *that the qualities demanded of women by society are the opposite of the qualities of creativity,* let us now go into a little more depth and detail. If we examine a list of creative behaviors, the contradictions are clearly visible.

What, according to academic consensus, characterizes creativity?

fluency of thought
flexibility
variability of ideas
verification
restructuring
rational control
ability to identify and
    transfer relations
ability to identify function
ability to identify form of
    communication
self-expression
strongly developed ego
    function
critical
socially introverted
leadership qualities
no adaptation to social
    demands
unconventional
unsocializable
asocial

aggressive
ability to bear conflicts
    arising from percep-
    tion and action (respon-
    sibility)
ability to bear a feeling of
    uncertainty
preference for complex,
    ambiguous stimuli
tolerance of frustration
energetic
willingness to be con-
    trolled by what one
    wishes to create
autonomous
association
rational productivity
self-assurance
positive self-image

Let's put this to the test:

Which mother can and may by controlled by what she wishes to create? If she left her child and husband, would she not be called a bad mother?

Which wife is permitted to have leadership qualities and be socially introverted, unconventional, unsocializable, even asocial, when she is supposed to conform to the demands of society, to cultivate social contacts, etc.?

Which girlfriend is allowed to have a positive self-image, devoting her time exclusively to realizing one of her own plans?

Which mistress is allowed to be autonomous, to show initiative?

Which woman is allowed to be at all self-expressive, critical, aggressive, to possess fluency of thought, if she is not to be robbed of all womanliness?

Let us sum up what we have said so far to get a conceptual handle on the relationship between women and creativity—a relationship that has been given little thought and whose articulation has often been all the more mangled as a result.

On the concept of CREATIVITY, the literature says the following:

Creativity is the ability to produce compositions, products or ideas of any sort which are essentially new or novel, and previously unknown to the producer. It can be imaginative activity, or thought synthesis, where the product is not a mere summation. It may involve the forming of new patterns and combinations of information derived from past experience, and the transplanting of old relationships to new situations and may involve the generation of new correlates. It must be purposeful or goal-directed, not mere idle fantasy—although, it need not have immediate practical application or be a perfect and complete product. It may take the form of an artistic, literary, or scientific production or may be of procedural or methodological nature.[VI]

To use a more German term, one might speak not of *Kreativität* but of *schöpferische Fähigkeit* or *schöpferisches Denken*. But the religious-philosophical background of these German terms made me prefer KREATIVITÄT, also for its links to creature, living thing.[VII]

The notion of creativity in its current psychological meaning was introduced by the American [J. P.] Guilford

in 1950. Guilford's results were inspired, however,
by the 1945 book *Productive Thinking* by German
researcher [Max] Wertheimer, so that creative thinking
can also be thought of as productive thinking. As this
clearly shows, *creativity in our culture is always directed toward a product*. The PERSONAL CREATIVITY
attributed to those whose greatest creative product is
their own life or the life of those close to them, and the
SOCIAL CREATIVITY attributed to those who shape
social relations in creative ways, are valued less than
the PRODUCTIVE CREATIVITY of those who by their
own individual thinking arrive at new results in the
field of science or art.

We must keep this in mind as we proceed to examine the creative achievements of women in our culture.
For although it is beyond doubt that women display
great amounts of creative behavior in shaping social
and family relations as they tackle everyday life, thus
possessing high levels of both personal and social creativity, they are generally credited with lower levels
of productive creativity and if we consult the history of
our civilization, we find nothing to contradict this view.
But we must contradict those who seek not a social but
a biological cause. For as the values assigned to the
different types of creativity show, such an explanation
fails to do justice to the social position and duties of
women in our society. These values are blind to the
necessary connection between the low productive creativity of women and their high levels of personal and
social creativity. From this specific socially determined
creativity of women that consists in keeping house,
raising children, keeping husbands emotionally satisfied, etc. (i.e., in fulfilling the many and varied demands
made by the social complex of the family, demands
that prevent them from freely and forcefully deploying
their productive creativity), male chauvinism and sexism have derived the theory of the biological inferiority
of women, a prejudice that was not only combatted in

122

Freud's time by Freud himself, but which is still going strong today. In 1962, research by T. W. Taylor showed that men are given higher ratings for creativity than women, a result that does not change when men and women of equal intelligence are assessed.

These contradictions go deeper than the level of prejudice and sexist ideology, however, lying in the structures and norms of our social system itself. Anthropologists have told us about societies that differed from ours concerning the social position of women, and even what was considered masculine and feminine, with things viewed as masculine in our society discredited as feminine and vice versa. I do not wish to speak here of matriarchal cultures, only to point to women's socially specific characteristics and the fact that these characteristics can and do change from culture to culture.

Margaret Mead confirms this claim that the sexes are subject to value judgments in every culture and form of society, but she stresses that certain socially determined traits and behaviors are attributed to both sexes. Rather than physical differences being the point of departure for the position the sexes occupy within the life of society, the behaviors shaped by society are attributed to one or the other sex in different ways.

This does not rule out changes in the way certain behaviors are judged within one and the same society. While certain traits are attributed to one sex from the outset, these same traits may become associated with another sex within the same social order. Mead sees these traits not as gender-specific but as universally human. Only a specific study can provide information about the outstanding traits of the people in question and how to differentiate between the sexes. Mead notes that in primitive societies, very different behaviors are observed sometimes in men and sometimes in women, meaning that gender roles are not strongly differentiated.

Among the Tchambuli, for example, the women are energetic, unadorned, and busy, working hard for the upkeep of the tribe, while the men like to gossip, cry easily, and practice dance steps while wearing jewelry. Here, the men are the so-called weaker sex.

Among the Arapesh, both women and men are what we would call feminine: women and men do the work together, during childbirth men are connected to the women via rituals that express pain in the form of moaning and screaming.

Among the Mundugumor, both the men and the women are aggressive, hostile, and argumentative. Motherhood is rejected, pregnancy reluctantly tolerated. With these descriptions of tribal differences in male and female behavior, Mead supplied material that refuted the view of essential differences between the sexes supposedly founded in biology.

Our society has fixed, specific ideas about what is female and male, ideas it idealizes and practices. Not just that a violin serves as a symbol of the female body due to its curved form: curves in general are automatically considered womanly, just as linear and geometrical compositions are considered manly. Ernst Bloch in *Traces*: "woman, around whom there is always a seething, even a phosphorescence, is, like music, the highest as well as the most undecided thing in the world." For our aesthetics, male characteristics can be derived from the streamlined functionality of weapons: straight lines, arrows, no ornament, etc. The opposite of this, e.g. the Baroque, counts as effete and effeminate, so that it is women, not men, who are likely to be called "Baroque." Mead's examples show that the distinction between male and female attributes is specific to each culture or society, but this shouldn't be allowed to obscure the fact that each culture and society "naturally" views certain qualities as female or male. If we look at just a short list of professions and activities, we can predict that most of our fellow human beings would describe mechanics, engineering, politics, banking, architecture, mathematics, chemistry, physics, etc. as men's professions—and housekeeping, healthcare, childrearing, show business, dance, etc. as women's professions.

They would also describe various behavioral traits as "male," such as: active, tending toward generalizations and principles, concentrating on objective matters, self-assured, aggressive, entrepreneurial, fearless, brusque, coarse in language and demeanor, boastful, earnest, desiring power, able to separate the physical and emotional components of love—and other traits as "female" such as: sensitive, modest, passive, submissive, following fashion and public opinion, gracious and gentle, empathetic and sympathetic, emotionally moved, interested in literature, protective, focused on personal matters, interested in family relations, irritable, impulsive, intuitive, altruistic, caring for helpless and abandoned people, crying, etc.

But it is not just average fellow human beings who think and feel, as one might say, that a man's life is "creating" while a woman's life is "being." Precisely the above-average pillars and creators of culture are responsible for such thoughts and feelings.

Nietzsche
Man shall be trained for war, and woman for the recreation of the warrior, all else is folly.
Thou goest to woman? Forget not thy whip!
The woman must obey and find a depth for her surface. Surface is woman's soul.

Strindberg[VIII]
Let man fear woman when she loveth: then maketh she every sacrifice, and everything else she regardeth as

worthless. Let man fear woman when she hateth: for
man in his innermost soul is merely evil; woman, however, is mean.

Nietzsche
Thus would I have man and woman: fit for war, the one;
fit for maternity, the other.
The best belongs to mine and me; and if it be not given
us, then do we take it: the best food, the purest sky, the
strongest thoughts, the fairest women.
You creators, you higher men! Whoever has to give birth
is sick; whoever has given birth, however, is unclean.
Ask women: one gives birth not because it gives pleasure. The pain makes hens and poets cackle.
You creators, in you there is much uncleanliness. That
is because you have had to be mothers.

Kierkegaard
There is an adjective that describes this crucial quality in woman. However great the difference may be
between woman and woman in various respects, this
quality is required of every woman. No abundance
hides, no poverty excuses, the lack of it. . . . This quality is the art of making a house a home. . . . We hereby
make the great admission to woman, that it actually
is she who shapes the house.

Strindberg
For the woman, you know, is the man's child, and if she
is not, he becomes her, and then the world turns topsy-
turvy.
Can you now grasp what woman is? Woman, through
whom sin and death found their way into life.

Otto Weininger
The enormous increase in dandyism, as well as homosexuality, in recent years can only be a consequence of
the greater femininity of the present era.

There is only "platonic" love. Because any other so-called love belongs to the realm of sows. There is only one love: it is the love of Beatrice, the worship of the Madonna. For coitus there is the Babylonian whore.
In W "thinking" and "feeling" are one, undivided, for M they can be separated.
Woman lives unconsciously, man lives consciously.
Woman has no original consciousness, only a consciousness bestowed on her by man.
W has only one class of memories: they are memories connected with the sexual drive and reproduction.
Woman is amoral.
Woman is false.
Absolute woman has no self.
Woman is indeed totally anti-social.

Baudelaire
Why does the man of intellect prefer prostitutes to society women, although both of them are equally stupid?

Theodor Roosevelt (in a speech made in Chicago in 1899)
We do not admire the man of timid peace. . . . The man must be glad to do a man's work, to dare and endure and to labor; to keep himself, and to keep those dependent upon him. The woman must be the housewife, the helpmeet of the homemaker, the wise and fearless mother of many healthy children.
Etc., etc.

In such valuations, every society ostensibly and supposedly starts from nature. It has always been the nature of woman or nature per se that destined women for the role of mother and all of their other roles. As a result, women are assigned "natural" qualities. No society is willing to see that it is not nature but society itself that assigns values, attributes roles, names qualities. John Stuart Mill was probably the first to point out, in his book *The Subjection of Women,* that so-called nature plays a dubious and noteworthy role in definitions of the essence of womanhood. In his view, the problem of woman hinged on this false view of nature. Correspondingly, serious research has found that female and male characteristics are not sexually specific, but merely expressions of a will to power. Mathias and Mathilde Vaerting attribute the formation and development of male and female traits solely to the position of power achieved by the respective sex among different peoples. Male and female behaviors, they conclude, are not innate but learned.

These insights may sound obvious, but in the brains of men they fall on barren ground. Otto Weininger driveled about the inborn feeblemindedness of women—the same Otto Weininger who, in his foreword to Arnold Schönberg's theory of harmony, counted the composer alongside Maeterlinck and Strindberg, another pathological misogynist, among the outstanding minds of his time.

Our main theory, then, is this: when we compare the list of qualities that characterize creativity with the list of qualities that our society demands of women, we see that the two are largely incongruent or incompatible.

EDITOR'S NOTES

I    Simone de Beauvoir, *The Second Sex* (1949).
II    No original source could be traced that exactly corresponds to the German translation of the quote in VALIE EXPORT's original text. This is a translation from the German.
III    The original German source for this quote could not be traced.
IV    From the lecture "Marxism and Feminism" given at Stanford University in 1974. Published in *Women's Studies* 2, no. 3 (1974), 279–288.
V    Individual texts cannot be clearly assigned to the authors and dates mentioned in this section; the dates probably do not necessarily relate to first releases, but follow-up editions.
VI    John E. Drevdahl, "Factors of importance for creativity" (1956).
VII This paragraph is included here for the sake of completeness, but it makes little sense in English. The German *schöpferisch* translates as creative, and the English creative/creativity similarly suggests the

religious notion of a creator (*Schöpfer* in German), as does the word creature. A classic example of the way loan words may take on different meanings in the language/culture that borrows them.
VIII This quotation is in fact not from Strindberg, but also from Nietzsche. We do not provide evidence of the easily accessible citations in this list, some of which show minimal deviations from the originals.

- - - - - - - - - - - - - - - - - - - - - - - - - - - - - - - - - - - -
## BODY CONFIGURATIONS
- - - - - - - - - - - - - - - - - - - - - - - - - - - - - - - - - - - -
### 1976
= = = = = = = = = = = = = = = = = = = = = = = = = = = = = = = = = = = =

Since 1972 I engage myself in drawing, photographing, filming and by making actions with the representation of body positions as expressions of internal conditions, represented in nature as well as in architecture, as adjustment, insertion, and addition to the environment. The parallelism of landscape and mind, architecture and mind is mediated by the body, on the one-side because this parallelism has its origin in that extreme confrontation between body and mind, and on the other side because the body is coined as the landscape, the landscape is coined by space and time, e.g. under more scrutiny, the arrangement of its parts as there are trees, stone, hill, etc. are such a coining. The arrangement of the members of the body are the body positions, they are coinings or else expressions of internal conditions; those analogue between scenic and bodily dispositions, those common forms of coinings are used as a projection screen for expression since the beginning of pictorial art: external configurations in the landscape, or in the picture (which becomes a landscape in this way) as expression of internal conditions. Therefore landscape is as much liked for a subject in painting (and in filming) as the body. Out of this reason one talks of "scenic moods." The landscape represents one mood in the same way as a body position expresses a mood. The expression of emotions does not only happen facially. A condition of the mind, firstly, can be expressed by the configuration of scenic parts, secondly by the configuration of body members—and thirdly, this is the innovation of my work, by body members in the landscape.

On a second level, the expression manifested by certain body positions is analysed in its historic coining. The paintings of the past have unintentionally left an archive of body postures. These are most expressive and of great informational value for examining the emotional condition and mythologies of their time. It becomes evident these frozen bodily movements demonstrate a canon, a doctrine. By reportraying these postures I attempt to extract the expression, to make it independent; by assembling these postures with contemporary materials I attempt to lay their expressive content open. At the moment I am dealing with feminine postu res viewed from the feminist standpoint and I use material from the feminine circle in order to thaw the standardization of the female body gesture and body language and their connected function of the female body in our culture.

-------------------------------------------------

## EX TEMPORE

-------------------------------------------------

### 1977

=================================================

In the year 1968, I was occupied with the Expanded Cinema, for example *Cutting* and *TAPP und TASTFILM* (TAP and TOUCH FILM). In the fourth part of *Cutting*, I shaved the chest hair of a nude male body (Peter Weibel) in such a way that a hairless line was developed. The pubic hair was cut with a pair of scissors. In 1971, I used a naked female body (Erika Mies) for the same action.

A small mechanical portion of the cinematographic pasting press is called body cutter. This part stands in direct relation linguistically to what I do to the human body: I cut, that is, the body is treated as if it were film, celluloid, as an expanse. The marks on this expanse are the hairs—just as writing is formed of signs on paper. In the first part of *Cutting*, screens of paper and cloth are sheered. In consequential sequence, the surface of the body is now used as a plane for projection and agitation, a screen made of skin to be used as a place for signs. Skin tracks and body drawings are developed. The body is the material for this painting. It is not, however, merely a theater for marks of a sexual, social, or rather nature (a medium for signals which could be additionally formed by clothing and body movements). The body itself is also a sign, one which our culture has heavily trimmed and made taboo. I have, therefore, always understood bodily analysis to be analysis of society as well because the signals (the communication function of the body) are not only individual but are socially codified. One can take as an example the embarrassment of having to raise one's hand to go to the bathroom in school (which I never wanted to do and therefore suppressed my urge). This alone demonstrates how the body irritates social communication when it makes itself known. The needs of the body form the language of the forbidden literature, one which embarrasses or oppresses mankind. The public announcement of so to speak intimate proceedings is denied by the institutionalized code, public speech, the sanctus. The natural enemy of an abstracted social system is the use of the human body with its concrete needs for interpersonal communication and perception. Society uses the body to fit people into its mythology and structure by equipping them with signs of belonging to sex, class, territory, breed. It is actually through the body that we are associated; this process of socialization deforms not only our awareness of our bodies but awareness itself. The cinematographic-theatrical work with the body is the expression of such reflections. The everyday world in which I situated my *TAPP und TASTKINO* elucidates the connection between body and politics (witness my 1974 action, *Body Politics*).

"Film and breasts" is a known and profitable equation, the victim of which is naturally woman since feminine traits in our culture are an object for male sexuality. I broke the boundaries of socially approved sexual communication by allowing, in the lingo of film, my body projection screen/projection screen body (breasts) to be handled in public by all. The breasts as an object of voyeurism will be withdrawn from the "society of spectacle." The society of spectacle will be deprived of the breast as an object of voyeurism, forcing women to become things. Furthermore, in this situation, the bosom is no longer the possession of one man. Rather, the woman attempts to independently define her own identity through free disposal of her body. This is the first step from object to subject. This first "true women's film," as I called it in 1968, is a mobile film (straßenfilm) as well.

The problem of emancipation of women, the step from object of a culture to subject, is strongly bound to the problem of sexuality which men have solved in their way. In as far as the woman's solution is still overdue, the women's movement is a struggle to form a basis for a new culture. In *Genitalpanik* (Genital Panic, 1968), I utilized actions pants, a pair of pants which leaves the vagina and pubic hair free for inspection. Wearing these pants, I forced myself through the narrow rows of a movie house thereby attempting to expose the nature of a culturally determined symbol and salvage the sexual characteristics from estrangement from meaning.

The body is not only a means of social integration, it is also integration itself, it is not the medium of expression and presentation, it is expression and presentation. Thus, a line may portray more than aggression, or anger, or tenderness. A line can itself be angry, aggressive, or tender. This is the same case with the body. The body is also the *notation* itself. It is the national institution which tattoo signs and symbols into our minds. The body is also sign and icon. It is tattooed from beginning on. *Body Sign Action* (1971), a tattooed garter placed on my left thigh, is a reminder of that fact (an attribute of feminity not determined by women). It is also a reminder that the future holds the duty of self-determination for woman.

In my 1971 action *Eros/ion*, emanating from the aforementioned problem of notation, I use the body as carrier and transferer of tracks, for a semantic analysis. I rolled over a large plate of glass, then up on a large pile of broken shards, and finally on a white paper canvas. The tracks which the broken shards caused bloody on my skin canvas, left tracks resembling an informal painting on the paper canvas. The glass shards became signs, in that they were reduced to the simple tracks of an aesthetic process upon the body. That is the warning of rented pain. I furthered this analysis in 1973 and used myself as an example for many by rolling first in water and then upon ice.

In the action *Kausalgie* (1973), the body shade of a man is burned into a large wax plate with a blow torch. I lay naked within the outline of this body shadow. My body warmth changes the bed of wax slowly; the image of my body flows into the cold wax. Slowly I free myself from the motionless state and begin to move on the borders of the shadow which are, nevertheless, bound with electric wires which injure me. I roll over the electrified boundary whereby the wax dampens. I free myself from the waxen model, from the—the adipocere (corpse wax)—tangible rigidity of the man. The traces left behind are covered with hot lead which slowly cools: my replica remains, the traces are covered. On the morphology: in *Eros/ion*, a paper canvas conveys body tracings, in *Kausalgie* a canvas made of wax.

In *Hyperbulie* (1973), I enter a corridor braced with wire bearing a current fed from two batteries. I move through the corridor. Every contact with the wire hurts me causing me slowly to fall to the floor, however, I conquer the pain and reach the end of the corridor. In the closed room of society which rules and parcels out all human energy with painful barriers, man, blanketed with the stigmata of the social matrix, becomes a tamed animal.

In *Homo Meter* II, a street action in which I have a loaf of bread tied to my stomach, passersby should take pieces. I view this action as a continuation of my examination "on mythology of the Homometer processes" (1971). Especially in that the bread is easily interpreted symbolically, the bread serves as a symbol for motherhood just as cereal grain for seed and life, the bread gives my body the appearance and aspect of pregnancy—a psychological experiment with symbol and behavior.

In *I Am Beaten* (1973), I lie on the floor, a mirror above me which, so to speak, visually doubles my existence. Near me on the reel of a tape recorder the words, I am beaten, persist and, in such a way, that

I also constantly said these words. My being is auditorily doubled. I am beaten: through myself? The situation in which man can only see himself as the image of all things and is himself mirrored in all things, this attitude is mirrored here. Since 1972, I have concerned myself graphically, photographically, and actionistically with the representation of body posture as an expression of inner realities. These are depicted in both nature and architecture, as an adaption, interpolation, as well as environmental cause. The parallels between landscape and spirit, architecture and spirit (see my expanded movie *Adjungierte Dislokationen* [Adjunct Dislocations], 1973) are meditated upon through the body.

Since 1973, as a second corollary, I've been examining body postures as a manifested expression of historical stamp. The paintings of the past have unintentionally left an archive of body postures. These are most expressive and of great informational value for examining the emotional condition and mythologies of their time. It becomes evident these frozen bodily movements demonstrate a canon, a doctrine. By reportraying these postures I attempt to extract the expression, to make it independent; by assembling these postures with contemporary materials I attempt to lay their expressive content open. At the moment I am dealing with feminine postures viewed from the feminist standpoint and I use material from the feminine circle in order to thaw the standardization of the female body gesture and body language and their connected function of the female body in our culture.

---

## INVISIBLE ADVERSARIES

---

### 1977

==========================================

For a long time, I have been working on artistic representations of physical states, on what the body feels when it loses its identity, when the self eats its way through tattered skin, when steel casings keep the joints from flexing and the exhausted identity is fastened to modern mythomania using steel nails.

My body actions since 1968 and my drawings show the loss of communication and withdrawal from language that occur when the body rejects the norms of expression—the body reduced to empty space, hiding its wounds, a mere element of a lifeless sculpture (photographed body configurations in nature and architecture). Space experienced via the body and via a consciousness deformed by constraining structures (my short films). Increasingly, I have had the idea and the wish to work with the social structures (strong current) and norms (mutilation) of life—these invisible opponents, the dictates of meaning—turning them into a metanoia of cinematographic images (sketches for films, 1972). As a result of my frequent, intense discussions with Peter Weibel, he became my collaborator.

Mannerist gestures of a deviant and crumbling identity, when a person wishes to escape the restrictive structures and damaged forms of communication. Female body language that gets the message while refusing behavioral roles: fear, heavy as a lead plate, forces the skin to slide down the glass walls of telephone booths, a deep lesion when the distinction between observer and observed breaks down, when the image in the mirror injures reality with its sonic idiom (breaking glass). When the mirror image presents a mask that she has already left behind. Viewing oneself as a stranger, deeply yearning for a last identification.

When sentences are spoken that are devoid of general meaning, when all the lights are switched off, opening up the dark abyss behind, never to return, when the lost one cannot part even in tears, when children become enemies, then it is no longer a matter of testing out a theory of existence, but of salvaging individuation, naked being in its reality of mindless destruction (even at the price of isolation).

A communication that conveys hate is resisted by a behavior of vulnerability. When dreams and sleep, the storage bed of unconscious thoughts, become a battleground where all preexisting images begin to be torn to shreds, then in the rents we see the real picture, the drama of human self-realization: in search of a home, the hangman's noose tightens round your neck.

- - - - - - - - - - - - - - - - - - - - - - - - - - - - - - - - - - - - - - -

## ASPECTS OF FEMINIST ACTIONISM

- - - - - - - - - - - - - - - - - - - - - - - - - - - - - - - - - - - - - - -

### 1980

= = = = = = = = = = = = = = = = = = = = = = = = = = = = = = = = = = =

Before discussing Feminist Actionism, we must look briefly at Actionism. What is Actionism, what are its origins and goals?

### *ACTIONISM*

Actionism is a movement in the visual arts which developed from Abstract Expressionism, Art Informel, Action Painting, and Happenings, with its earliest source in Dada. Actionism has been a major influence on performance art and Body art.

This historical background already suggests some characteristics of Actionism: Dada's criticism of society and art, Art Informel's expression of psychic or even automatic contents, Body art's focus on the body. In his 1965 essay, "On the Possibilities of a Non-Affirmative Art," Peter Weibel wrote:

> Regression to the material as the general principle for the development of the graphic arts during the last decades signals a method of perception that aims through one body to another body and takes place in this world rather than in the realm of the fine arts' false semblances. Centered in the body and in this world, the body is the artistic medium. The human body itself is the work of art, the material.[1]

The equation material = body typifies Viennese Actionism, which anticipated Body art and certain forms of performance art. In other countries, there are forms of action in which it is not the body but things that serve as material—automobile tires, fat, electronic devices, etc. Using the body in actions corresponds to using these other materials (as, for example, in Beuys's actions). In any case, a specific awareness of material characterizes Actionism, the drama of material acting in and against itself.

> The free handling of artistic material also freed material of its old, repressive meanings and made new, prospective meanings available. Freed, extended material extends awareness and frees people from old and restrictive meanings and conditions.[2]

Regardless of whether the material consisted of the body or objects, in reality the drama of material was a drama of meaning. Material was the stage for various meanings, not only processing and integrating people's experiences, but also activating their ability to experience and sharpening their awareness of the meanings the material called forth.

> A way of thinking that sets material free and keeps it free and a use of artistic material that sets thoughts free and keeps them free aims at creativity as the significant form of experience and thus of life. The activity freed by the creation of new sign combinations in the artistic process is not only a self-affirmation but, what is more, a new self-creation.[3]

Given the way some of the key terms—"body," "development the meaning of the material," "self-affirmation"—relate to the following passage, it is easy to understand why Feminist Actionism has become so important for feminism.

> But it is not only through the sentiment of personal dignity that the free direction and disposal of their own faculties is a source of individual happiness, and to be fettered and restricted in it, a source of unhappiness, to human beings, and not least to women. There is nothing, after disease, indigence, and guilt, so fatal to the pleasurable enjoyment of life as the want of a worthy outlet for the active faculties.[4]

## FEMINIST ACTIONISM

Just as "material thinking shall free human products from their thing-character," one might suggest,

Feminist Actionism shall free men's products, that is, women, from their thing-character. Just as action aims at achieving the unity of actor and material, perception and action, subject and object, Feminist Actionism seeks to transform the object of male natural history, the material "woman," subjugated and enslaved by the male creator, into an independent actor and creator, subject of her own history. For without the ability to express oneself and without a field of action, there can be no human dignity.

Human history is without dignity because it is solely male, a story of masculine activity. As long as women have not escaped and been liberated from male history, the history of humanity has not fulfilled its claim of humanity. "The million tears which have flowed over canvases of pain, fear and despair are the Niagara Falls of women's servitude."[5]

Feminist Actionism shares the artistic sources of Actionism, but has other, new ones as well. Just as Abstract Expressionism has some roots in the psychic automatism of Surrealist artists like Yves Tanguy, André Masson, Arshile Gorky, and others, Feminist Actionism can be traced back to Tachism and Surrealism, which, in its techniques of automatism, articulates the repressed and unconscious. Women artists of the Surrealist movement will therefore be given special consideration. Those familiar with their works can find the insignia of a mutilated enigma in their automatic messages: under iridescent waters, bleeding fish dream of birds. It is part of the pathology of female repression that female desire is still often expressed by the inhibition of travesty—this is true even for Feminist Actionism, hence the Surrealist traces. A further source of Feminist Actionism is Action art itself (Happenings, Fluxus, music and dance performance, etc.), but its primary source is the history of female experience. A specific style of representation is connected to a specific content, women's experience. Women's history is made visible to give women their future. For if, as Brecht said, "the repression of women makes itself invisible by assuming enormous proportions," it is necessary to show this repression. "The blood trail inscribed in us all with invisible ink as sex-specific taboo"[6] is the material of Feminist Actionism. And there is no lack of material; it is abundant.

## BLOOD TRACES[7]

There is no need to evoke a psychology of the sexes when role behavior and forms of life created by socialization and education provide more suitable testimony. The battle of the sexes has always already been won by men. The fondness playwrights have for this theme characterizes the exploitation as exploitation of a corpse, for women have already lost entirely different, more important struggles before even beginning their fight with men. The defeat in house and home is only the last in a series of battles lost, from the right of inheritance to the right to a name. World conquest, the acquisition of continents by force of weapons and force of intellect—those were the decisive battles, the domain of men. Women's marital struggles, which so delight male playwrights, are only a very poor substitute for men's maritime battles. Clytemnestra shows that women, lacking any real political power, have their only power in bed, the weak power of refusal. In conjugal battles, in battles between brothers and sisters, women are toy soldiers. Their uniforms are made of the despair and bitterness which result from the fact that they are acting the drama of deprivation in the dressing rooms of the great men of state rather than on the stage of world affairs. Women were deprived of more than their human rights in matrimony. She, who had no right to her name, how could she have had a right to herself and her abilities? The Austrian poet Friederike Mayröcker's "Text with Continents" substitutes "grandfather, grandmother," for continents. Those are the true inscriptions in women's military cemeteries, the memorials of great defeats.

Let us read the inscriptions on some of these tombstones: Dorothy Wordsworth, the unusually gifted sister of William Wordsworth, sacrificed herself for her brother's career. Her escape from dependency was a private literary career instead of a public one: her letters. She remained an amateur so that her brother could become a professional. The price: internal conflict, self-destruction, confusion about herself which showed in her stammering, among other things.

Jane Carlyle was married to Thomas Carlyle, who said himself that his wife had sacrificed her talents in order to help make his career.

Caitlin, wife of Dylan Thomas and also a writer, published a book after his death significantly titled *Leftover Life to Kill*.

Louise Bryant, poet and revolutionary, wife of historian John Reed (*Ten Days That Shook the World*) died forgotten, having escaped into alcohol.

The tragedy of Zelda Fitzgerald, who wanted to publish "a work of her own" at any price and died in a fire in a mental hospital.

And what price did Virginia Woolf pay for "a room of her own?" Did she find the space she needed in the waves in which she drowned herself?[8]

Sylvia Plath: her poems—"death, rage, blood, cuts, deformation, pain, suicide, torture, mutilation"—her words. Was her suicide self-punishment?

These women poets' words—cuts, deformation, blood—can also be found in Feminist Actionism, but not as reflections of sadomasochistic needs, of abnormal drives. They are historical scars, traces of ideas inscribed onto the body, stigmata to be exposed by actions with the body. If they are interpreted as pathologies of self-hatred, poor self-esteem, sorrow, subjugation, or even identification with the oppressor, then

they are part of the truth of women's history. And the
truth is such that only very few women are ready to
scrape away the veneer concealing it. Many prefer
the illusion of meaningless glamour to the sovereignty
of fully exposed pain and to the *painful energy of
resistance.*

But the long history of woman's constant "double
bind" (G. Bateson), which is both within herself and
with men, has caused deep injuries, disorders, estrangement to the point of alienation in the feminine psyche.
Women have long preserved and sealed off their damaged identity under the emblem of pain's deformations.
To prevent submission from becoming women's eternal
destiny, the wounds of actual historical submission
to men must be unhesitatingly revealed. This avowal,
this *confession publique*, will free women from the ills
men have inflicted on them. Only knowledge prevents
contagion. Doesn't the best indictment, the true victory, come from withstanding one's own merciless self-
accusations?

## SURREALIST TRACES

Feminist Actionism is an objective artistic movement,
a movement in the morphogenesis of art. It is exactly
what male colleagues refuse to admit. The male adversaries of Feminist Actionism, whether critics, artists,
or museum directors, ignore the fact that Feminist
Actionism is not just a remake of 1960s Actionism, or
just an independent extension of it. By virtue of its
inclusion of new sources (Surrealism and kinetics) and
its use of new media (video and film), Feminist Actionism is an objective historical force in its own right
within a broader artistic context.

Part of its historical force derives from the revival
and deployment of certain aspects of Surrealism and
Art Informel. The works of women Surrealists will
therefore be more closely examined, as these are, so

to speak, "first papers," immigration papers, preliminary identification cards.

The surreal material fetishism of Meret Oppenheim was especially effective: her fur-covered breakfast china of 1936, her demon with animal head of 1961, her dress and furniture designs (e.g., the table with bird legs, 1939). The illusions and reversals of her masks and objects (which anticipate aspects of Pop Art) sensitize the feminine imagination and show feminine creativity and sensitivity. The fetishlike character of many of her objects points to repressed sexuality and tells of the contradiction between inhibition and desire, between development and limitation, a contradiction which only by disguising itself escapes the taboos of our civilization. The meaning suggested by material fetishism later becomes the associative link in the material drama of action.[9]

Meret's concern with fauna symbolism, which feminist Actionists Carolee Schneemann, Lygia Clark, Rebecca Horn, VALIE EXPORT, Nancy Wilson Kitchel, and others carry on,[10] is also found in Dorothea Tanning's Surrealist works and in Isabelle Waldberg's airy sculptures made from willow branches or metal rods. Waldberg's work especially anticipated Art Informel's dynamics of movement, for example in *Le dernier rôdeur* of 1945, or *The Swallow Built Herself a Cage with Her Wings*.

The works of Dora Maar, Marie Laure, the poet and painter Eileen Agar, Sophie Täuber-Arp, the poet Valentine Penrose, Grace Pailthorpe (automatic drawings), the poet Mirna Loy, the poets and painters Kay Sage, Leonora Carrington, Maria Cerminova, Valentine Hugo, Varo Remedios, and others[11] are especially revealing of women's self-definition. Three Surrealist heroines deserve special attention: Nadja, the protagonist of Breton's novel; Bataille's companion, Laure (*Les écrits de Laure*[12]); "Aimée," subject and case (of self-punishment) of Lacan's thesis, *De la psychose*

*paranoïaque dans ses rapports avec la personnalité*.[13]
Kay Sage's picture *Tomorrow Is Never* (1955) shows a
landscape of rigid scaffolds veiling a female figure
under amorphous scarves and dresses. This escapism of
the feminine self is also expressed in one of Dorothea
Tanning's pictures, *Happy Birthday* (1942), in which
she stands before a flight of open doors, roots of trees
dangling from her body. Mimi Parent's picture *The Age
of Reason* (1961), subtitled *An Imaginary Self-Portrait*,
shows the outlines of a black figure. Only her extremi-
ties (hands and feet) are white, her raised hands struck
by lightning—a woman electrocuted by the unremitting
contradiction of the double bind. A bird with folded
human hands on a fence of glass fragments marks *The
Dangerous Hour* for Maria Cerminova Toyen (1942).
But this bird has huge wings and an eagle's beak. It
is not C. G. Jung's feminine bird of Anima. The dog
breaking out of the wall of Château Lacoste (title of her
1946 picture) is a fox with sharp fangs holding a bird
in its paws. The Animus-Anima relation is interpreted
aggressively. Fauna, nature, rooms, the sea, ordinary
things become the motifs of a disturbed balance in the
works of women Surrealists. They announce the end
of the *Galas of Silk* (a 1962 picture by Toyen showing
empty silk dresses) to the women and men of our century. The preeminence given to the unconscious, understood as the historical as well as the individual locus
of oppression and repression, has helped thematize the
historical oppression of women.[14] In serving revolution,
Surrealism also served feminism, which male Surrealists did not realize at all, and even female Surrealists
did not fully comprehend. The revolt of the unconscious
included the insurrection of women against their own
lack of consciousness and revealed the repression of
women: significantly, a 1930 publication by the androgynous Salvador Dali was titled "La femme visible."[15]
Feminist Actionism has further developed many Surrealist techniques and motifs, such as automatism,

fetishes, mannequins, eye symbolism, dreams, chance, transformed objects, provocations, blasphemy, sexuality, etc.

## ART INFORMEL

The appearance of feminist content in Art Informel follows logically from the emergence of Informel from automatic Surrealism in the works of André Masson, Georges Malkine, Arshile Gorky, Wols and others. Feminist content can be conveyed in even the most abstract Expressionism. Here, Niki de Saint Phalle and the Austrian Maria Lassnig, pioneers of Art Informel and Action Painting, will be examined more closely. Maria Lassnig's abstract-expressionist drawings are self-expressions, as their titles indicate: *Selbstporträt als Zitrone* (Self-Portrait as Lemon) (1949), *Wörthersee-selbstporträt* (Wörthersee Self-Portrait) (1949), *Informelles Knödelselbstporträt* (Informal Self-Portrait as Dumpling) (1950–51), *Primitive Selbstdarstellung* (Primitive Self-Representation) (1956–58), *Tachistisches Selbstporträt* (Tachistic Self-Portrait) (1961), etc. The titles in her later naturalistic period are: *Thiwahn-Selbstporträt* (Thiwahn Self-Portrait) (1970), *Lady im Stuhl* (Lady in a Chair) (1970).

However, this series of self-portraits, which has lasted through decades and styles, is not an expression of "narcissism and self-love" as Lassnig puts it,[16] but rather of the "loneliness of the critic." This loneliness of women, their withdrawnness, is viewed critically. "Women are especially prone to withdraw into themselves, and still are. Thus it became their strength."[17] For Lassnig, Art Informel's problem of boundaries, of surpassing the canvas's edge, is always a psychic challenge "to walk the borders of the extended self."[18] Lassnig's graphic fusion of self and surroundings (lemon, lake, couch), with its reification and objectification, its incorporation of the outside, actually expresses

an extreme and constantly self-challenging body awareness. Her 1950 *Exkremente des Kolibri* (Excrements
of a Hummingbird) the title of which recalls Surrealist
pictorial symbolism soon to become her own. Lassnig's
Art Informel paintings and drawings and even her later,
more realistic drawings, share Feminist Actionism's
fundamental concern with the identity of the body:

> The introspective experiences of 1949 were already "body-
> awareness" drawings. I have not since abandoned introspection,
> whether the period was Art Informel, abstract or partly realistic.
> When I tired of representing nature analytically, I searched for a
> reality I could possess more fully than the outside world, and so
> encountered my physical shell as the most real reality. I had only
> to become aware of it in order to project its image with its center
> of gravity onto the canvas. One can become aware of one's body
> through pressure, tension or overtaxation of one of its parts in a
> certain position. This awareness may manifest itself in sensations
> of pressure or tension, of fullness or emptiness, etc.[19]

Simone Forti, a dancer and performance artist who
first appeared in the 1970s, has deepened this experience of body awareness and her art in kinesthesia, body
sensation.

> Ann Halprin taught me that our medium is our bodies and their
> movement possibilities. The way we work with our bodies depends
> on the way we want to work with them. Thus, we have developed
> certain problems. One technical problem concerned suddenly chang-
> ing the position of the spine or running quickly and changing the
> position of the spine in various ways in succession. It is impossible
> to improvise completely because it is impossible to predict exactly
> how body form will change given its measurements and the change
> of torque in space.[20]

The tension of the female body which Lassnig projected
on the canvas's surface is transferred to the legs and
dance floor in Simone Forti's work. Here, too, aspects of
locating the center of gravity play an important role.[21]

It is remarkable how similarly women of various
cultures and times describe becoming aware of their
bodies: Lassnig's *Introspektive Erlebnisse* (Introspective
Experiences) (1949), Carolee Schneemann's kinetic

theater of the mid-1960s, Simone Forti's kinesthetics of the 1970s.[22]

Niki de Saint Phalle's aggressive pseudonym[1] already reveals the tural morphology she investigates in her highly abstract works of Informel. Her first tachistic action was to fire a gun at paint-filled bags suspended in front of a canvas. The bags burst, spraying the canvas with color. The sexual aggressivity of this early voluntaristic identification with male symbols (the gun as phallus, the spurting colors as ejaculation, the chase, the kill, the bags as scalps, etc.) revealed hatred as the actual motivation. In her 1973 film, *Daddy* (script written with Peter Whitehead), she furiously demolishes the phallocratic kingdom and its symbols. She discloses her previous identification as a forced collaboration, a desertion stemming from fear of the adversary's superior strength, and reveals the actual source of her work: refusal. Parallel to this refusal, she also resurrects female symbolism. Examples would be the large female sculpture *Hon* (1968) in the Stockholm Moderna Museet (made together with Tinguely), which can be entered through the vagina, and the creation of numerous large and small colorful buxom female figures named "Nana."

Yayoi Kusama's 1964 environment *From the Driving Image Show* [*Driving Image Show*] was also animated by this shifting identification: banal objects of women's daily life such as chairs, tables, gloves, make-up tables, paravents, and plates are painted white and covered with handsize phallic cloth structures. The artist stands beside a mannequin and brushes her own hair as well as the mannequin's. Marina Abramovic used this hair brushing motif in her action *Art Must Be Beautiful, Artists Must Be Beautiful*, brushing until she drew blood. Not only the title but the action itself shows the shifting identification which was already described in Niki's case, and which also characterizes most of Abramovic's actions: the ambivalence

151

of conformism and refusal, of suffering and revolt. Women's adaptation to the masculine ideal of beauty, even if it is so deeply internalized that women experience it as their own, is already soaked with the blood of self-abandonment and identity loss. Insofar as the tide displaces this problem of adaptation onto the male artist's problematic of identity, the action acquires a further social dimension: the artist himself very often adapts to the mechanisms and ideals of society, very often loses his identity, which would consist in a challenge to that society. He repeats in his sphere what woman must do in hers: he adapts. And the artist, himself oppressed, becomes an oppressor. To be sure, the dialectic of adaptation and refusal, as they derive from mutual identification, is in danger of appearing as an affirmation, in spite of its cynical style.

Lygia Clark (born 1920), who from 1959 to 1964 constructed aluminum "animals," made objects which were to produce body awareness in the viewer. The process of the "internalization (*Verinnerlichung*) of the object" began with women Surrealists' fetish objects. They selected material in accordance with their own psychic sensations, so that it would evoke analogous sensations in the viewer. In Clark, this has led to an unusual anthropomorphization of objects: her objects become bodies intended to activate people as bodies.

She built *Organische (Organic)* and *Sensorielle Masken (Sensorial Masks)* and *Dialog (Dialogue)*, an object exclusively for eye contact between (male-female) pairs. The sensorial mask, which is worn on the head, reflects the wearer's eyes in small, roundish mirrors. *Dialog* connects endlessly intersecting gazes. The gaze dims as soon as the distance in the constructed object, which the partners wear like glasses, decreases too much. The machine also permits the wearer to find his own gaze in the other's, at the appropriate distance. *Dialog* is not to establish a (technical) order but a human connection, enabling the exchange of equal and unequal. It is interesting that in one presentation, a man operates the mechanism of this *Dialog*/machine, which was built at the high point of the May 1968 events in Paris.[23]

The search for consciousness separate from a language permeated by male culture, in which female consciousness can only articulate itself in a mutilated way, had already moved Gertrude Stein to create a theatrical form in which the action is not held together and developed by the usual meaning of words. Thus her first play (1913) poses the question: *What Happened: A Five Act Play*.[24] It is not by chance that the word "happening" appears here for the first time, since the play uses a new equivalence of elements to find a new syntax, a language which escapes rational, phallocentric discourse. Stein's other plays also have this instantaneous quality and are imagistic like the happenings of the 1960s.[25]

Dominance of the body, sensuality, repetition, and illogical events characterize Ann[II] Halprin's pieces. Her total theater includes the spectator in the communication so that "a process takes place that develops out of the moment the interaction with the audience." In *Rites of Women* (1961), kinetic communication becomes a ritualized presentation which hardly distinguishes between life (spontaneity) and art (planning).[26]

Ann Halprin's work shows that the sources of American Feminist Actionism and performance art not only include Surrealism, Abstract Expressionism, Art Informel, and Happenings but that there is a strong connection to dance, ballet, and singing as well. Dancers Trisha Brown, Simone Forti, Yvonne Rainer,[27] who had all studied in Ann Halprin's workshops for experimental dance, and performance artists Laurie Anderson, Julia Heyward, Tina Girouard, Jana Haimsohn, among others, demonstrate this.[28] However, the younger generation has focused its work solely on their own bodies, experiences, and pasts. The physicality of dance is well suited to body-centered Actionism. Dance and ballet, art forms traditionally reserved for women, offer a

natural starting point for revolt, for the changed role
of women. Standardized feminine movements, condemned to gracefulness, which had no other purpose
than pleasing male eyes and obeying male ideals of
fragility and sexual charm, are decoded and liberated.
Bodies produced by years of discipline actually come
alive and move according to their own laws. Trisha
Brown, Simone Forti, Yvonne Rainer, and others create
examples of feminist dance actions, of Body art which
escapes phallocracy.

"Body motorics, automatism, the labyrinthine en-
gravings of Action Painting mark an attempt at counter-
training around the mid-1950s. They express a central,
individual stance."[29] Feminist Actionism arose from
this movement as much as from Surrealism. "By the
end of the 1940s, Jackson Pollock had already begun
to develop further Mallarmé's 'écriture corporelle,'
by transferring his own movements to the canvas."[30]
The artists of Feminist Actionism have taken écriture
corporelle beyond the canvas, written it onto their
own bodies, and posited their own individuality against
the culture around them.[31]

The abstract expressionist concept that any material
can become content if it is transformed by a sufficiently
active and gesticulate style of painting is adapted to
the body in Carolee Schneemann's work. She links the
equivalence of materials which characterizes Action
Painting and early Happenings to the idea of an equivalence between gesture, text, music, etc. Again, a certain
style, a certain intention, and a future-oriented concept
of art and female experience become the source of
inspiration: the kinetic theater of Carolee Schneemann.
In a series of photographs, *Eye Body* (1963), she regis-
ters her bodily sensations, how random fragments of
her memory and personal elements of her environment
are superimposed on her perception. The photographs
show her naked body as a body environment collage
with furs, lamps, paintings, snakes, water, plastics. Her

well-known play, *Meat Joy, Kinetic Eye-Body Theater* (1964), staged in Paris, London, and New York, was a visual and tactile extension of this project. As the title *Meat Joy* suggests with its allusion to "meet joy," the play deals with a conspiracy against the evils of asceticism and develops the feminine dream of a warm, sensual, meaningful, fulfilled life. During the Paris production, it almost came to an untimely end when a man tried to strangle Schneemann during the action. Schneemann's theater of body movement in space is an investigation into and clarification of the feminine sphere involving group experiences. Her texts and theatrical actions are full of sexuality; for her, the obsession with flesh, the carnal celebration of all kinds of material is joyful. By freely admitting self-defined feminine sensuality, other women artists' sexual martyrdom becomes cheerful aggression. But as her 1976 performance *Up To and Including Her Limits* shows, Carolee Schneemann's concerns reach beyond sexual freedom for women. Since 1974, she has taught feminist art history and fought against male culture as a theorist. In her essay "The Pronoun-Tyranny," she points out the extent to which male mania has influenced our culture, so that only the masculine is used in proverbs, phrases, compounds, etc.: mankind, chairman, man of the moment, man on the spot, to be one's own man, a man of letters, cameraman—an endless collection. Woman is the "missing gender," and not only in the grammar of everyday language.[32] Schneemann writes: "As long as we are not able to give language back to ourselves, we will not be able to see up to what extent our integrity has already been deformed."[33] Her rejection of male language has led to an insistence on physical experience and sensation, paralleling the linguistic perception that "man" is the disconnected suffix of "woman," and "male" the disconnected suffix of "female."[34] Estrangement from male verbal language becomes mute female body language in the younger generation of feminist Actionists: VALIE EXPORT, Hermine Freed, Ulrike Rosenbach, Friederike Pezold. In VALIE EXPORT's work, fear of the damage male language does to women is extended to an analysis of the damage done to the body language of women, as evidenced in paintings by men.[35]

Alison Knowles has likewise contributed to a feminization of male culture through her imaginative and innovative Fluxus pieces, happenings, collages, and performances since 1962. The work of Eva Hesse (1936–1970), which anticipates much of Arte Povera, is significant, even unique, for the creation of a feminine material language. With the title of her 1966 exhibit, *Abstract Inflationists and Stuffed Expressionists*, she takes a definite stand. The artist, who was born in Germany but lived in the United States, created material images (*Materialbilder*) with figurations resembling breasts and nipples. For her sculptures, she preferred limp, flexible material—rope, chain, string, net, hoses, crumpled plastic sheets, hanging accidental forms, organic tree structures. Another exhibit was titled *Eccentric Abstraction* (1966). The concern with nature, which goes back to Sophie Täuber-Arp's work, culminates here in the use of natural materials or materials close to nature. Whether non-natural objects are inserted into nature, as in Clark's work, or whether parts of the body are interpolated into nature in drawing and photography, or whether natural elements are substituted for parts of the body, as in the work of Rebecca Horn, VALIE EXPORT, and Barbara and Michael Leisgen, uncultivated nature is always a challenge to feminine self-determination.[36]

Just as the female body serves men as a "musical" instrument—see, for example, Man Ray's 1924 *Violon d'Ingres* in which Kiki's naked back is painted like a violin—music itself is a masculine domain. Charlotte Moorman (USA) has tried to shake the rigid frame of masculine conventionality with her numerous actions.

In performing with her breasts bare or playing a cello of pink ice (Bremen, 1978), she shows that masculine culture is merely gestural. Christina Kubisch (FRG) also protests against music as male eros insofar as her musical performances ridicule it by using undisguised phallic or vaginal symbolism and metaphors. After all, the pleasurable musical instrumentalization of women hides much more insidious instrumentalization.

## WOMAN AS INSTRUMENT: FEMININE MORPHOLOGY

> When, however, we ask why the existence of one-half the species should be merely ancillary to that of the other why each woman should be a mere appendage to a man, allowed to have no interests of her own, that there may be nothing to compete in her mind with his interests and his pleasure; the only reason which can be given is, that men like it.[37]

In the search for a feminine morphology, that crucial project in the exchange between art and feminism, one does well to keep Harriet Taylor's words in mind. Since women's history is stamped in this way, it is small wonder that the morphogenesis of art showed and still shows traces of that history.

Goethe's sister, Cornelia, serves as an example of what happens when women no longer want to live for men. Passive failure in all feminine roles in order to no longer be a woman necessitates the renunciation of life itself. If a woman no longer wants to live for men and the functions they assign her—sex machine, birth machine, cooking machine—then there is no life for her, or, like George Sand, she lives as a man (masculine clothing, masculine name, masculine habits). The ordering of the feminine role and the demands she did not want to satisfy broke Cornelia Goethe. She rejected her child, refused her feminine sexual role, became frigid and depressed, and stayed in bed until she died. Cornelia Goethe's life was without joy, dignity, and happiness because she refused to be the means for other

people's ends. She wanted to live according to her own
will, rather than submitting to the will of others, to
live for herself, as men do. But this was so drastically
denied her that lack of joy and meaning finally deprived
her of life itself. Her fate was lifelessness. But the fate
of women will not always be submission; being a woman
will not mean being lifeless. Male rule will not succeed
in destroying all identity.

The first revolt: the mirror motif indicates the
search for a new and autonomous feminine identity,
free from the so-called "natural" characteristics men
have imposed on women as their so-called "inner
nature." Changing and refusing roles are some of the
cures.

## "THE CLINIC OF TWO MIRRORS"

Self-will and self-assertion form the type of what are designated as
manly virtues, while abnegation of self, patience, resignation, and
submission to power . . . have been stamped by general consent as
pre-eminently the duties and graces required of women.[38]

The mirror motif is intended to end alienation, the
alienation which even Harriet Taylor, who named
and explained it, was forced to endure. Her essay,
"Enfranchisement of Women," was attributed to her
companion, the philosopher John Stuart Mill, and
male executors suppressed her collaboration on *The
Subjection of Women*.

The mirror, which so few men and so many women
carry and consult in a sad routine of control, dis-
plays both feminine appearance and feminine tension,
women's constant, insecure need for reassurance. Thus
in many works of art, the mirror represents more than
narcissistic mirroring. It is ambivalent, a symbol of
broken dreams and utopias, of broken identity, but also
of hope, the retrieval of fragments of a tortured soul,
the summons to independence. The return of repressed
emotions, the longing for self are expressed in mirror

rites. The magical significance of the human body and the magic of mirrors, pleasure and prohibition of narcissistic mirroring are united in the "mirrored" work of art.

Since this section is named after a poem, the following works may be seen as parts of it.

"The Clinic of Two Mirrors"[39] is inhabited.

Alexis Smith's mirroring tears or tear mirrors confront the world with the history of woman. There could be no more authentic articulation in this epoch of a paradigmatic breach between the sexes, in which for the first time women conceive of a consciousness of their own, and so lose many of their traditional, conditioned pleasures (compare also VALIE EXPORT's actions *I Am Beaten* [1973] and *Bewegungsimaginationen* [Movement Imaginations, 1974–75]). These works articulate the pleasure of resisting, of tolerating and overcoming pain, of overcoming others' resistance, seeing and feeling the loss and smiling about it. For one thing is certain: if women depart from official male history, the independence of their feelings and wishes makes them a departing majority.

In *Mirror Check* (1970), Joan Jonas destroys the *closed* image of feminine objecthood. Standing naked on a stage, she slowly mirrors her body in the spotlights. As the audience watches, she fragments the female body, decomposing it into many tiny images, partializing the fetish "woman" and its symbolic-voyeuristic connotations. The monogamous male glance is diverted, vainly seeking sexualized "areas," sex-bits. Jonas attempts something that exceeds the male's alienated powers of comprehension: she is absorbed in the pleasure of looking at herself.[40] Lilli Dujurie rolls around in front of a video monitor. The eye of the monitor supplants men's voyeuristic glances and shows women to themselves. In *Class Pieces, Life Slices* (1977), the Brazilian artist Jole de Freitas smashes seven mirrors with a kitchen knife. The object of her inverted

narcissism is the mirror as "daily criterion of women's
sexual struggles." (Cf. the mirror in the fairy tale
of Snow White.) Visitors to the exhibition *Künstlerinnen international* (*International Women Artists*)
in Frankfurt's Kunstverein, 1977, were to grind the
remains of mirrors, the abysmal milestones of super-
seded history "with their shoes and disperse the
dust and fragments by carrying them into the city
streets.")[41]

## THE MUTE LANGUAGE OF THE BODY

To find one's own words.[42]
The House of Disease, Forbidden Rooms.
One is not allowed to go into all rooms. . . . From the beginning,
I decided on the chamber of the solar plexus and the closet of
the hands. I meticulously avoid the hall of the bellies and also the
bosom room.[43]

The revolt against male language has already been
identified as one source of Feminist Actionism.
The work of women artists like Annette Messager,
Gina Pane, Friederike Pezold, Yvonne Rainer, VALIE
EXPORT, and Carolee Schneemann in developing a
women's body language has been discussed. It was
not possible to "find one's own words," because words
belong to men. Nor was it easy to find one's words in
body language, because it too was mainly occupied
by male fantasies. The oppression of women is reflected
in male ideals of women. The history of images can
therefore be connected with the history of women.
Both are a history of oppression.

The Middle Ages scornfully classified the graphic arts among the
low arts, because they were prelinguistic, and because of a religious
prohibition of images. Therefore, the oppression of women as especially low beings, who could be reduced to mere physicality, can
only be seen in the context of the history of images. Because whenever more freedom was promised from the lifting of the prohibition
on the image to the tempting pictures in advertisements more freedom became more oppression for women precisely because those
images promised more freedom for men. Women's history, more so

> than men's, is the history of physical oppression. And because part
> of this physical oppression is accomplished through images, because
> they participate in the deformation and standardization, the deper-
> sonification of the female body as merchandise, the presentation of
> the female body is immensely important.[44]

VALIE EXPORT's drawings and video work examine the historical meaning of certain female poses. By deforming women into objects,

> men have succeeded for thousands of years in bringing their idea
> of eroticism, sex, beauty, their mythology of power, strength and
> severity to sculptures, paintings, books, films, dramas, drawings,
> etc., and influencing everybody's consciousness. . . .I try to unmask
> this humiliating expression by drawing or arranging these female
> poses anew and inserting them into our present social environment
> by using materials from the current feminine environment.[45]

The distortions of anatomy, the unnatural dislocations in the darkness of male-imagined transfigurations, as seen for example in classical painting, show the degree of women's deformation. A feminine body language that no longer follows the rules of advertising and classical grace is needed. Everything from female sex characteristics to female body functions can be used as material for free artistic articulation. Thus, a new time and space will be inscribed with women's body language, an age where for the first time, human beings are at home. The echo of the breasts and the belly reverberates not only in the mass media, but also in the valley of hope. Beginning in 1973, Friederike Pezold has developed a "new, living sign language of gender based on principles of anatomy, geometry and kinetics." It consists of a series of photographs and video pieces with titles such as *fußwerk* (foot work), *scham werk* (pubic work), *nabel werk* (navel work), *mund werk* (mouth work), *arm werk* (arm work), etc. and is rooted in her *Sinnliche Architektur* (Sensual Architecture) of 1969, in which "the female body is the measure of all things."

In her photographs and videos, she thinks about her body geometrically, using lines and primary forms.

She selects camera angles and body parts that may be applied in this sign language. By cutting and rearranging photographs, body parts such as eyes, nostrils, breasts, and thighs become decorative patterns—a body language which her medium (photo, video) geometrizes. In her videos, which are partially composed of drawn-over film script or picture book pages, she abstracts the sex-specific areas of her body to make partly Informel, partly geometric signs. The sparseness of her movements before the camera induces a meditative state in the viewer.

Rebecca Horn, whose work shows strong Surrealist and Informel traits, has also produced pieces which may be discussed in terms of a feminine body language. In these pieces, with their fan and mask extensions of the body, she examines the relationship between the body and civilization: body ornament as law of civilization, the body as object of socialization. She writes about her 1973 action, *Bleistiftmaske* (Pencil Mask):

> My head was bandaged with 3 vertical and 6 horizontal ribbons,
> and a pencil was attached at each intersection. The pencils were
> 5 centimeters long, forming a three-dimensional profile of my face.
> I moved my head rhythmically in front of a wall. The pencils reg-
> istered my movements on the wall with increasingly concentrated
> lines.[46]

These works, as well as those of Lyn Hershman, Ulrike Rosenbach, and others, connected persona and performance, not merely to adjust images of women or show the attitudes inflicted on them by culture and mass media. Rather, they deconstructed the cultural coding of women, from art history to mass media. For example, in photographs, films, performances, or even life itself, Lyn Hershman played on images of women's roles. Feminist theory and performance in the 1970s used the performer/theorist herself to represent and shatter different socially coded female identities. Interestingly, a strong post-Informel movement has appeared with the continued development of Actionism in Feminist

Actionism. Informel and lyric abstraction, which had seemed dead after Pop Art, were reanimated by Feminist Actionism and indeed to such an extent that general interest in abstract expression was renewed and (some) men have also used it in their work.

## ECHO OF THE BREASTS

Friederike Pezold showed her action *Brustwerk* (Breast Work) during the Styrian Autumn event of 1973. She distorted her naked breasts by wrapping them in transparent tape and pressing them with her hands, compressing them or pulling them apart. By destroying perception, she both stressed the givenness of the breasts as objects, and approached a self-determined body language representation.

VALIE EXPORT's 1968 *TAPP und TASTKINO* (TAP and TOUCH CINEMA) captures the violence of the patriarchy through acts of self-chosen demonstration. In this "expanded cinema," the code with which she counters the frustration induced by the media is quite evident. In the long run, however, this campaign of women's sexual self-determination, which clearly demonstrates the shift in the relationship between the sexes, occurs at the expense of the woman Actionist. Art—any art— needs its breaks. The event was repeated several times and then stopped. In the future, the goal of "getting out of the established trade as an object of exchange" (Luce Irigaray)[47] should be pursued much more radically.

In Varo Remedios's picture, *L'agent double* (The Double Agent) (1936), there is a wall of breasts, an early testament to a "society of the spectacle," in which women's breasts serve as voyeuristic objects of the profitable identity of film screen and breast. In this first true film for women, the breast is withdrawn from such exploitation. It is no longer exposed to view, but only to tactile communication. By having control over their bodies, women attempt to determine their identity independently: the first step from object to subject.[48]

## ECHO OF THE BELLY

Kirsten Justesen and Jytte Rex, the most important Danish feminist Actionists, have performed many actions. For example, they ran naked through a public bank. They have used motifs of pregnancy in posters and films, and Justesen sculpted her pregnant body. Justesen and Rex's 1972 film, *The Sleeping Beauty*, glorifies the beauty of the pregnant body.

EXPORT's action *Homometer* (1973) continues her investigation of the mythology of civilizatory processes. Her area is the interpretability of symbols, the fact that different meanings are projected onto the same emblems and signs.[49] In *Homometer II*, passers-by cut a slice from a loaf of bread (symbol for motherhood, as grain is for life) placed in such a way as to make EXPORT look pregnant.

In her book *En bas* (1945), Leonora Carrington describes a breakdown: she experienced her belly as a mirror of the earth, and wanted her vomitting and stomach convulsions to spew out the evil of the world.[50]

## ANDROGYNY AS ALTERNATIVE?

Barbara Bloom deconditioned habits of viewing with a minimal shift: she directed the gaze to unclear pictures on deceptively clear surfaces. Subtle estrangement sensitized consciousness for a break in the female image which initiated a landslide. In early 1975, she placed posters in the streets of Amsterdam that showed a (vaguely perceptible) woman behind glass (as if cleaning windows). On April 4, 1975, in the de Appel gallery, the well-dressed visitors waited in darkness for a long time, when suddenly they saw the following scene, briefly illuminated: a woman on a ladder behind glass.

The scene on the poster was repeated live in the gallery. A picture on a poster, which was difficult to interpret since posters usually show very different images of women, acquired its full meaning in the gallery through the negation of an expectation (the usual image of the woman in art). The actual snapshot as the conclusion of a long-lasting poster performance, the blurred boundaries between reproduction and reality: silent pinpricks of attention in the "big sleep," the big sleep of public awareness. Minimal, sensitive gestures to the nature of culturally conditioned seeing, to a cultural commonplace: the role of women in the media, the image of women in visual media communication. Such ironic treatment of feminine ideals is an essential part of the activities of contemporary feminist Actionists.[51] In their photographs, Katharina Sieverding and others approach the mythology of androgyny—since Virginia Woolf, the search for the androgynous spirit has been regarded as an escape from the history of female self-alienation. Through the possibilities of make-up, the alienated presentation of sex-specific appearances, the transfer of sex-specific characteristics using make-up and photographic retouching, estranged gestures and mimicry, Katharina and others break through the limits of the physical definition of gender. Our culture, however, is still far from the androgynous spirit that listens to the echo of the belly, for men too would have to revise their ideals: "As soon as the wife of a Jambim man feels she is pregnant, her husband no longer goes fishing. The sea, the endless amniotic fluid, is not to be disturbed by the strokes of the oar."[52]

NOTES

1    Peter Weibel, *Kritik der Kunst/Kunst der Kritik* (Vienna: 1973). All translations from the German are my own.
2    Weibel, "Material Thinking as Freeing People's Products From Their Thing-Characteristics." *Kritik der Kunst*.

3    Weibel, "Material Thinking."

4    John Stuart Mill, *The Subjection of Women* (London: Virago, 1983).

5    VALIE EXPORT, "Those Who Are Not Painted Are Stupid," *Kronen-Zeitung*, 16 June 1973.

6    Gertrud Koch, *Frauen und Film* 13 (1977).

7    See VALIE EXPORT's action *Blutwärme* (*Blood Warmth*) (1973):
On the beach North Sea, Belgium, two parallel grooves (man and woman) dug in the sand, one filled with blood, the other with gasoline, are to be lighted. In one groove blood, in the other fire (warmth of blood, union, life).

8    Virginia Woolf, *A Room of One's Own* (London: Penguin Books, 1945). *The Waves* is the title of a novel by Virginia Woolf.

9    Also see Sarah Schumann, "Fragen und Assoziationen zu den Arbeiten von Meret Oppenheim," *Künstlerinnen international 1877–1977* (Berlin: Schloß Charlottenburg, 1977).

10    Fauna symbolism: Meret Oppenheim, *Déjeuner en fourrure* (1936); Isabelle Waldheim, *Le dernier rôdeur* (1945); Lygia Clark made aluminum sculptures between 1959 and 1964, which she called "animals," for example *Caterpillar* (1964), green rubber mounted on a tree like a caterpillar; Nancy Kitchel, *Men & Dogs* (1976) in Galerie Magers, Bonn.

11    Collections of poems by Kay Sage: *Demain Monsieur Silber* (Paris: 1957); *The More I Wonder* (New York: 1957); *Piove in giardino.* Collections of poems by Valentine Penrose: *Herbe à la lune* (Paris: 1935); *Le nouveau Candide* (Paris: 1976). Books by Leonora Carrington: *En bas* (1945; Paris: 1973); *La maison de la peur* (Paris: 1938); *La dame ovale* (Paris: 1939); *Le cornet acoustique* (Paris: 1947); *La porte de Pierre* (Paris: 1976).

12    (Paris: 1976)

13    (1932; Paris: Seuil, 1975)

14    "Up to now art was decided and administered by men and it is, therefore, male art. Women were said to have no creativity of their own." VALIE EXPORT, interview, *Kultur speziell*, ORF, 30 Dec. 1972.

15    This may be compared with *The In/visible Woman* by Penny Slinger (London: 1971), in which surrealistic methods are actualized for the feminist movement in collages, fetish objects, etc. As above: the dominance of the unconscious in Surrealism anticipated much of the present feminist art movement, because for the first time women became aware of creativity, and because the techniques of Surrealism are well suited to women's introspection. Therefore, there are objective historical reasons beyond the sphere of subjective influence for the evident correspondence between Surrealist and feminist art. Just to mention a few examples: compare Man Ray's *Vénus réstaurée* (1936), with Friederike Pezold's bound breasts in *Brustwerk* (*Breast Work*) (1973).

At the international Surrealist exhibition in London, Sheila Legge used one of Dali's ideas, and walked around as *Woman with Flower Head*, her face hidden in a bunch of roses. She stood in Trafalgar Square, as pictured in the *Bulletin internationale du Surréalisme* (Sept. 1936) with pigeons on her outstretched arms. Compare this with the videotape (1973) of Ulrike Rosenbach's *Kohleinwicklung* (*Cabbage-Wrapped Head*). The difference is that Dali presents the woman as a revered object, while Rosenbach presents her as an exploited one.

The Surrealists both radicalized the image of woman and also darkened it by making it mythological. See, for example, André Masson's *Doll* of 1938: a mannequin's head in an aviary, a flower in her mouth (woman = bird).

16   Maria Lassnig, catalogue of the Albertina exhibition, 1977, in Vienna.

17   Lassnig.

18   Lassnig.

19   Lassnig.

20   Simone Forti, "Kinästhetik," interview by G. Nabakowski, in *heute Kunst* 8 (1974).

21   "Yes, what I've learned from Ann Halprin is mainly the feeling for one's own body perceptions (= kinaesthetics), the visual and audible sensations of the body, the nerves, muscles and the skin. What we learned was to undisturbedly move in the sensations of our movements. It was a deep harmony between torque and center of gravity in the piece 'Sheila in Progress,' Cologne 1974, especially towards the end" (Forti).

22   Copenhagen, 1975.

23   Gislind Nabakowski in "Tod der Fläche," an unpublished manuscript. "The title was taken from Lygia Clark's pamphlet of the 1960s wherein she announced that she had turned away from Constructivism."

24   G. Stein, *What Happened*. "Act three: A cut a cut is not a slice, what is the occasion for representing a cut and a slice. What is the occasion for all that." Also see VALIE EXPORT's *Cutting* (1960) and Gina Pane's *Sentimental* (1973).

25   More on Stein by VALIE EXPORT in: *Neues Forum*, Jan. 1973.

26   More on Ann Halprin in: VALIE EXPORT, "Feminismus & Kunst," *Neues Forum*, March 1973.

27   See especially Rainer's *Lives of Performers* (1972); *Film About a Woman Who* (1974); *Kristina Talking Pictures* (1976). Rainer wrote of the latter film: "its main themes: the undefined relation between public acting and personal fate, the difference between publicly directed conscience and private will. . . . Nothing can secure our remaining honor nor save us from treason and death."

28   More on these people in *Kunstforum* 24 (1977) and *Documenta 6 Katalog* v. 1, Kassel.

29   Nabakowski.

30   Nabakowski.

31   Nabakowski: "Happenings and Actionism envisioned romantic, dreamlike and fantastic pictures of freedom, happiness and autonomy in the early 1960s. They were extravagant longings for the undoing of instincts and for reconciliation with 'everybody.' The co-actors in Carolee Schneemann's *Meat Joy* affectionately mingled everybody, but still they remained in a collective, remained non-personal and without subject. Most actors even agreed on (unintentionally) not attacking the social differences between men and women, their social-conventional conflicts. Carolee Schneemann, the artist who drew attention to the 'missing gender' in the early 1950s, which were especially hostile to women, was, together with Lygia Clark, the first to integrate matriarchal symbols (spirals, snakes, uteri) into her work even before "the éclat" of

the artistic feminism in the 1970s pictures that got lost too soon because they did not become central metaphors."

32  Zinaide Hippius, the uncrowned queen of literary life in St. Petersburg before World War I, author of "The Eternal Woman," gave masculine endings to all Russian possessive pronouns. She used the masculine forms to emphasize her status as human being as a woman. See *The Selected Works of Zinaide Hippius*, ed. Temira Pachmuss (University of Illinois Press, 1972).

33  Carolee Schneemann, "The Pronoun-Tyranny," *The Fox* 3 (1976).

34  Schneemann.

35  In this context, it should be mentioned that the male art scene does not shrink from applauding artists who want to take advantage of body language, this privileged domain of women, her finally conquered autonomous territory. One example of this would be James Collins, whose photographic sequences domesticate women to nice nothings under his view. Eyes roaming over colored beds also degrade woman to a sex object without any will of her own. This modern contorted variation of the bourgeois depiction of the nude that surrenders the woman, under the cover of art, to the voyeurism of the ruling, a tradition thought to be already extinct, is also revived by Arnulf Rainer. In a series of photograph overdrawings of 1977 with the title "Frauensprache" (language of the woman) and the subtitle "Ekstasen" (ecstasies)—what else, the man is in control of his feelings and cool—one can see photographs of naked women in pornographic poses painted over by Rainer in the same chance manner as other poses. A more cynical and despicable exploitation of women and their experience, one that is furthered by market strategy and the intention of being à la mode, can hardly be imagined.

36  Cf. the text of Germaine Richier (1904–1959) who got the award for sculpture at the Biennale in São Paulo in 1951: "Nature! The animals, the insects. I took cocoons to look for silkworms. I had a whole regiment of grasshoppers." *Künstlerinnen international 1877–1977*.

37  Harriet Taylor Mill, "Enfranchisement of Women," in John Stuart Mill and Harriet Taylor Mill, *Enfranchisement of Women & The Subjection of Women* (1851; London: Virago, 1983), 23–24.

38  Harriet Taylor Mill 24.

39  Since I found the title of this poem by Peter Weibel (1975) very appropriate for this part of the essay, the author was kind enough to let me use it.

40  Joan Jonas also made several other mirror pieces. In 1968 she wore a costume of variously sized mirrors. Later on, her performers wore large mirrors indoors and outdoors (e.g., on the beach). She also used video as a mirror machine.

41  Nabakowski.

42  Danielle Sarréra, *Arsenic Flowers* (Munich: 1978), 70.

43  Unica Zürn, *Der Mann im Jasmin* (Frankfurt: 1978), 177.

44  Gertrud Koch, "Unsichtbar macht sich die Unterdrückung der Frauen . . . ," *Frauen und Film* 13 (October 1977).

45  VALIE EXPORT, "Women's Art. Ein Manifest," *Neues Forum* 228 (1973).

46  Rebecca Horn, in *Magna. Feminismus: Kunst und Kreativität*, ed. VALIE EXPORT (Vienna: Galerie nächst St. Stefan, 1975).

47   Quoted in Nabakowski.
48   Cf. also "Der befreite Busen," *Der Spiegel*, 24 July 1978.
49   VALIE EXPORT, *Zur Mythologie der zivilisatorischen Prozesse* (Vienna: 1971).
50   Leonora Carrington, *En bas* (Paris: 1945).
51   See *Die Löwen*, Dec. 1975.
52   EXPORT, "He Who Is Not Painted Is Stupid."


EDITOR'S NOTES

I   In fact, only the Niki part was an "alias," she was born Catherine Marie-Agnès Fal de Saint Phalle. The false notion that "Saint Phalle" was an artist's name was widely shared at the time though.
II   Halprin started using the first name Anna in 1972.

- - - - - - - - - - - - - - - - - - - - - - - - - - - - - - - - - -

## KUNST MIT EIGEN-SINN: FOREWORD[1]

- - - - - - - - - - - - - - - - - - - - - - - - - - - - - - - - - -

### 1985

= = = = = = = = = = = = = = = = = = = = = = = = = = = = = = = = =

"Art can be a medium for our self-determination and this offers art new values. These values will change reality by means of the cultural symbolic process, towards adaptation to feminine needs. The future of woman will be the history of woman." (1973 [written 1972])

These lines, written more than ten years ago, have raised questions, demands and prophecies which have been provided with massive answers and confirmation in the 80's. The society of today is no longer one where women, faced with a discourse, are isolated without answers. The subversive strategies and provocations of the 60's and 70's have transformed the profile of this society, have made its face more humane. In the cracks, a new meaning has risen like a periscope. Woman has emerged in the wings of the empire as the aquanaut of symbolic order and has abducted the energy of the myth of power. What she sees is what he has not recognized. The pole of conquest is melting, the Earth is turning toward the pole of discovery in order to find balance. Image by image a different legibility is being created.

The view that social cohesion is based on the familial victim is losing its pathos. The obligation of fear as the legacy of religion is forfeiting its persuasive power. The home is no longer the place of socialization, parents are no longer the subjects of self-realization.

In this context woman's emancipation from her status as victim is the revolutionary action of women in constructing society anew. As a response to the destruction of man and beast, women have developed an aggressive energy, an aesthetics of resistance, of anger, out also of distance and repose which denudes the body of society of the traces of the colonization of all kinds and degrees. Society is becoming naked, the naked woman is turning the mirror around. The subversive energy of past decades has become a movement that no longer wants to dispose of the allegory of classification, but to float free of definitions.

Transition to the realm of equality is not attainable as the mere result of quantitative progress. It necessitates the development of a different quality. Stratification of social processes as the cause of inequality cannot be abolished quantitatively, but must abolish itself. Equality has more mouths than the welfare state has plates. Nevertheless, the values and ways of life which transcend existing society must also be mirrored in the struggle for economic and cultural equality.

So, art with a meaning of one's very own (Kunst mit Eigensinn) is an implosion of stratification, a grappling with the different quality. Its representations of reality convey values which are the antitheses of the prevailing ones. The flayed or glossy skin of the world is not replaced with new plumage, but stripped off. Skinless— the new values.

Matter grows more sensitive without the wrappings of form, the pain of matter greater. In her historical denudation woman experiences history as skin, as a form of deformity. In her perception of this variability she is taking a new history from the future which will be a medium for self-realization, just as art with a meaning of one's very own is now. In the presence of this artistic practice one by no means earns individual margins but visualizes the self-realization of the human community.

For, according to Hegel, history is primarily the history of freedom. In the texture of this history of freedom the individual and society are interwoven. So the image of freedom appeals on the screen of mutual conditioning. Art is also inscribed in the history of freedom as a "medium of self-determination," as a process of progressive individuation. Progress, the concept and existence of which are readily denied in art and politics, is tied to history as a figure of meaning. For this reason conservatives declare the era of post-history (*posthistoire*) so as to be able to abolish the concept of progress. Yet, progress and freedom are inseparably connected, precisely in Hegel's definition of world history as "progress in the consciousness of freedom."

If we understand freedom as the meaning of history and individuation as the meaning of art, individuation and freedom converge in the concept of a meaning of one's very own, just as art and history. With progressive individualization, where the characteristics and uniqueness befitting a person increasingly evolve from what is general, hence where every person increasingly finds himself/herself and so finds what is alone his/hers and belongs to nobody else (nor is enslaved to anybody else), the meaning of history will be individualized: one's own meaning as the echo of one's own voice in the world.

A free individual also has the liberty to give history and the world a meaning different from the general one and peculiar and unique to him/her alone. This individual meaning, this meaning of one's very own, as the expression of the individual and society, is the aim of self-realization beyond power, violence and exploitation. So, a meaning of one's very own is a kind of individual expropriation of the general meaning in so far as the latter is inscribed in a history of inhumanity and derives from it. I must plant a meaning of my very own where the meaning of the world is perverted in destructive meaninglessness.

So, art with a meaning of one's very own (Kunst mit Eigensinn) is a kind of twin statement, for both art and a meaning of one's very own have the freedom of the individual as telos and statement. In this respect art is a meaning of one's very own and a meaning one's very own is identical with art. A meaning of one's very own is an emphasis of what is already inherent in art itself. This emphasis is made in the knowledge that the history of art has the obscuring features of a history of mastery. The twin statement formulated in an art with a meaning of one's very own is postulated and presented in the sense of "progress in the consciousness of freedom" and is the "joy of being a woman."

EDITOR'S NOTE

I    The title of this exhibition and its accompanying publication plays with the German word *Eigensinn*, which translates as independence of mind or self-will, but also as stubbornness or obstinacy. By inserting a hyphen between the two parts of the word, VALIE EXPORT highlights various possible readings, since *Sinn* can mean not only meaning, but also sense (as in the senses of sight and smell), and mindedness or will (the *Eigen* part means own). While translated here as "art with a meaning of one's very own," *Kunst mit Eigen-Sinn* could also be translated as "art with a will/mind of its own," "art based on a distinct sense/perception of the world," but also "headstrong art." It has been translated elsewhere as "Art with a Sense of One's Own/Art with a Sense of Its Own," see p. 194.

The English press release for the exhibition, issued by Museum Moderner Kunst, Vienna, offers the following translation and explanation of the German word Eigensinn:

"*Eigensinn*—willfulness
*Eigen*—own characterists (sic!)
*Sinn*—sense, meaning

This title has two levels of reference. On the one hand it terms the differentiated and complex nature of contemporary artistic production by women, on the other, the emancipatory potential which has brought about changes not only on the artistsic scene over the last two decades, changes which are still being made. The title 'KUNST MIT EIGEN-SINN' refers to the self-confidence which expresses itself as freedom of artistisc movement on the ground already gained. This freedom of movement is articulated in many dynamic ways, it takes new courses which are followed single-mindedly and expressively."

----------------------------------------

## CORPUS MORE GEOMETRICO

----------------------------------------

### 1987

==========================================

"The body is to be compared not to a physical object, but rather to a work of art," Maurice Merleau-Ponty wrote in *Phenomenology of Perception*. He thus pushed the body out of the level of the object into the realm of the symbol, out of physics into the psyche. This is possible since the body as artwork as well as medium of art was never an object or mere instrument alone. Rather, the body always appeared simultaneously as image of the body, as double-image or as double-sculpture.

Therefore, in one famous picture, Leonardo stretched out the human body in a circle and in a square, i.e., in a double image. This geometric representation of the body, these two body configurations derived from two phases of motion, namely standing at rest and in motion (cartwheel, circle), display in an unmistakable manner an affinity between geometry and body, which is compulsory for European culture and which finds expression in the term "human measure." For how can the human body serve as a yardstick, as a measuring instrument, if geometry and body, world and experience, don't mark out a secret relationship, a mysterious ratio, indeed, the human measure? Humanism blew up this human measure as anthropological principle into the cosmological constant.

Between one's own body and the world of objects, between the body and surrounding bodies, between body configuration and (the cultural, social, physical) context, a secret proportion thus arises. That is the sense of the double image by Leonardo, inasmuch as geometric figures and human body (in two-dimensional representation) stretch over one another like bridges. The Corpus More Geometrico proclaims a doctrine of proportions, a possibly common measure, not only of geometry and body, but also, following Merleau-Ponty, an affinity between geometry and experience, between spirit and matter, between soul and body.

My photographic presentations of body positionings, in which the geometric processes like perspective and proportion are also expressive figures of the body, are built upon the portrayed parallelism. As plastic poses, as living pictures and sculptures, my photographic body configurations signify not only the double images of the (geometric and human) figures but, instead, the body writing is also always sociography and cultural history. The body pictures yield images from cultural background figures. As, namely, with double sensation, where the touching of my right hand with the left hand arouses sensation in the left as well as in the right hand, so too the body images arouse not only images of the body but also images of the culture, of its secret models, patterns and codes. Man as physical ornament in the modern world reveals a double model; body model and relationship model. The inner worlds of the body and of the culture become visible in this double refraction.

I use the photographic fixing in a physical context (house, city, country) not because it is the movement of the body that should articulate its meaning, but because I want to extort the body code from the frozen history of the culture which is a history of silence concerning the body. I want to avoid the kinesthetics of the body, since in it the human body too easily and too often degenerates into a machine or a metaphor for a machine in a masculine discourse (from laying hens to advertising).

My photographically frozen pictures, my stills, unmask the cultural body code and show the logic of the body within the social structure in a type of double exposure. In the metaphor of the body as machine the body decays into a gruesome economics and functionality. In the body configuration as a chain of linked geometries and geometric ornaments, there breaks forth from the standardization of the body, not from a deceptive intoxication of the expressiveness whose actual raw material is narcissism, bare self-reflection, where one's own mirrored image (albeit distorted) is taken as standard, the body is sacrificed. Instead, the true logic and language of the body unfolds only in the above-mentioned double images, double mirrorings and double exposures of spirit and matter, consciousness and body, experience and world. The double meaning of the word figure as form (as phenomenon of visual perception), already refers to the dialogue of the objects and members, to the morphs as roots of the body's signification. The body's sense thus articulates itself not in the self-body, or in the mirror image of the body—the body sense also gets lost if the body becomes distanced as instrument and apparatus—the sense of the body speaks to us MORE GEOMETRICO.

## MAN & WOMAN & ANIMAL

### 1987

The images of woman that our civilization has produced are representations of a reality that is not the same for all, but a social construct that advances certain interests. The camera, which has produced the image lying in the cultural developing tray, is the masculine eye. The image that is developing itself now in the culture (developing tray), is it the "real" image of woman? Is it the image of woman at all? And how can the feminine object of portrayal develop itself into a photo of itself, the photo of woman into the subject woman?

- - - - - - - - - - - - - - - - - - - - - - - - - - - - - - - - -

## THE REAL AND ITS DOUBLE: THE BODY

- - - - - - - - - - - - - - - - - - - - - - - - - - - - - - - - -

### 1987

============================================

In a famous passage in *Civilization and Its Discontents*, Sigmund Freud laid an unexpected foundation not only for an adequate theory of media, but also for the contemplation of the relationships of body and technology, of bodily functions and tools, and of natural organs and artificial prostheses:

> With every tool man is perfecting his own organs, whether motor or sensory, or is removing the limits to their functioning. Motor power places gigantic forces at his disposal, which, like his muscles, he can employ in any direction; thanks to ships and aircraft neither water nor air can hinder his movements; by means of spectacles he corrects defects in the lens of his own eye; by means of the telescope he sees into the far distance; and by means of the microscope he overcomes the limits of visibility set by the structure of his retina. In the photographic camera he has created an instrument which retains the fleeting visual impressions, just as the gramophone disc retains the equally fleeting auditory ones; both are at bottom materializations of the power he possesses of recollection, his memory. With the help of the telephone he can hear at distances which would be respected as unattainable even in a fairy tale. Writing was in its origin the voice of an absent person; and the dwelling-house was a substitute for the mother's womb, the first lodging, for which in all likelihood man still longs, and in which he was safe and felt at ease.

Freud thus defines technological tools as expansions, perfections, and transgressions of the human organs of sense. From the motor to the camera, from the microscope to the telephone, all technical tools/media are extensions of the functions of natural physical organs as well as conquests of their limits and weaknesses. With the help of an army of auxiliary organs that are, however, not just artificial substitutes but also incredible advancements in the performance of natural organs, humankind has not only surpassed the natural limits of its own body, but also the boundaries imposed by nature, such as gravitation, for example. Freud calls the use of tools the first acts of civilization: "all activities and resources which are useful to men for making the earth serviceable to them, for protecting them against the violence of the forces of nature, and so on," are recognized as cultural (CD 90).

Hence, tools are the result of cultural development and the perfecting of the natural organs of humankind. The perfecting consists of removing limits to the performance of these organs. With the help of tools mankind can overcome the natural limitations set by the body. The triumph of tools over physical organs belongs to the logic of cultural development in the fight against nature to shelter mankind. Civilization itself is nothing other than "the whole sum of the achievements and the regulations . . . which serve two purposes—namely to protect men against nature and to adjust their mutual relations" (CD 89).

So the apparent paradox results, that tools, inasmuch as they perfect, complete, and augment the natural organs and hence follow the functions exhibited by the natural organs, overcome and ultimately replace the natural organs themselves, the more complete and civilized the tools become. The house replaces the mother's womb, not only because the embryo has become an adult, but because civilization begins to replace and repress nature in the imposition of the reality principle.

Technology as the sum of all tools serves thus not only the cultural transformation of nature, but also has the tendency to transform and dissolve the body itself, precisely inasmuch as technology is cultural activity. The civilization of the body is at the same time its replacement and absence. Like all technology and civilization, culture is a "language of the absent." As language of the absent, the body belongs to the rhetoric of the real—that is its crux. The crucifixion has therefore ascended to a central phantasm of our culture, because it demonstrates the role of the body in our culture. The body is the medium of the real and the social, of control. The body is the "kairos" of the subject. Precisely because the body represents the real insertion into the world, the insertion of the subject into the real, the body can be nailed to the cross and the son can be forced to submit to the law of the father, to the reality principle. The soul escapes from the tortured dead body as salvation of the subject into the imaginary.

The language of the present mixes itself with the language of the absent in the triumph of technology *as* body, which is also a triumph *over* the body. To define the body as the exclusive site of nature is therefore an abundantly naïve conception. Because culture, which we all do insist on, also always means the civilization of the body, the technical extension and transformation of the body.

This transformation begins, moreover, long before the acquisition of tools, namely, at the moment of the development of the ego, with the separation of the self from the outside world. Not only in cultural development does the mother's womb become a house, but also in psychic development. With the formation of the self, the body itself ultimately becomes the outside world.

The replacement of the mother's womb by the house and of the house by a lodging of one's own belongs to the stages of development in the formation of the ego, where, in the end, even the body can no longer be perceived as home of the ego.

The progressive perfection and replacement of natural organs by artificial tools, which themselves can again produce new tools and artificial organs, effected a cultural progress, created a cultural elevation, a civilizatory pyramid, on whose summit man sits as a sort of prosthetic God.

> Man has, as it were, become a kind of prosthetic God. When he puts
> on all his auxiliary organs he is truly magnificent; but those organs
> have not grown on to him and they still give him much trouble at
> times. Nevertheless, he is entitled to console himself with the
> thought that this development will not come to an end precisely with
> the year 1930 AD. Future ages will bring with them new and prob-
> ably unimaginably great advances in this field of civilization and
> will increase man's likeness to God still more. But in the interests of
> our investigations, we will not forget that present-day man does not
> feel happy in his Godlike character. (CD 91–92)

The concept of the prosthesis cannot be separated from the cultural process, from civilizatory development. Freud himself introduces this concept of the prosthesis in the discussion of cultural progress. Cultural discourse itself produces the artifacts and prostheses that do not stop with the body; on the contrary, since the body is the point of departure for tools, one must perceive every "made object as a projection of the human body."[2] It is thus the logic of the body that generates the prostheses. The body produces its own technology.

Any technology which plainly deals with God's monopoly, namely, with the engendering of life, doubtless belongs to the "unimaginably great advances in this field of civilization" that Freud foresaw and that were to "increase man's likeness to God still more." Technologies of reproduction pose the question about the body, and above all, about the female body, most radically.

## THE FEMALE BODY

Women are ambivalent in their reports on how they experience their bodies. If ecstasy and pain are the two forms of experience where we apperceive the body most distinctly and directly, and if we develop from this binary polarity strategies of ego development, of physical awareness and of the relationship to the outside world (and even actually construct the outside world, body and ego conceptually from this apperception, namely, as a defense against the pains that reality forces onto the body and as a search for the satisfaction of pleasures which the body grants us) then the images and works of language by women that speak to us about the experience of the female body have the tendency to be more discerning and independent when they deal with the pain of the body. For a patriarchally structured society that is built on the gaining of pleasure by men, this comes as no surprise. If women speak of the body's pleasure, then their vocabulary is, as with Erica Jong or Anäis Nin, a stereotype of trivial masculine pornography. "To find her word," her language, the problem of the missing gender, is valid here, too.

In literature and art, on the other hand, the reports are numerous and self-willed about how women perceive their bodies as disturbing, and about how the physical functions that are expected from the female body are perceived as oppressive. The body appears as a burden, as a piece of the outside world, or even as illness.

The French lyricist Danielle Sarréra,[1] who committed suicide in 1949 at the age of seventeen, describes as murderous the transformation of the "woman child" into a woman: "My belly was a prayer drum. The . . . sex of a violated virgin howled, carved-up on a roof, bloody. Facial wounds flared up in incandescence, flowed like lava down the entire breasts."[3] A tone strikes us, a metaphysics of agony, of denial, of emptiness, whose sound has been recorded as early as Sappho, and which describes the physical and psychological tortures of female puberty. Sarréra rejects as destructive birth, belly, and body—all these synecdoches of femininity which she should, or rather must, embody to qualify as a woman in our society. She doesn't want to have to destroy her Self in order to become a female body. She rather destroys her body (in suicide). In this crisis of female adolescence, in this "dark spring" (Zürn), we hear the cries of the female body, terrible moments of truth, that later become mute in the accommodated consciousness, in the conventional feminine "pariah-awareness" (Elisabeth Lenk):

With one soul and one body, with this single swing which breaks the sling and shatters the skull, breaks in the windowpanes, from this damned loneliness where the putrid ravens of the entirely deranged spirit gather, from this spot too small for our unfulfilled expectations where we have seen worlds of good will with henceforth unaffordable sources inconsolably live and die, from this icy shut-up room where no childbearing is possible, I, the proud handmaiden of a death which is much deader than you can believe, direct this greeting to you, hoping from the bottom of my heart that it will make you thoroughly wretched and let you sink steadily deeper, down to the mute hour of the legally sufficient violation that will create a final world with monstrous muteness from the chimera that you are. (Sarréra 15–17)

In her book *Das Haus der Krankheiten* (The House of Illnesses), written and illustrated in 1958, Unica Zürn, a German living in Paris, writes about "forbidden rooms": "From the beginning I decided on the alcove of the solar plexus and on the chambers of the hands. The hall of the bellies and also the breastroom I carefully avoid."[4] In the phenomenology of pain, the body becomes the house of illnesses. Breastroom and hall of bellies are shunned as architecture of the feminine. From them "wafts a sickly-sweet hot odor that makes me ill" and "thus the breastroom instilled in me only despair" (Zürn, Haus 62). It is thus especially the prototypical sexual characteristics of the feminine and the organic functions of the feminine—breasts and belly, milk and childbearing—that instill in Zürn terror and despair. Zürn spent the years 1960–62 in Jacques Lacan's psychiatric clinic of St. Anne, and committed suicide in 1970, at the age of fifty-four. It is not the body itself, but its femininity—the social doctrine of the body as definition of woman, the identification of woman's being with her physical sexual characteristics and sexual functions, that makes the body into the house of illnesses, into the place of death.

Rot winde den Leib,
Brot wende in Leid,
ende Not,
Beil wird Leben.
Wir, dein Tod
weben dein Lot dir
in Erde. Wildboten,
wir lieben den Tod.

Red wind the body
bread turn in[to] suffering
end need
ax becomes life.
We, your death
weave you your lot
in earth. Wild messengers,
we love death.[5]

Thus goes an anagram of Zürn who was fascinated by anagrams during the last decades of her life. "Anagrams are words and sentences that have arisen from the rearrangement of the letters of a given word or sentence," Zürn herself writes. The object is, by purely formal language, to draw out hidden, repressed meanings, to restore the distorted meaning. That, in the end, death comes from the body in an anagrammatic poem, reveals the sense—that the construction of the feminine from the body means pain for the feminine Self, and ultimately, because of this pain, the extinction of the body itself. Zürn often felt herself an ally of the American Indians, a member, so to speak, of an oppressed race threatened with extinction. Life itself, therefore, couldn't endow her with a sense of her own. In 1958 she writes, "this life hasn't become my life." The "search in one sentence for a new sentence" is the search for a new meaning; it is the attempt to give, even if not to life itself, at least to sentences about life, a new sense of their own. Even if life hasn't become her own, one

187

that sets her identity free, then at least language, the word, should become her own. The search for a new sense in a sentence, the anagrammatic activity itself, is the way out from the house of the body, from the obstructed life. In terrifying texts the pain of the body—of the female body—is articulated. The construction of the subject upon the female sexual characteristics of the body in our patriarchal society has effected her tortures and left her no way out. Zürn's thought, her sensibility, and her Self were disfigured and disarranged by the socially defined female body, so that she became "a woman affected" and acted "conspicuously." To look anagrammatically for a new implicit sense in sentences became an obsession with her after 1953, when the sense of the construction of the feminine upon the body began to vanish.

Mental illnesses, as deconstruction of this female body, or as dissolution of the socially determined female body, have belonged for a long time to the strategies of female insurrections. That Zürn lived together with Hans Bellmer, who made a name for himself with his artistic dolls, is a providence that supports our interpretation and that is called fate when it is a matter of deep predetermined affinities. Bellmer's dolls are, namely, likenesses of a dismembered and newly recombined female body. Hence, Bellmer does exactly the same thing in his visual art that Zürn does in her language. As the body is divided into organs and then repeatedly reconstructed, so the sentence is split up into its letters and reassembled anew. Objectual or verbal anagrammatizing results from the inadequacy of the body as social construction of woman. The interchangeability of the body parts and the sentence parts stands for the interchangeability of the Self of women as body. Via her body, woman becomes an element of the social grammar of masculine desire. Through the social grammar of the body, where the female set pieces such as breasts, belly, bottom, legs, and the like are interchangeable linguistic elements, the woman herself becomes interchangeable, obliterated, and in this sense doesn't exist, as Lacan says.

Precisely through reference to the body, to the female characteristics of the body (e.g., the womb as opposed to the phallus), woman surrenders herself for her own extinction in the patriarchal structure of our civilization. Deconstructed, Zürn's texts show us how the persistence of the body as nature, as site of the feminine nature, as site of woman (as it is expressed in the ideology of childbirth, of motherhood, etc.) follows exactly the track laid out by patriarchal society, namely, obeys exactly its construction of the feminine, where woman is a castrated man. Precisely because woman doesn't exist, she must be constructed. Precisely because incompleteness (the lack of a penis, the anatomical difference) became the determining feature of femininity, the insistence on these features (breasts, vagina), even if contorted into the positive, follows the masculine logic of the construction of the feminine. Disembodiment and avoidance of the body are thus not synonymous with avoidance of the feminine. Only there, where the feminine is identified with the female physical characteristics, as Freud set it out, can the avoidance of the body (as house of illness) or the escape into illness (as with hysteria) be understood as the avoidance of the feminine. In truth, it's a matter of how (as the history of hysteria, interpreted from a feminist point of view, demonstrates) to break up the social identity of body and woman, to release the feminine Self from the female body and its female biological bodily functions, in a word, how to cancel the social construction of the feminine by patriarchy.

In a phallocratic culture, woman, the being that has no phallus, can be defined only as deficiency and defect, as nonexistent, since with her there doesn't exist what the man has—the penis. Her physical, sexual characteristics are the negative form of the man's, marked by emptiness and absence (of the penis). Whoever presumes to be able to found her determination of Self on the feminine physical characteristics and sexual functions only deepens the masculine determination. This is why the more phallocratic and fascist in its male bonding a society is, the louder the hymn of praise for the woman as mother, as nature, as childbearer is sung. The hymn is sung to the female sexual characteristics and bodily functions because it is praising the woman as negative of the man. If woman is the negative of man, characterized by lack and absence, then she is, logically, virtually nonexistent and must therefore be constructed. In phallocratic society the woman therefore discovers, as far as she traces her own voice, that she is, by way of her body, determined by others. If we want, then, to concern ourselves with the technologies of reproduction, we must take as our starting point that the natural body of the woman doesn't exist.

We have now already indicated two social determinants that not only frame the picture of the body (of woman), but also simultaneously fashion its content as frame of reference. These two determinants are structurally interconnected with each other. The one is the cultural prosthetic-like quality of the body, the other is the gender determination of the body. If Freud designated mankind, the crown of creation, as a prosthetic God, then this illustration of cultural progress as increasing summation of prostheses is comparable to his pronouncement that "where id was, there ego shall be." In "The Dissection of the Psychical Personality," the thirty-first lecture in his *New Introductory Lectures on Psycho-Analysis* (1933) he adds to this imperative the sentence: "It is a work of culture—not unlike the draining of the Zuider Zee [sic]."[6] Here, too, the work of culture is compared with a technologically civilizing work, which in turn is compared with the work of psychological development. Before that, Freud wrote: the intention of therapeutic effort "is, indeed, to strengthen the ego, to make it more independent of the superego, to widen its field of perception and enlarge its organization, so that it can appropriate fresh portions of the id" (DPP 80). Ego formation, identity, sovereignty of the subject on the one hand, and technological extension of the body, transformation of nature through prosthetic auxiliary organs, and technological improvement on the other hand, thus stand for Freud under the same yoke, namely, that of the work of culture.

Is it my destination to come into being there where id was? But how, if id is the object and the phallus the subject of the unconscious? Then woman, who has no phallus, can only be a lost signifier, characterized by castration and hence by "lack of being." If being is related to a signifier—the phallus, the symbol for the libido—then it follows that woman has no being and must be constructed.

Reproduction technology is, therefore, to be viewed ambivalently. On one hand it is a progression of the work of culture—the prosthetic transformation of the body, the expropriation of the body, discorporation, and the "traversing of the phantasm," the separation of the subject from the object, the development of the ego, the breakthrough into being. But as this happens under a masculine signifier, reproduction technology is, on the other hand, a continuation of the masculine construction of the feminine. Precisely because woman doesn't exist, or does so only as body, science can experiment unhindered on nature, on the body of woman. So woman is in a double-bind, in a no-exit situation; her *passe* (Lacan), her traversing of the phantasm is broken. Because on the one hand woman must pursue the process of the transformation of the id into ego, the formation into subject, so that "I am not" will be overlaid by "it is I." But on the other hand, the exposing of castration, of penislessness, (i.e., for the woman the return to the object, to "I don't think") stands at the end of the analysis. The traversing of the phantasm is thwarted by the phallic signifier. The body of woman is thus the site where "culture" manufactures the blockade of woman. Right in the very body of woman herself, "the world" establishes the rupture, the contradiction, and the incongruity of id and ego that express limitless pain of inner distortion. Hence it comes that women perceive their bodies as mirrors of the world in those "mentally ill" phases, where the subconscious articulates itself, where there is rebellion against the thwarting by the phallic signifier. In the body itself they experience their test of tensile strength in the workings of the signifier, which decides their being or nonbeing.

The painter and writer Leonora Carrington writes in *Unten,* where she reports her perceptions as she lay bound hand and foot as "incurably insane" in a sanatorium in Santander in 1940:

> I had induced the vomiting knowingly, inasmuch as I drank the water of orange blossoms. At the time, I hoped to be able to divert myself from my pain through the violent cramps that tore my stomach like an earthquake. Now I know that this was just one aspect of the vomiting: I had become acquainted with the injustice of society, and wanted first to purify myself and so leave its brutal stupidity behind me. My stomach was the seat of this society, but also the location in which the elements of the earth united with me. It was, to use its image, the mirror of the earth, whose original image has the same reality as the one reflected. This mirror—my stomach—had to be purged of thick layers of filth (of the generally applicable formulae), so that it could again provide an accurate mirror-image of the earth. . . .[7]

The identification begins to waver. The body detaches itself from the subject and identifies itself with the objects of the outside world:

> To begin with, the drive proceeded without incident, until the car, twenty kilometers beyond Saint Martin, stopped with the brakes jammed. I heard Catherine say: "The brakes are jammed." "Jammed!" I, too, was jammed inside, by powers that weren't accessible to my conscious will, and I was convinced that the force of my anxiety had carried over to the mechanism of the car and had lamed it. This was the first time that I identified myself with the world outside my body. I was the car. (15)

Gliding along the chain of signifiers, the ego identifies itself in a logical sequence first with the body, then the body with the objects of the outside world, and finally the ego with the object ("I am the car"), from which the ego had originally set out to differentiate itself. There is no ego at all without this differentiation. "I am the car" is thus forfeiture of ego and being.

In the aporia "I am the car," in this logical contradiction, the whole dead-end street into which the body steers woman in our culture becomes recognizable. The *passe* becomes for woman a dead-end street—an *impasse*. The misery of the culture is increased still more, inasmuch as the cultural work of woman counts for little in it, and must necessarily count for little. Because if the "work of culture" indeed contributes to the mutilation and the disappearance of woman, then it certainly can't at the same time be her forum. Culture, as we know it today, is not the arena of the woman; she is exiled from it by definition. This explains why Shoshana Felman (of the Lacan school) in her book, *Writing and Madness*, addresses only writings by men (Nerval, Flaubert, Balzac, Henry James), although the "insane" texts by women are the most relevant and revealing. When Felman writes that "the madness silenced by society has been given voice by literature," she continues the silence of society about the "insane" literature by women.[8] Literature has given a voice to masculine madness, because even in their aberration, men are part of civilization. But literature has as yet to grant female madness a voice.

## THE ENIGMA OF WOMAN

Freud sees "the riddle of femininity" as based on its sexuality, on "the influence of lack of a penis on the configuration of femininity."[9] The anatomical sexual difference, interpreted as lack and defect, has far-reaching psychological consequences and constitutes the being of women, which is largely "determined by their sexual function," even if "an individual woman may be a human being in other respects as well" (135). Here psychoanalysis articulates the consciousness of the civilization, the cultural code of the woman. Thus it becomes clear that in a phallocratic society the definition of woman through the sexual function of the body not only excludes woman from the culture, but even obstructs her Self-actualization. No wonder that woman, in her ambivalence between insurgence and accommodation, between id and ego, and between completion and fragment, becomes an enigma. Civilization produces the enigma woman. In all feminine attempts at rebellion against the alien classification by the masculine logos, as through hysteria or anorexia, the site has been, therefore, the body.

In the exhibition of topical art by women I organized with Silvia Eiblmayr, Monika Prisch-Maier, Cathrin Pickier, and Heidi Grundmann in 1985 at the Museum of the Twentieth Century in Vienna—*Kunst mit Eigen-Sinn* (Art with a Sense of One's Own/Art with a Sense of Its Own)[10]—I presented artworks which, as the exhibition's title indeed already says, pose the question about feminine identity, about a life of its own and a sense of its own (see Zürn), and especially, stage the interpretations of the ego status of woman via the body. These stagings of the ego—via the body, via images of the body or via a fragmented body—showed the tendency to leave the status of sacrificial victim behind, inasmuch as the social construction of woman, the wounds of the defect woman, the destructive ambivalence, the cultural codes of woman, the blockade of the *passe,* and the cultural portrayals of woman herself were made the theme. For one thing should not be mistaken: there is hardly a feminine imagination or a feminist aesthetic that intends to inscribe itself into the "culture" that would not have been written from within the arena of patriarchal discourse. Hence, I wrote as early as 1973: "Art can be a medium for our self-determination, but only if we change art. This offers art new values. These values will change reality by means of the cultural symbolic process towards adaptation to feminine needs."[11]

In ego-stagings via the body or in feminine objects (like the bed), one is able to recognize how the feminine tries to escape that ambivalence of the work of culture between transformation of the body (the ego as object) and transformation of the id (the id as ego) in order to achieve a specific feminine aesthetic, an art with *Eigen-Sinn*, a feminine Self.

The Swiss artist Miriam Cahn, who illustrates gigantic sheets of paper while lying on the floor, achieves this work of culture in that position which culture attributes traditionally to her gender. In the pictures of cultural history, woman usually lies stretched out in bed or on a sofa or somewhere else. This gender specific past which is made apparent in a physical position, this prescribed passivity, is, however, ruptured by very wild sketching. Her corporal technique causes Miriam Cahn to call her drawings "spatial work." The spatially encompassing tendency of the female body under conditions of ego insurrection is indeed familiar to us from Carrington's texts. Inversely to the masculine optics that, according to Freud, makes every made object *a projection of* the human body, the feminine optics annexes the environmental space, the objects, *into* the human body. Cahn therefore names her work "spatial work," since her physical drawing on the floor also includes the space.

The Czech artist Eva Kmentova says: "I move in the microcosmos of myself, my body and the things that surround me." So here we find again the typical triad of self, body, and objects, which allow the feminine identity to float and which make it diffuse, whereby the woman doesn't identify herself "with something in particular, with never being only one" (Luce Irigaray). She becomes the sex that is not one, in order to evade

the impasse erected by the phallocracy, to evade the
prohibition of the *passe*. Laura Carlotta exhibited a
chest of drawers in which photographs of body parts
lay in the open drawers. The body becomes furniture,
metonymically, a house in which the Self, the ego lives,
but at the same time it becomes a car where the ego
loses itself. Hence the disintegrated representation of
the body in the photographs. Because with the feminine
assimilation of the environment through the body, or
with the regression of the body into object (see also
the Austrian painter Maria Lassnig's 1977 self-portrait
as a chair, *Niagara Chair Self-portrait*) the representation of the body takes place in parts, fragments, or
mechanisms ("I am the car"). This indicates that woman
views her own body from outside as alien. To view the
body from inside would mean to experience it through
expressions of its needs, as [Elaine] Scarry correctly
describes (285), but these needs of the female body are
in this culture indeed made taboo, cut off. So this is
not possible for woman. Maria Lassnig speaks of body-
awareness-drawings, "the first self-representations of
an introspection," but shows us only objects and animals with which her body has grown together. With her
"inside-views" she refers back to the "reality of body-
housing," because a house as a metaphor for the body of
woman not only corresponds to the female experience
of the body imposed by our culture, one experienced
from outside—although the opposite is occasionally
claimed by women themselves (the artists I have named
indeed always speak about space and the objects which
surround the body, never about the viscera or needs of
the body)—but also because in patriarchal civilization
woman is actually a house: "The dwelling-house was a
substitute for the mother's womb" (Freud, CD 91). The
woman as house, as shelter for the baby, is the reduction
of woman to the uterus, the mother's womb. Society, in
fact, assigns only to woman the role of the house, i.e., the
biological function of childbearing, the carrying of the

fruit. Freud certainly doesn't say: "The house was a substitute for the father's body," as the metaphor would be senseless without the analogy giving meaning to house and mother's womb, which the metaphor makes possible. Similarly the French sculptress Louise Bourgeois (who lives in New York) often depicts women as houses and the vagina as entrance and thereby confirms the masculine *idée fixe* about the being and function of woman.

The bodily awareness of woman is characterized by the experience of the body as boundary, as difference. Precisely because the Self merges with the body under the pressure of culture, this urge is present to give the body what it wasn't possible to give the ego — autonomy and delineation from the outside world, the superego. In order to detect the difference between itself and the outside world, the body must first detect itself. The corporal experience of the difference, which the anatomical gender difference repeats, becomes important. From it arises the ontological experience of the body as difference. The anatomical difference of the sexual body is the original difference. Through her body woman becomes difference. So the body also becomes an instrument to experience and express her difference. But as we have seen, the female body doesn't present itself as a unity with itself, as autonomous, but rather as heteronomous, associated with physical objects and animals. In appearance, the difference is obliterated, the boundary diffuse. In truth, hidden behind it is a problem of representation.

## THE ENIGMA OF THE IMAGE

In order to represent themselves as difference, the heteronomous elements (the body as well as the objects) must be present at the same time. The difference can't be demonstrated otherwise, for if I were to show only the body or only the objects, I wouldn't be portraying the difference. In the representational fusion of body and objects, of body and space, in the annexation of environmental body into one's own body, it is not confusion which is represented, but rather the merciless difference which is the real experience of the female body. The ontological experiencing of the body by woman is the simultaneous experiencing of the personal and the alien. Kafka's words, "the only reality is pain,"[11] apply because the experiencing of the body as the experiencing of difference is painful. Through this representational fusion the external world is, of course, robbed of the privilege of being inanimate. A consciousness of one's own being alive transfers itself in this feminine extension/projection of the body to the environment. Here is to be seen the source for that "animism" that is so fondly attributed to women: their feeling for plants and animals and inanimate objects. Nevertheless, this animation of inanimate objects, which is defamed as animism when it applies to a feminine extension or projection of the body, is nothing other than the direct business of culture. The technotransformation of the world, the replacement of organs by prostheses, is indeed a type of (inverse) animism, where living organs are equated with lifeless objects. The "animistic" ability of the woman (especially the witch) is thus the negative form of the masculine Proteus-like creativity. It is therefore not surprising that fetishism is to be found in the animistic as well as in the technical world, since their common origin is the projection of the human body into the environment, or vice versa, so that man can appear as a machine and machines can appear human. The structure of representation is a structure of fetishism, Stephen Heath (following Barthes) therefore correctly writes in *The Sexual Fix*.[12] The bijective association of animism and technotransformation hence focuses in the human body their common dream of the creation of the artificial human, of the final triumph of the animation of the inanimate. It is of special historical importance in this connection to indicate that the image of the most popular artificial human, namely Frankenstein's monster, was created by a woman, by Mary Wollstonecraft Shelley, in 1818, at the beginning of the machine age and the industrial revolution, and with the descriptive subtitle, *The New Prometheus*. Creations from the test tube, artificially engendered life, or reproductive technologies are thus not alien to "animistic" women, even to women of the age of romanticism.

We recognize that the representation of the difference in the image, which exhibits the female experience of the body in its ambivalent double structure, creates not only the enigma of woman, but the enigma of the image as well. In the representational system of phallocratic culture, where woman only exists as body or as image (or not at all), the representation of man is transparent, that of woman, however, opaque, since woman is always trying to be more than body and image. Perhaps one could even say that our culture has produced only images of women and that the only place where women can recognize themselves is in images. But images made by whom? The postmodern practice of questioning and deconstructing the images of women which have been begotten in the culture and realized in paintings and print media—of investigating them down to their feminine identity—is an assignment whose difficulty, if not to say aporia, could be formulated thus with reference to the passage from Freud with which I opened this essay.

The images of woman which our culture has produced are the portrayals of a reality that isn't the same actuality for everyone, but which, as socially constructed, represents different interests. The camera, which has produced the image lying in the cultural developing tray, is the masculine eye.[13] The image that is developing itself now in the culture (developing tray), is it the "real" image of woman? Is it the image of woman at all? And how can the feminine object of portrayal develop itself into a photo of itself, the photo of woman into the subject woman? How does the ego (of woman) form itself obliquely through the typical identifications of the subject, where it can recognize itself, if society either blocks the goals of identification for woman, or makes them diffuse or randomly variable? Freud answers with the reality principle. But we must ask, is it the reality of the body or the reality of the images (since these often converge with women)?

Therefore the feminine aesthetic takes recourse almost exclusively to the (naked) body of woman or the decoding of the image of woman. We have seen how both—the experience of the body and the representation in the image—are opaque because of the social impasse in which woman finds herself. The representation of the difference in the experiences of the body, like the representation of the difference in the image, are opaque and ambivalent. The opaque representation (of the difference) produces the enigma of woman and the enigma of the image. In the image, in the representation, the key to the enigma woman conceals itself. The woman is covered by images, by projections, by codes. Hence the almost manic passion in the feminist aesthetic of the postmodern to deconstruct woman, to disrobe her of her images, and in performance, to disrobe the body of woman. This deconstruction and decoding of reality in images and of images of reality cannot shake off the virus of the masculine discourse (because of the mentioned problematic of representation) and thus stand in danger of landing in a no-space, in black empty-space, as the experiences of women artists show us.

In the catalogue to the exhibition "Kunst mit Eigen-Sinn," the Portuguese photographer Helena Almeida writes apropos of her self-portraits, where her body, covered with black clothing, merges seamlessly into the black-painted background:

> Now I wanted to immerse my own body in black—just to see. This "experience in black" gave me the sensation as if I were expanding into infinite space. It was as though my inner self had fled to the limits of my body and, since it could not stay here, had left me and

dispersed itself in all directions, in an undefinable outside. It was the sensation to consist of nothing, to give myself up and at the same time to feel an abundance that led to this sort of floating-falling-space.

The theme already familiar to us returns again: the identification of the Self with the body, the boundary, the expansion of the ego into space and the simultaneous loss of ego, the consciousness of nothingness and of emptiness. The arena of woman is thus the empty space, the virtual space, the no-space. The portrayal of woman by means of the woman collapses into a black hole, so total is the impasse. The photo developing under the feminine eye is black; it yields no image of woman at all. The British artist Helen Chadwick's "Ego Geometria Sum Incubator," a photo installation, shows photos of her body in positions of the turn of the century together with childhood objects or geometrical solids; the photos are subsequently mounted attached to the geometrically reduced childhood objects, which are again repeated along the walls. This installation tries to reconcile two discourses—the body (the natural anatomy) and the machine (geometry), the organically alive and the lifeless. But in her geometric splintering of her own body she shows us again the ego dissolution, the virtual space, the virtual absence of the woman, who as "sex that is not one" (Irigaray), avoids every definition, classification, or identification. The question is only whether this avoidance happens voluntarily or as escapism under the pressure of the one signifier—phallocratic civilization. The feminine stagings of her own corporality are stagings of dissolution, of opacity, of indeterminacy, of ambivalence, of bare virtuality.

## THE REPRESENTATION OF THE BODY AND ITS ABANDONMENT

May one conclude from this that the feminine Self must detach itself from its own body as from its own images? Doesn't the black virtual space of woman tend towards the demonstration of the disappearance of the body, as in Almeida's photography? If woman doesn't exist and her space is invisible, therefore black, then her reality cannot be the visible body, nor the image of reality. Woman must undermine and overwhelm the forms of representation—body as well as image count among them—under which she has been abased. In an era characterized by what Martin Heidegger said in *The Age of the World View* in 1938 (published in 1952 [1950])—that the world is but an image, that the world only exists through the subjects who believe they create the world inasmuch as they produce its representation—woman must ruin the representation, the apparatus of representation of our society, in order to achieve Being. But she must also deny her negative forms derived from the masculine, the so-called feminine, i.e., she must accept that woman doesn't have to be a mother, doesn't have to be passive, doesn't have to be body, a feminine self for some other self. In the phrase "my belly belongs to me" woman again identifies the ego as body, as exactly that which the masculine definition of woman intends anyhow. If women are against the dissolution of the body, as it is being introduced through in vitro fertilization, then they thus confirm the masculine identification of woman as body. The woman must therefore break away from the body and these images of woman.

The great feminine forms of rebellion, such as hysteria and anorexia, teach us this as a rejection of the body as well as of its images. Hysteria derives its power precisely out of the ambivalence which the social impasse of the woman prescribes. In her book *Nicht Ich— Ich Nicht*, Christina von Braun writes: "The Hysteric 'disrobes' herself, strips off the body with which she had provided herself in the fight against the logos, as one would get rid of a disguise or a second skin."[14] Georges Didi-Huberman showed in his book *Invention de l'hysterie*,[15] in many displayed photographs, how hysteria was a fabrication of images, a theatrical production for the director, the doctor, the man. Charcot was likewise a stage artist, a conductor, who provoked, directed, and led the *mise-en-scène* and *en-images* of hysteria. In anorexia we see the strongest feminine rejection of the body, which doesn't, however, mean a rejection of the feminine, but rather the rejection of the masculine identification of the feminine with the female body. That anorexia ultimately leads to death, to the extinction of the body, only indicates that the anorexic woman prefers the disembodiment of the body to a disembodiment/forfeiture of the spirit and of language. Before her Self is disembodied in the body, she prefers to disembody herself. A change of paradigms in the gender role is prepared: "the body, the matter, which once were attributed to womanhood have become 'masculine.' The 'illness of the will to resist' on the other hand, has seized on the former characteristics of "masculinity": immateriality, spirituality of 'pure reason'" (von Braun 453). The hysteric, too, has already made a fiction out of her body. The real body becomes a stage for simulation in the hysterical drama. In anorexia the disembodiment, the dematerialization becomes total. The body appears as prosthesis, as "clone," as artificial organ. In the denial of nourishment, the total repulsion of the forces of the stronger succeeds from a position of powerlessness. The mother, too, is repulsed. The power of the mother, of the father, and of the real is canceled, inasmuch as they are given no more power over the body and no more power is given to the body itself. The delineation from the outside is total. The body, too, becomes outside. The body no longer intermingles positively with the environment, as in the previous examples. Rather, because the body belongs to the environment, from which the power comes, the body is rejected. The body appears as accomplice of the real and of power. Disembodiment, the dissolution of the body, is the triumph over the reality principle and over representation. The catch is clearly that this happens from such an extremely weak position that the resistance and the refusal can lead to one's own extinction. But isn't the position of woman, of the weaker sex, just that powerless in our culture?

In the denial of the body we recognize the denial of the real because it is a real of the masculine power or of the phallic mother. The actual double of the real is the body, anorexia teaches us. Its fight against the body is a fight against the real that represents the power of the man. The insistence of women on the body as their property, their real, not only contradicts the experiences of the highest feminine forms of representation like hysteria and anorexia, and contradicts the experiences represented in feminine artworks, but also consolidates the power of the real, the power of the masculine culture.

Against this background, flashy journalistic books like *The Mother Machine* by Gena Corea, which view reproductive technology as a mere "product of the male reality," as "exploitation of women"[16] are scarcely "fertile," to stay within the jargon. Because not only patriarchs want to "clone." The technology of reproduction can also be viewed as a softer version of anorexia, as an emancipation from the burden of the body, as a chance to release the Self of woman from the body of woman, beyond the mother image and beyond the reality principle that is a power principle. The social-patriarchally prescribed role of the sexes, the *idées* and *images fixes* of woman have become a reality, a materiality, whose double and accomplice is the body. As the anorexic struggles against it to establish and preserve her Self, her own identity, so too the cultural work of woman struggles. The desertion of the body as a double of the real belongs to the internal logic of subversion: how woman can reassemble, overcome, change, reconcile, and make effective for herself the transformation of the body and the transformation of the id, the dual axes of the cultural work that normally lead to an impasse for woman. From representation the front shifts to reproduction, where the sovereignty of the Self doesn't seem within reach for woman, if she isn't ready to abandon the image of the body in which the enigma of woman and the enigma of image unite and must unite, because for woman in the system of representation of our masculine culture, the image and the represented object have the same reality (see Carrington).

The image has always been handled as the double of the real. As image, woman became a victim of the phallocultural strategies of representation. The rejection of the representation of the body through the image, the hiding of the body (or the excessive exposing of the body) and the denial of the image therefore belonged to the emancipating art forms of the feminist aesthetic.

The insurrection defamed as specifically feminine—hysteria—was already a revolt against the body as the real, as embodiment of the reality principle (of the logos)—as in the denial of the sexual, bodily functions by Goethe's sister, who didn't want to leave her bed. Image and body are thus the two doubles of the real. Just as with the image of woman before, the woman as body is now in danger of becoming a victim of reproductive technologies. But since we at the same time agree with Freud, that the increased prosthesis-like quality arises from the progress of civilization, we cannot refuse disembodiment. In this dilemma the abandonment of the body is the way out for the feminine Self.

The mirror function of the body for the woman makes even the body into an image. Body, image, and portrayed objects become infinite reflections of the same level of reality. Because the transformation of the id presupposes the disappearance of the id and the transformation of the body presupposes the disappearance of the body, the retention of the body as the reality of woman is an obstruction which originates in the masculine phantasm and which hinders both transformations, and thus the ego-discovery and self-actualization of the woman as well.

The contemporary art of women shows us that woman has for a long time already viewed her body from the outside, almost as instrumental, although women artists still sometimes believe themselves to be portraying the body from within, to be producing images of the inside through the body. They hide themselves in the works as if behind the body. Hence the urge to expose the body. The instrumental view of one's own body from the outside is comparable to the minutes before the ascension of a balloon. It requires just a couple of steps more and the body will be dropped, left behind. Women have prepared, therefore, since Mary Wollstonecraft Shelley, in their own way, the prerequisites for the cloning of the body, for an artificial technology of reproduction.

The American performance artist Laurie Anderson shows herself in one of her latest videos as her own clone. In our phallic culture and in its system of representation ("Forces that [aren't] accessible to my conscious will," Carrington), woman doesn't have the possibility to simultaneously achieve autonomy of the body and autonomy of the Self, as the "case histories" and artworks show. In the experiencing of the body as difference, which is, however, represented in the media language and image (of the masculine logos) as a "mixture" of body and environment, the ego (its autonomy) only perishes when it has identified itself with the body, because then the ego apparently mixes with objects. The "mixture" of the heteronomous elements in the images of the body already indicates the tendency to sacrifice the autonomy of the body in order to achieve the autonomy of the Self, since only when feminine identity separates itself from the body and ceases to base itself on the attributes and functions of the female body, and ceases to define womanhood as mother, childbearer, wife, etc., then the blockade collapses and woman (as sovereign) begins to exist. As I have written elsewhere, "the biological order that is still forcibly imposed in our society by making physical attributes determine how we live, can only be expunged once the force of the body over the mind has been overcome."[17]

Technology and body are the bijections of a work of culture from which woman can't extract herself, not even in the radical case of the technology of reproduction.

NOTES

1    Sigmund Freud, *Civilization and Its Discontents* (1930), *The Standard Edition of the Complete Psychological Works of Sigmund Freud*, trans. and ed. James Strachey (London: Hogarth Press, 1961) 21: 90–91. Abbreviated in the text as CD.
2    Elaine Scarry, *The Body in Pain* (Cambridge: Oxford UP, 1985), 281.
3    Danielle Sarréra, *Arsenikblüten* (Munich: Matthes & Seitz, 1978), 75.
4    Unica Zürn, *Das Haus der Krankheiten* (Berlin: Brinkmann, 1986), 61.
5    Unica Zürn, *Hexentexte* (Berlin: Galerie Springer, 1954).
6    Freud, "The Dissection of the Psychical Personality," *New Introductory Lectures on Psycho-Analysis* (1933), *S.E.* 22:80. Abbreviated in the text as DPP.
7    Leonora Carrington, *Unten* (Frankfurt: Suhrkamp, 1981), 10–11. First published as *En bas* (Paris: NP, 1973). See also VALIE EXPORT, "Feministischer Aktionismus: Aspekte," *Frauen in der Kunst*, ed. G. Nabakowski (Frankfurt: Suhrkamp, 1980).
8    Shoshana Felman, *Writing and Madness* (Ithaca: Cornell UP, 1985), 15.
9    Freud, "Femininity," New *Introductory Lectures on Psycho-Analysis* (1933), S.E. 22:115, 132.
10   VALIE EXPORT, *Kunst mit Eigen-Sinn: Aktuelle Kunst von Frauen, Texte und Dokumentation* (Vienna: Locker, 1985).
11   VALIE EXPORT, "Women's Art: Ein Manifest (1972)," *Neues Forum* (Jan. 1973). A manifesto of the exhibition "Magna. Feminismus: Kunst und Kreativität." An overview of the feminine sensibility, imagination, projection and ambiguity, suggested by a tableau of images, objects, photos, lectures, discussions, readings, films, videotapes and activities. Compiled and organized by VALIE EXPORT, Galerie nächst St. Stephan, Vienna, 1975.
12   Stephen Heath, *The Sexual Fix* (London: Macmillan, 1982).
13   VALIE EXPORT, text on *Mann & Frau & Animal*, film, 1973.
14   Christina von Braun, *Nicht Ich—Ich Nicht* (Frankfurt: Neue Kritik, 1985), 453.

15   Georges Didi-Huberman, *Invention de I'hysterie* (Paris: Macula, 1982).
16   Gena Corea, *The Mother Machine: Reproductive Technologies from Artificial Insemination to Artificial Wombs* (New York: Harper, 1985), 4, 7.
17   VALIE EXPORT, "Feminismus und Kunst," *Neues Forum* (June–July 1973).


EDITOR'S NOTES

I    The Sarréra texts first appeared in French in 1976 and then
in 1978 in a dual language edition in Germany with drawings by VALIE
EXPORT. Doubt as to their authorship arose shortly after, and many
assumed that the editor, Frédérick Tristan, had adopted the name as a
pseudonym. A Danielle Sarréra does not appear to have existed.
II   Probably a synopsis of a diary entry by Kafka, February 1, 1922:
"Looked at with a primitive eye, the real, incontestable truth, a truth
marred by no external circumstance (martydom, sacrifice of one's self
or for the sake of another), is only physical pain."

- - - - - - - - - - - - - - - - - - - - - - - - - - - - - - - - - - - - - -

## FEMALE BODIES[1]

- - - - - - - - - - - - - - - - - - - - - - - - - - - - - - - - - - - - - -

### 1988

= = = = = = = = = = = = = = = = = = = = = = = = = = = = = = = = = =

The images of women generated by our culture are likenesses of a reality that is not the same for all, a socially constructed reality that represents different interests. One of the most important image-making media in today's culture is film. In German-speaking film, seventy percent of the parts are parts for men. What does this mean? The absolute majority of key functions and positions in the German and Austrian film industry, the state institutions devoted to film, the film schools, etc. are occupied by men. What does this mean?

Firstly, it clearly means legal and social discrimination. The question is: Can this discrimination be tackled by purely legislative means, by amendment bills and constitutional decrees? One answer is obvious: such legal approaches are necessary preconditions. In my view, however, one must actually ask: How, in our system governed by the rule of law, did such a fundamental social discrimination of women, that is at odds with our basic laws, come about in the first place?

The answer to this second question lies within the culture itself, in the way the current circumstances are constructed, how they are represented, modelled, and *depicted* by this culture. Accordingly, we must look at two things in parallel: on the one hand, the social development, the building of modern society with the help of science, technology, and politics, what we might call the social body, and, on the other, the cultural development, the creation of the modern body since 1800, since the beginning of the industrial revolution, a modern body based essentially on the establishment of sexual difference, on biological difference; and the use of this modern body in pictures, in a visual culture that was produced for the purpose of performing and perpetuating this work, this separation.

The French philosopher [Nicolas de] Condorcet, the English anarchist William Godwin, the English economist Adam Smith, the English philosophers David Hume and Thomas Hobbes, and the English economist Thomas Malthus took metaphors and analogies between body and state, in different and sometimes contradictory ways, as the basis of their social theories. Metaphorical correspondence between the body and the state: "Healthy bodies in a healthy state" was the slogan a few decades ago, and today's cult of fitness repeats this in its own liberal fashion. Precisely this notion of society as "the body of the people," which is preyed on by parasites and pests, leads to this parallel view of the development of the body in modern society and the development of modern society itself—not only because this body metaphor helped to found modern society, its laws, its ideology, but also because this body metaphor is still a potent force within society. In perhaps the most famous work of social history in the nineteenth century, *London Labour and the London Poor* (1851) by the English sociologist Henry Mayhew, economic terminology is already applied to the body. Mayhew speaks of productive and nonproductive bodies. As shown by the book's subtitle, "A cyclopaedia of the condition and earnings of those that will work, those that cannot work and those that will not work," the capitalist definition of labor is applied to the body. In his "Essay on the Principle of Population" of 1798, at the beginning of the industrial revolution, Thomas Malthus, too, described the distinction between productive body (e.g., that of the proletariat) and nonproductive body as the logic of modern society. Within this logic, it is clear that the reproductive body, as the word itself states, cannot be a productive body. And Mayhew unashamedly referred to nonproductive bodies, such as those of nomads, as parasites by which the *apparatus* of production, circulation, and consumption is weakened.

In this equation, then, the merely reproductive body is a parasitic body. Declaring women responsible for reproduction, as housewives and females, implemented a division of labor that gave them a marginal place in the construction of society, an activity represented not by the female but by the statesman—the man who is, who builds and realizes states and societies and their contents; beyond this, women were even degraded to the status of a profiteer, a parasite on the body of the state.

The drivel about reproductive biology that began at that time must therefore be seen in the economic context of the establishment of modern industrial society where women, as reproductive bodies, weaken production and circulation, where references to absence from work due to pregnancy and similar "breaks" serve to justify women's inferior social and financial status. But even today, we see the construction of a female body that is not fully capable of work, not fully productive, because this body is assigned reproductive tasks, and we see how this biological definition of a woman's social body is used to legitimize her social degradation.

The myth of reproduction, then, was devised as a mechanism of subjugation in connection with the construction of capitalist society. As a reproductive body, as a body that is not truly healthy because not truly productive, a woman cannot participate fully in the construction of modern society.

In this analogy of body and society, in the transferal of economic categories to physiological-corporeal ones, in this distinction between productive and nonproductive bodies, we see the first step towards the erasure of women: because within this system they become a reproductive body; because this class struggle, this social struggle, forms the basis for the myth of reproductive biology with which the social disadvantaging of women can be legitimized.

A physiological basis was constructed, a physiology of the body, with which women could be excluded from the construction of society and thus from the construction of culture. For the body of the state, the reproductive body has limited economic relevance. The aim of this metaphor, the analogy of state and body on which modern society is founded, was therefore to exclude a specific body from the state, from society, or at least to banish it to the lower regions. The construction of the modern body was thus also a suboperation in the construction of modern society, with the aim of stigmatizing and socially condemning the female body as the site of reproduction, of nonproduction.

The images in art that draw, paint, and characterize women as bearers of children, as mothers, as great forces of nature, right up to Lulu, have proved their servility to the system and contributed to its formation and stabilization, to its construction and representation.

In this way, women secretly become a disease of the social body, its fate, *femme fatale*. In the redistribution of female and male that began in the nineteenth century in the age of the mechanical revolution and continued in the postindustrial age—a task actually carried out by culture in the construction of the modern body and modern society—the female body became an allegory of modernity. The worship of prostitution, in the work of Baudelaire for example, the mythologization of mass sexual intercourse, while assigning these things to women, to women's bodies, must be viewed as a response of the nascent mass production of goods, what Lacan might call a "père-vers" reflex, a reflex directed toward the father. Mass production as a fundamental trait of the body of modern society is projected onto the female body as mass consumption of sex (as sin, as something harmful).

The extent to which the separation of bodies into productive and reproductive, male and female, is a purely social construction—the extent to which the separation of the sexes on the basis of biological, physical differences is a socially constructed myth—is laid out in Anne Fausto-Sterling's book *Myths of Gender: Biological Theories About Women and Men* (Basic Books, 1985), where biological, genetic, evolutionary, and psychological evidence is used to show how insubstantial gender difference based on biology and the body is and that it can only be explained in social terms, as socially intended, as a social economy of the body.

In her book *The Woman in the Body: A Cultural Analysis of Reproduction* (Beacon Press/Boston, 1987), Emily Martin, too, shows how even today the female body is judged by medicine in terms of productivity, how economic metaphors still flourish in so-called medical science, alienating women not only from their bodies but, as bodies, from the state, from the body of society.

In cultural grammar, the same applies to the view of childbearing as women's sole productivity. The uterus is the machine, the child the product, the mother the worker. Menopause thus signifies the end of productivity, and menstruation is failed production. In this logic of the body as a marketplace, as a factory, in this view of reproductive processes in terms of production, a woman who refuses to reproduce, who does not conceive a child, is thus worthless, because unproductive, ergo not really a woman. As this shows, those who content themselves with the role of woman as the bearer of children, and who even pride themselves on this, are actually defining themselves in terms of productivity and thus from a man's viewpoint, as a result of which childless women themselves often feel worthless, in addition to being considered worthless by society. As long as she defines herself purely in reproductive terms, then, a woman defines herself as a nonwoman.

This is why separation from the body, refusal of the body, is part of a great struggle for liberation from the patriarchal family and from the patriarchal state. The self-imposed periods of starvation undergone by holy women in the Middle Ages can be understood as states of longing for autonomy within a culturally redefined social body.[1]

What does this have to do with the visual medium of film, with the social status of women in film? The answer lies in the fact that culture has taken over the work of sociology. The metaphor of body and society has been replaced by the analogy of body and culture.

The economic categories for the definition of the body that were seemingly founded on physiological and biological ones, are now perpetuated by cultural categories that continue to refer to physiological and biological legends and myths in their construction of gender difference. I would like to refer here to my 1976 contribution to feminist theory under the title "Women and Creativity": "creativity in our culture is always directed towards a product. The *personal* creativity attributed to those whose greatest creative product is their own life or the life of those close to them, and the *social* creativity attributed to those who shape social relations in creative ways, are valued less than the *productive* creativity of those who by their own individual thinking arrive at new results in the field of science or art."[2]

The economic apparatus, for example, was replaced by the "cinematic apparatus" because the representative apparatus of the cinema is that best suited to the technique of the imagination, as Christian Metz has shown in his essay "The Imaginary Signifier."

This cinematic apparatus, referred to and discussed as such since 1978, as a part and element of the cultural apparatus, now constructs images of women that perpetuate the social definition of woman as a reproductive body. In "Through the Looking-Glass," her contribution

214

to *The Cinematic Apparatus* (St. Martin's Press, 1980), the volume she co-edited with Stephen Heath, Teresa de Lauretis writes:

"Insofar as the cinematic apparatus operates in history, is traversed by and in turn produces ideological effects in social practice, the current debate on representation, identification, subjectivity, gender and sexual difference not only occupies a critical space within a historical materialist theory of the cinema, but directly invests its basic premises."

Woman as spectacle, woman as naked body, as a commodity image in cinema, is the new economy of the body, the logic of capital in culture. The sexualization of the female body in film, the idealization of women as bodies in film, is the continuation of the forced labor, the separation begun around 1800. The image of women created by cinema underpins sexual difference afresh via the body. This image not only represents the social condition of women, it not only depicts the social position of women, but, by the force of this representation, of its imaginary function, the image also shapes the biologically justified sexual difference that perpetuates the early-capitalist distinction between productive and nonproductive bodies. The image thus constructs the discrimination of women. In film, the female body becomes the image of woman, to such an extent that the history of cinema and the history of the female body are virtually identical. The image of woman in cinema becomes the woman's body.

This ongoing classification of the female body as a marketplace, as an economy, as exchange value in visual culture, as we already know it from the early days of social theory, is characteristic of the way culture marginalizes, parasitizes, and excludes the existence of women. Just as at the beginning of the construction of modern society women were excluded by biological classification from the construction of the social body itself, women have been excluded from the construction of modern culture by the same mechanisms, via an almost inescapable logic because culture, visual culture, has ecstatically celebrated the female as a body.

Today, then, the work of constituting the modern body as a mechanism to repress the other half of the human race[3] not only continues unabated in our culture, it has actually gathered pace. A brief note on this subject: When the exhibition of contemporary art by women in the context of feminine aesthetics that I initiated in 1981[4] finally took place at the Museum des 20. Jahrhunderts in Vienna in 1985,[5] Jürgen Hohmeyer wrote the following in *Der Spiegel* under the title "Waiting for Josephine Beuys":

"So: a limited gratification for the beardless, menstruating, and childbearing half of humanity who have had less success than men not only on the football pitch but also, to date and for whatever reason, at the chess board. If we are going to talk about a comparison of intellectual achievement, then the latter is a less innocuous claim (because it can be more objectively checked) than any claim of inferiority where art is concerned."[6]

Cinema in particular thrives on celebrating, shaping, representing, modelling the physical beauty of women. It is visual culture, then, that unrestrainedly exploits the female body today, like capital before it. The exploitation of the body takes place not only in reality, but also in the media, via images.

This results in the paradox that the image of woman is directly linked to the image itself. The images of women generated by our culture are likenesses of a reality that is not the same for all, a socially constructed reality that represents different interests. May we conclude from this that the female self must detach itself both from its body and from its images?

Women must subvert and override the forms of representation under which they have been bowed down—including both the body and its images. In an age marked by a phenomenon noted by Martin Heidegger in 1938 in "The Age of the World Picture" (first published in 1950), namely that it is characteristic of our time that the world is now only a picture, that the world only exists via subjects who believe they create the world by producing its representation, women must ruin representation, our society's apparatus of representation, in order to gain access to being. But they must also negate the negative forms derived from the masculine, the so-called feminine, which means accepting that a woman does not have to be a mother, does not have to be a body, does not have to be a female self for another self.

In the representational system of phallocratic culture, woman exists only as a body or an image (or not at all). In fact, one could almost say that culture has only generated images of women and that women recognize themselves in images only. But who made these images?[7]

The image has always been treated as the double of reality, and the image celebrates the woman as a body, thus excluding her from culture.

In a real sense, women live in exile within culture. According to the logic whose development I have outlined here, a woman cannot produce culture because she has never been a productive body.

Women must therefore transform culture, transgress it even, because in the real existing culture constructed by men they really don't have a place. Only in the transgression of culture can women gain consciousness and produce art, produce their own image.

NOTES

1    For more on this, see Rudolph M. Bell, *Holy Anorexia* (Chicago: University of Chicago Press, 1985).
2    VALIE EXPORT, "Frau und Kreativität," in *Zur Situation und Kreativität der Frau*, exh. cat., Forum für aktuelle Kunst (Innsbruck, 1976).

3    Anna Wheeler and William Thompson, *An Appeal of One-Half the Human Race, Women, Against the Pretensions of the Other Half, Men, to Retain Them in Political, and Thence in Civil and Domestic, Slavery* (London, 1825).

4    I conceived this exhibition as an extension of the show *MAGNA. Feminismus: Kunst und Kreativität* at Galerie nächst St. Stephan in Vienna in 1975 and the 21st International Art Talks with the same title (concept and design of both exhibitions: VALIE EXPORT, organization: Dr. Erika Patka).

5    *Kunst mit Eigen-Sinn: Aktuelle Kunst von Frauen.* Title of the exhibition and of the accompanying publication, edited by Silvia Eiblmayr, VALIE EXPORT, and Monika Prischl-Maier (Vienna: Locker, 1985.)

6    Jürgen Hohmeyer, "Warten auf Josephine Beuys," *Der Spiegel*, no. 18 (1985).

7    VALIE EXPORT, *Das Reale und sein Double: Der Körper* (Bern: Benteli, 1987).


EDITOR'S NOTE

I    The original title, "Women and the Real: The Social Repressed" was replaced by "Weiberleiber" ("Female Bodies," the German "Weiber" being a rather pejorative term for "women") by the editors of *Neues Forum* without the author's knowledge.

---

## EXPANDED CINEMA AS EXPANDED REALITY

---

### 1991

==================================================

"Expanded Cinema," i.e. the expansion of the common-place form of film on the open stage or within a space, through which the commercial-conventional sequence of filmmaking—shooting, editing (montage), and projection—is broken up, was the art form that I chose in the mid-1960s when I realized that the course of my life would lead me through the history of art. During this period I had already completed a course of study in painting, and it was clear to me that I would turn towards the image, but this image would be the living, expanded one. I had been particularly impressed during my student years by Cubism, Constructivism, and Futurism, and thus with the form and extension of artistic expression in(to) space, and the related element, time; the interconnection between light and movement, processes that irritated my educated way of seeing; and above all the image, and an "actionist" method for dealing with the image. Today I make feature films, to the extent that the situation—and by this I mean the financial situation— allows it, but in all of my films there always occur elements of the film medium that I have won through my own experiences with, and deliberations on, expanded cinema. I always see film as a sculpture that, for me, has varying levels of ways of observing it.

I have also found a way to continue expanded cinema in my physical performances in which I, as the center-point for the performance, positioned the human body as a sign, as a code for social and artistic expression.

Today, expanded cinema is the electronic, digital cinema, the simulation of space and time, the simulation

of reality. The expanded cinema of the 1960s, as part of
the Alternative or Independent Cinema, was an analysis
carried out in order to discover and realize new forms
of communication, the deconstruction of a dominant
reality. Expanded Cinema must also be seen within the
context of the development of the political situation
in the 1950s and '60s—on the one hand, in the revolts
of the student movement that waged an attack against
dominant oppressive state power, and, on the other,
in the artistic developments of this period that sought
a new definition of the concept of art. Its aesthetic was
aimed at making people aware of refinements and shifts
of sensibility, the structures and conditions of visual
and emotional communication, so as to render our
amputated sense of perception capable of perception
again. It was a matter of abolishing old, outdated aesthetic values.

The bankruptcy of European culture in 1945, the
attempt to jump over the graves of twenty-five years
of political darkness and to find a connection with the
avant-garde movements of the 1920s and the avant-garde
that had been exiled left their imprint on the efforts
of the artistic groups of the postwar period. While the
majority of the European population turned blithely
toward a purely economic project of restoration, groups
of artists and intellectuals attempted to uncover the
foundations of European crisis and culture, and to find
new constellations by connecting with oppressed and
forgotten movements in art and thought, from Dada to
Surrealism, from linguistic philosophy to constructivism.
This mood also redefined concepts of cinema and film.

In 1916, Marinetti, Arnaldo Ginna, Giacomo Balla,
Bruno Corra, Emilio Settimelli, and Remo Chiti wrote,
in the manifesto "Futurist Cinema," that

> cinema is an autonomous art, one must face the cinema as an expres-
> sive medium in order to make it the ideal instrument of a new art,
> immensely vaster and lighter than all existing arts. It must become
> deforming, impressionistic, synthetic, dynamic, free-thinking.

We are convinced that only in this way can one reach the poly-expressiveness toward which all the most modern artistic research is moving.

The rediscovery and incorporation of modern linguistic philosophy, psychoanalysis, modern music, etc., served as nourishment for (re)building a culture that had been destroyed. The period of the 1950s and '60s was a segment of history marked by artistic innovation and political provocation. Young artists ransacked antique shops and archives to find spiritual nourishment beyond the groundwork that had been laid waste. The purpose of these innovations and provocations was to break out of traditional artistic representations, the inclusion of reality as a means of expression, and to overstep the limits of individual artistic categories vis-à-vis one another such as language, painting, film, and theater. Art is brought radically into question so as to bring artistic thought and intention to new forms for communication. In 1966, Stan Vanderbeek wrote in *Film Culture*'s "Expanded Arts" edition: "Everything expands, in all directions, there is a interconnection between all of the arts, literally between them all, and this is what it is about. I mean, let's say that art and life really should be one, and let's see what happens if we really make them one."

The term "expanded cinema" means just that—an expanded or broadened cinema. It is, as Birgit Hein writes, "not a stylistic concept, but rather a general indicator for all works that go beyond the individual film projection." I.e., it means multiple projections, mixed media, film projects, and action films, including the utopia of "pill" films and cloud films. "Expanded Cinema" also refers to any attempts that activate, in addition to sight and hearing, the senses of smell, taste, and touch. Nicolas Beaudin spoke in 1921 of a poly-level poetry which transmits the poetic synchronism of thoughts and sensations as a sort of film with images, smells, and

sounds." In the mid-1920s, Moholy-Nagy had suggested
rippling screens in the form of landscapes of hills and
valleys, movable projectors, apparatuses that made it
possible "to project illuminated visions into the air, to
simultaneously create light sculptures on fog or clouds
of gas or on giant screens."

The concept of "expanded cinema" was established
in Europe in the mid-1960s within the context of the
far-reaching movement of Expanded Arts and is a part
of the structural film inquiry which grappled above
all with the foundations of the medium.

In Expanded Cinema, the film phenomenon is initially split up into its formal components, and then put
back together again in a new way. The operations of
the collective union which is film, such as the screen,
the cinema theater, the projector, light, and celluloid,
are partially replaced by reality in order to install new
signs of the real. The cinematic image is freed from its
traditional image character through the exchangeability
and simulation of its signs. The filmic artwork was no
longer understood only in its symbolic expression, but
replaced by signs of the real; the media-technical separation of image and sound was transformed into reality. Sound was no longer a trace applied to the image
material, but originated in the gasps in front of the
microphone. The figures were not created on celluloid,
but through holes in the celluloid; the breasts were no
longer a sign on the screen, but were themselves the
screen. The mission of the Futurists was fulfilled in the
multimedia, intermedia activities of Expanded Cinema
under the motto of the expanded concept of art. It made
it possible to engage individually in every element of
the collective form "cinema" to re-form and re-interpret
context in such a way that not only the apparative art is
liberated from the confining mechanism; rather, it also
frees image-connected thought from its constraints.
The Expanded Cinema, which can also be referred to as
the liberated cinema, is part of the tradition of liberated

sound whose project was initiated at the turn of the century. Expanded cinema is a collage expanded around time and several spatial and medial layers, which, as a formation in time and space, breaks free from the two-dimensionality of the surface.

In 1967, Peter Weibel and I developed our Expanded Cinema in Vienna. We examined the relationship between reality and the apparatus that registered it. The media of expression and representation were themselves brought into this discourse. The expansion of our film work proceeded initially from the material concept; thus the "illusion" film was transformed into the *material* film, and in this way the foundations of the film medium were reflected. Film was brought back once again to its value as a medium, liberated from any linguistic character which it had taken on in the course of its development. The formal arrangement of the elements of film, whereby elements are exchanged or replaced by others—for example, electric light by fire, celluloid by reality, a beam of light by rockets—had an effect which was artistically liberating and yielded a wealth of new possibilities, such as film installations and the film-environment. In the production of the film medium, celluloid is only one aspect that could (also) be deleted. The freeing of this radicality from the illuminated film material was also a prerequisite of the expanded cinema. Instead of the projected image, the film strip itself can become a site for expanding the medium and, consequently, if the celluloid becomes a filmic image as material rather than through projection, a transparent PVC-foil, held before one's eyes, can supply the desired image of the world onto the foil, he sees the world in accordance with his own image. This was the "Instant Film" that I invented together with Peter Weibel. We wrote the following at the time about it in 1968:

> "Instant Film" is a meta-film that reflects the system of film and reality. After the development of instant coffee and instant milk, we have finally succeeded in inventing the "instant film," which is

In any case, the axiom that "film requires celluloid" was
destroyed, just as the axiom, "film is dependent on the
screen" was repudiated, since the represented object—
such as furniture, a field, an animal or man—can itself
become a projection surface, which is perceived by the
subject, and the environment centered by the camera
is projected onto the subject itself. The film itself can be
completed by the life action of the filmmaker.

In my 1968 film, *Auf+Ab+An+Zu*, not only was the
celluloid painted on, but so was the screen. The materials used were a paper screen, drawing utensils, and
the pattern film. Instead of technical reproduction
into infinity and through celluloid, there was a shift in
production to a new sense of time. Only portions of the
projected image were visible on the screen; the re-
mainder was painted over in black on the celluloid and
was supplemented with drawings on the screen. In a
circular movement, the inked-over part of the celluloid
wanders over the screen; the portion which is thereby
freed is again supplemented by the actor. The initial
starting point is finally reached again, where the completed drawing could now be seen as image. This film
is a learning film, an excursion into painting, a rejection of painting; it is an echo of the cubist desertion of
painting. Space is conceptualized as a moment of time.
In that the camera circles around the reflected image
and transfixes all sides of a body into one and the same
place—namely, the screen—an overlapping of static
images results. The emancipated viewer, who must take
part in the production of the film in order for the film to
be realized at all, uses the drawing pencil to supplement

what has been painted over on the celluloid. The simultaneity of the projection and the montage which takes place on the screen rather than on the celluloid shows that montage is drawing. After the film is shot, montage; after the montage, the projection: so goes the rule. Any attack on this rule, on the continuity of the phases of production, robs the production companies of their conventional success. Here montage and projection take place simultaneously. The film is painted over, not glued together; in the end the strokes and lines of the reproduced reproduction remain within the projected square. Editing in film is the equivalent of painting; metric film editing that tries to capture time as music is an echo of painting.

The site of film is not the layer of emulsion on the celluloid, the screen, or the cinema screening room, but the system of signs. Peter Weibel reinforced this point through his theoretical statement: "The ontological difference between the representation and the object becomes the point of departure and at the same time the identificatory transfer occurs again: the reflection and the object overlap one another in a newly arranged process-oriented presentation of the filmic media." He demonstrated the identity of the representation and the object as the identity of the site in a performance in Vienna in 1967 in which he projected a film onto his own body. Weibel:

> Whenever the site of the film is not the screen, houses can be projected again onto houses or bodies onto bodies, the representation and the object overlap one another, the representation and the celluloid become superfluous. Technical reproducibility is replaced by immediacy, and with this the objective character of the film is transcended; state-reality is not reproduced, but rather the subject and its experience predominate. The "world" is no longer simulated; rather, the possibility of producing "world" is demonstrated.

My/our works were/are always intended to be seen within the context of a social struggle, as an attack on state reality so as to destroy the limits of state reality and the traditional concept of art, for expanded cinema also means expanded reality. Transformed media produce a transformed world, and a world pressing toward transformation presses toward transformed media. Expanded cinema was not only an expansion of the scale of the optic phenomenon, but also was intended, in this phase, to do away with reality and with the language that construes it.

In my film *Ping Pong* (1968), a feature-length film ("Spielfilm") or a film to be played, in which points appear on the screen in an alternating rhythm, the actor who stands before the screen must hit these points with a ping-pong paddle and ball. I wrote the following about it in 1968:

> Independently of semantics, the relationship between the viewer and the screen is clear: stimulus and response. The aesthetic of the conventional film is a physiology of behavior, its means of communicating a phenomenon of perception. *Ping Pong* makes explicit the dominant relationships between the producer/director/screen and the consumer/viewer. What the eye tells the brain in this case is a release of motor reflexes and reactions. *Ping Pong* renders visible ideological relationships of domination. The viewer and the screen are partners in a game whose rules are dictated by the director, whose demand is that of making screen and viewer into a single unit of trade. To this extent, the consumer reacts actively. Nothing illustrates the dominant character of the screen more clearly as a medium to be manipulated by the director than this; no matter how much the viewer also enters into the game and plays with the screen, his status as a consumer is altered very little. The screen only appears to be a partner of equal value; the one who reacts is only the viewer, not the screen. The emancipation of the screen, which emancipates the viewer to become a producer, has not yet occurred; the viewer deals with the screen, and yet it does not react.

Here a film projection developed out of the function of the screen; the apparatus shifts between the image of reality and the experience of reality. Without the action of the viewer, the film remains incomplete. The intention is not that of achieving a psychic condition, but rather a direct experience of codification.

If the material itself is the experience, one also arrives at the thesis that "film without film," i.e., without celluloid," also originates an image in the examination of the film medium, its laws, its prerequisites. In accepting this thesis, the Viennese filmmaker Hans Scheugl made his film ZZZ *Hamburg Special* in 1968. The "film" consists of a strand of thread, which is run through the projector instead of celluloid, the shadow of which wanders back and forth on the screen in the form of dark stripes on the white-beamed screen by the projectionist. Scheugl wrote: "In this way the viewer is forced to think about whether the thread is really on film or whether it is really running through the projector. Thus an important requirement of intermedia is fulfilled: the creative input of the projectionist."

A year earlier, in 1967, I created the image on the screen through simultaneous real procedures in *Abstract Film No. 1*. The materials for this expanded movie were a mirror, water, thick and thin liquids, flashlights, and the screen. I wrote this about it in 1968:

> Here abstract patterns are created by concrete materials; there is no differentiation between nature and sign. Technological effects are achieved using simple means. A flashlight shines on a mirror, over which the various liquids are poured. This phenomenon is projected onto the screen through the reflection of the projector light; abstract moving patterns are created. The image on the screen is the result of the traveling of the light, for we only see what the light transports. This is of course true of every film. The recourse to natural means such as water, light, and mirroring, the reduction to elements, and the departure from technology creates above all unexpected and yet fundamentally illuminating connections with minimal art, land art, art povera. The same phenomenon can also take place in nature; the projection surfaces here are nature's screens.

After this came *The Magic Eye*, also made in 1969 together with Peter Weibel. *The Magic Eye* is an auto-generative screen that, through selenium cells, converts light and non-light into sound. The sound usually originates in the projector. In the light/sound process invented by Vogt and Engel between 1920 and 1930—their optical sound film process, photographed sound—the sound frequency is transformed into corresponding light frequencies, which on their part influence the light-sensitive layer of a film strip that is run at a constant speed. When it is replayed, a beam of light is modulated by the frequencies of brightness indicated on the edge of the filmstrip. A photographic cell accepts the light frequencies, which, after having been appropriately amplified, control the loudspeakers. In *The Magic Eye*, the sound develops on the screen, since it is prepared with photo cells, relays, etc., so that the light creates the sound. As film, a film with abstract patterns is used; if it is dark, the sound is deep, if it is bright, the sound is high-pitched. Since, however, the gauging of the light value is not the composite of the entire surface, but rather an individual impulse of the diverse cells modified depending on the light that falls upon them, an intense sound collage develops. It is not the sound trace which supplies the fluctuations of brightness; rather, the projected film or the public itself or the lighting in the room, etc., create it themselves. To each film at each moment its own sound.

Emancipation from the industry is also possible through the subjectification of film, through the abandonment of the industrial standard of presentation. The human body becomes a skin screen. The modification of the projection surface tends to eradicate as much as possible the difference between the object and the sign, and to emphasize the reality of the medial character of the film vis-à-vis the reality outside the movie theater. It shows us a way of undertaking contextual changes and expansions through the subject of the artist himself and thus also of the concept of the sign.

In *TAPP und TASTKINO* (TAP and TOUCH CINEMA), which I made in 1968, I examined the breasts as a central theme within the film industry. The *TAPP und TASTFILM* is a street film, a mobile film and the first real women's film. The performance takes place as usual, in the dark. Only the movie theater has become somewhat smaller, there is room in it only for two hands. In order to see the film, which means in this case to sense and feel it, the "viewer" must put both hands through the entranceway to the theater. Thus the curtains which previously had been drawn up only for the eyes is also finally raised for the hands. Tactile reception counteracts the fraud of voyeurism. In state-sanctioned cinema, they sit in the dark and see how two people make it with each other, and they themselves are not seen. In *TAPP und TASTKINO*, social prescriptions are no longer obeyed; the intimate sphere of what the state permits is forced open into public space. Since the consumer can be anyone—child, man, woman—it is an unveiled intrusion into the taboo of homosexuality; the morality of state prescriptions, the state, family, property, is exploded. For as long as the citizen remains satisfied with a reproduced copy of sexual freedom, the state will be spared a sexual revolution.

As Metz writes, for classical film theory, "film is the product of photography and the phonograph, i.e., of both of the modern technologies of mechanical doubling." In the conventional debates on film, the concept of similarity, of analogy, is defined not so much through sensuous experience, i.e., through an individual category, but much more through abstract identification, through re-recognition as a necessary condition of communication—i.e., through a social category. If one consciousness wants to communicate with another, and this communication is filmically coded; if reference is made to a process of analogy, an analogy is required that does not produce the subjective experience that would be one of freedom and fantasy, but rather through a process that constitutes social communication: identification. Identification means that, through the construction of a conceptual system that everyone can relate to equally, the reactions of the users of this system are predictable and controllable.

Identification is a process of the adaptation of consciousness to a concept that can be a concept for everyone. Sociological models are reinforced in the cinema. Yet film, photography, and the phonograph are not mechanical replications, but extensions and expansions of our structures of time and space, of our experiential structures, of our interpersonal communication—they are expansions of our reality and our independent consciousness. Voices address different places at different times, the past is made visible, space and time can be transported, spaces and times, hierarchies and values disappear. In a *total art*, the boundaries between artificial and natural reality, between actual and possible reality, between the products and the producers, between man and object are transcended. Gene Youngblood writes in his book on expanded cinema: "Today when one speaks of cinema, one implies a metamorphosis in human perception. Just as the term "man" is coming to mean man/plant/machine, so the definition of cinema must be expanded to include videotronics, computer science, and atomic light." This was written in 1970.

The forms of strategy in the 1960s and '70s that were internationally and nationally dominant continue into the 1990s in multimedia performances, by expanding and adapting the electronic media. The electronic cinema bids farewell to the commercial fairy tale of film as mimesis, for in the electronic film, the image has no place: it occupies space.

## THE RENT IN THE PICTURE OR RUPTURES IN SPACE AND TIME

### 1995

In my presentations of the rent in the picture, in the medium, I would like to start with my expanded cinema works of the 1960s, such as *Cutting*, where words are cut open or out, the cut in the screen between the material and the transparency, the cut in the skin—*the suture* between the *media*.

Something is cut out of the screen (1, 2), the locus of the phonetic sign separates from its track, language is no longer on the soundtrack, but used in reality. The screen-skin is cut, the technical term "body cutter"—a part of the splicing press where edited strips of film are put together—is translated into reality true to its nature. This actually means dealing with the way perception is encoded by the machinery that depicts and represents. Breaking up the suture in the visual arts also started in film theory, and forms part of the theory of Expanded Cinema.

Cinematographic techniques, such as space-time intersections, editing, montage, fade-overs, non-linearity, contextual variations, as well as intermedial techniques, such as destruction and abstraction of the material, have been introduced into the visual arts. The depicting apparatus is the suture; the technical equipment such as the camera in cinematography, photography, and video as well as the computer has made the difference between image and object, between the object and the way it is constructed, and between sensory reality and constructed reality particularly dear.

The space of the picture is the sign system of the
real, the symbolic, the imaginary. Irritation of the gaze
(3), haptic communication—the sense of touch is placed
vis-à-vis the visual representation.

The female subject within the symbolic order: opposition, refusal. One engages with the self and the body
and thus begins to engage with the image—and with the
gaze designing the "body," for that matter.

The broken suture, the cut within formal and aesthetic processes is one of the structural issues at stake
in Expanded Cinema. Its aesthetic shows the shift,
the abolition of sign construction. The concentrations,
the blanks, the areas of friction within the system
of the medium are what makes the visible features of
expression pertaining to the medium especially clear.
The events take place in the interstices, the media,
the images explore themselves at the intersections, in
the cuts. The context of the image is important because
the images are not supposed to reflect imaginary unity,
but the *difference*.

The way reality and perception are encoded by the
depicting and representing medium is thematized: two
families sit opposite one another, one on the TV screen,
the other in the apartment. (4) What can be seen is
not a program (because the screen at which one family
looks is at the same time the screen of the other one;
the specifics of the movie screen are thus transferred
to the TV screen), but the response to the program.
This response is the same as the audience's reaction
because the response of the family is also/still the program watched by the other family (TV in the family,
a family on TV). The TV set functions as an imaginary
screen, representing precisely "the interface where the
subject experiences separation and difference" (Silvia
Eiblmayr).[1]

Delayed reproduction in *Zeitspalten – Raumlücken*
(Time Fissures—Space Gaps) (5, 6) results in the par-
ticipating viewer reaching the monitors at the moment

when he/she moves on screen, but due to the diagonal arrangement of the cameras and monitors he/she proceeds from one monitor to the other in imaginary motion. He/she can see him/herself approaching on one monitor and—here is the rent, the rupture—walk away on the other; thus, past, future, and present converge where the rent is, while the body is really in mid-motion.

The camera shows the upper half of the room while the monitor stands in the lower half. The media apparatus divides the room, which is split in yet another way: between full shot and detail as mediated by the camera, the field of vision. I jump as long and as often as it takes until the body is visible in the mediated image.

The wound of the room is closed when the body appears on the monitor. *My body is the suture, my body is the interface.*

The image is considered the stand-in for reality. The suture joins the reality of the medial space with the reality of reality, with sensory reality, pitting one against the other at the same time. The body bears signs, conveys information. The female body is the locus where "culture" creates a barrier to block out woman.

In the 1970s I was concerned with visualizing the history of alienation from ourselves, including myself who I wanted to look at as alien because, for me, true action is always outside what happens. The physical awareness of women is always characterized by the feeling of boundaries, of difference. Thus, the female body becomes an instrument to experience and express difference.

*...Remote...Remote...* (9, 10, 11) is a performance for the film, but also a film in which the suture, the seam as a cut in the body, appears as a cut-up spot, as the picture of a cut or to be cut, as the seam of action between past and present, as the gap in identity, which reveals itself as a cut of the body, as a bleeding wound.

As the language of that which is present, the body forms part of the rhetorics of reality; the influence of culture on the body causes its substitution and absence.

The body is the *locus where civilization takes hold*, it reveals the signals, the signs of social influence, it is the medium of the real, of control. Precisely because the body represents our real being in the world, it is able to show the cuts left by injuries; is that the price to be paid for the evacuation of the subject to the realm of the imaginary?

The culture we insist on invariably comes with the influence of culture on the body, the *transformation of the body*; the stigma on the body is the visible energy, with the will behind it being sacrificed in the cultural discourse. The events of the past have a bearing on human behavior, no matter how far removed these experiences may be in the past. Therefore, there exists a para-time in parallel to objective time; in this para-time, deformations, bound to the principle of reality, have a constant impact.

*In the rent, in the cut we see the real picture—the drama of human self-development.* However, the questions "Who am I?" and "Where am I?" continue to be posed if that which characterizes me is an "incarnated and reproducible construction." My answer is: "I am where I stage 'disappearance.'" *Existence passes the test in the suture, in the rent.*

The following quote by Jean Laplanche is taken from the book *The Practice of Love* by Teresa de Lauretis, in which de Lauretis goes into even greater detail when she deals with the same theme I looked at in my film *...Remote...Remote...* dating from 1973, a theme which I also see in the context of the presentation of my works: the rent in the picture, not only in the visual image, but also in the psychological one, the rupture in the psychological process, the split between subject and object, the initiation of the subject/object separation which can no longer be kept up. The subject/object separation dissolves in the object and the subject of a sign. "On the one hand there is from the beginning an object, but . . . on the other hand sexuality does not have, from the beginning, a real object. It should be understood that the real object, milk, was the object of the function, which is virtually preordained to the world of satisfaction. Such is the real object which has been lost, but the object is linked to the autoerotic turn, the breast—become a fantasmatic breast—is, for its part, the object of the sexual drive. Thus the sexual object is not identical to the object of the function, but is displaced in relation to it. . . . The object to be rediscovered is not the lost object, but its substitute by displacement; the lost object is the object of self-preservation, of hunger, and the object one seeks to refind in sexuality is an object displaced in relation to that first object. From this, of course, arises the impossibility of ultimately ever rediscovering the object, since the object which has been lost is not the same as that which is to be rediscovered."[2]

The images are not designed to express imaginary unity, but difference. The ontological difference between image and object becomes the point of departure, the suture. (12)

There is no such thing as the wholeness of the body, the difference only appears to be blurred by the digital suture. It is only in the symbiosis with the foreign body that difference can be experienced—in an experience of oneself and of that which is foreign while the body of one's surroundings is incorporated in one's own body, something is made possible by the digital suture. (13, 14, 15)

To be able to represent a difference, the parts, bodies, objects, surrounding bodies, body surroundings have to be there *at the same time, simultaneously*. This is the only way there is to show differences, to trigger off an experience of oneself and that which is foreign.

[ILL. OF WORKS BY VALIE EXPORT IN THE TEXT:

1–2 *Cutting. Expanded Cinema*, 1967/68
3 *TAPP und TASTKINO*, 1968
4 *Facing a Family*, 1971
5–6 *Zeitspalten – Raumlücken*, 1974
7–8 *Bewegungsimaginationen – Implementation*, 1974
9–11 *...Remote...Remote...*, 1973
12 *Syntagma*, 1983
13 *Twi – Topon*, 1991
14 *Rot winde Leib*, 1991]


NOTES

1    Silvia Eiblmayer, in *Suture – Phantasmen der Vollkommenheit*, exh. cat., Salzburger Kunstverein (1994), 15.
2    Jean Laplanche, "Life and Death of Psychoanalysis" (1976), quoted in Teresa de Lauretis, *Practice of Love* (1993).

- - - - - - - - - - - - - - - - - - - - - - - - - - - - - - - - - - - -

WITH SARA ROGENHOFER AND
FLORIAN RÖTZER

- - - - - - - - - - - - - - - - - - - - - - - - - - - - - - - - - - - -

1988

====================================================

**SARA ROGENHOFER AND FLORIAN RÖTZER:** Under the banner of the vaunted postmodernism, it is common today to read diagnoses spelling the end of a modernist avant-garde that has failed in its intentions. But feminism rose up in the wake of the student movement, as an emancipatory movement in both the old and modern senses. Is there any indication that the avant-garde concept has continued in feminist art?

VALIE EXPORT: The avant-garde has been discussed to death and wished it would die by people on all sides. In my opinion, the patient still shows strong signs of life, but is not lying there where might be expected—in the hospital of the art business. For a long time it was assumed that feminism could take over the concept of the avant-garde, as it has done, but it must also devise new concepts through the ideas of postmodernism. Feminism is a movement which in its specific postwar form came to a close as such in the 1970s, before being revamped in the 1980s—above all by American feminism—in a form closer to popular mass media than art history. American feminism drew on the theories of Freud and Lacan, feminist theory from France, semiotics, art theory, image theory, linguistics, and the possibilities of reproductive technology, and examined the cultural gender image of woman through an amended theoretical agenda. The ideas of postmodernism are reflected in this undertaking. An avant-garde concept that also gives women space and location can only be developed through a new art or, better, through counterart.

SR/FR: It is noticeable that the younger generation of women distances itself from feminist art, from the "tampon art" of the 1970s. On the strength of past experience, what problems now confront a feminist concept?

VE: They are still by and large the same old political and social experiences. Not a lot has changed. There are merely apparent changes. Obviously there are now more women artists on the market, and more women museum directors and gallerists, but when one looks at the large, important exhibitions, the proportional representation is still just as low, or only marginally higher. And one must note with sadness and dismay that only a small percentage of the female gallerists and heads of museums who have managed, as we say, to establish themselves at these cultural interfaces look at the work of women artists and promote them. But these selfsame women have been able to gain their positions as a result of the feminist awakening in the 1970s, with help, that is, of countless women in all fields who fought in those years for women's self-determination in the face of humiliation, ignorance, and misplaced criticism. The task facing feminism in the 1980s is not only artistic creativity but above all inquiring into social creativity. The political and social appraisal must continue, more so than ever, because there is every sign that the 1980s are becoming increasingly reactionary. When people talk of the tampon, menstruation or vaginal art of the 1970s, it is a great slur on women's art. What is being cited is in fact the weaker side of feminism. Obviously 1970s feminism worked to combine a specific form of representation with a definite expressive content stemming from the world of female experience. But there were also other, strong sides. I merely wish to recall here the work of the Austrian Friederike Pezold, or the American artists Yvonne Rainer and Joan Jonas. Here, as with Lynn Hershman, Ulrike Rosenbach, and myself, person and representation were united in the 1970s in such a way that women's cultural coding—from art history to the mass media—became the point of departure. The image of woman was not simply reconstructed or presented in the poses imposed on her by the culture and the mass media, but also deconstructed. The aim of feminist theory in the 1970s was to depict woman's various socially coded identities and explode them through one's own self. This was continued in the 1980s by Cindy Sherman. Alongside this there was another path that I considered legitimate, which occupied itself with female mythology to arrive at mythological representations and even symbols taken from the world of biology. That of course was seen as reason enough by feminism's opponents to give a derogatory assessment of feminist art and deny its strengths. In addition, this "vaginal art" fitted more easily into the male view of feminism. I was never particularly fond of that kind of art because I was aware of the great dangers that lay in its reception. But recent women artists have distanced themselves not only from this kind of art, but by and large from feminism as a whole. Two years ago we organized an exhibition at the Museum des 20. Jahrhunderts titled *Kunst mit Eigen-Sinn*, featuring national and international female participants. And the replies we received said, for instance, that some were more interested in promoting the Green Party or ecology than feminism. I can't understand that. Feminism is on a downward slope in society, but the image of woman in public has gone unchanged, and broadly speaking women have once again fully adapted to the image that had already been made of them. Nothing has changed, the image is exactly the same. It has merely become hazier, with a few added concessions, but feminism is far from having achieved the goals that militant

feminism erected in the 1960s. The departure from
feminism is moreover a sign of the times, an expression
of the 1980s because people no longer want to be political, because art no longer wishes to tackle the present.
After the disappointments in the 1960s, or the failure
of the rebellion, the younger generation was no longer
incited to continue. Moreover, the conflict of the generations that we still had then is no more. Generations
now follow on from one another at an incredible speed,
so it all gets blurred equally fast, while previously
things got bottled up much more and more resistance
developed.

SR/FR: Feminism as a political and social goal is still
clearly a necessity, but what forms of representation
would belong specifically to feminist art?

VE: Feminist art is now moving away from the specific
topics and issues of the 1970s. Its task now should be
backing the quality concept in art to such an extent that
the question of whether a work can be assigned to a
man or a woman is no longer at the forefront. Art is one
medium among others for female self-determination,
but only when the definition of art has been changed,
because only then can other values come into being in
art and art saved from disappearing. Eighties' art is
a capitalist art. Which presents the problem of which
works will enable a woman to find her place in the system, because under capitalism not only the picture
but also the woman is circulated as a mere commodity.
The one important thing is that art tackles the theoretical issues that should always be raised, and that they
are recognizable in the artworks. The quality is most
certainly not decided by the art market or the museum.
A great many women worked with the Russian Con-
structivists, for instance, apparently on an agenda of
equal opportunities. That for me is the right approach,
because it was under the premise that the product was

created with the same abilities and had to meet the same demands. The demand today is for women artists to not subject themselves to a marketing strategy, to the requirements of those galleries that finance it, or to a museum program, because the aim today must be to work once again on the fringes of art history, on the borders between image and reality, where again specific feminine topics would flow into the creative process. Admittedly this is not conveyed as directly as it was in Body art in the 1970s.

SR/FR: So would you now distance yourself from the question of whether there's such a thing as a specific feminine aesthetic, as perhaps still informed the exhibition you organized? The emphasis on overall quality goes at least beyond establishing gender differences and female self-assurance.

VE: This question has been posed in literature and the visual arts. I think that the question about the female aesthetic is answered in the depiction, in the way, for instance, the woman depicts herself, because the chief source is female experience as such, which incidentally was also the point of departure for the women Surrealists. They produced wonderful works that shed light on women's self-definitions, but at the same time there are countless testimonies in literature and the visual arts on the destruction and alienation women experience in our culture.

That can be taken to the point where the woman presents herself as an object that is not present and cannot be portrayed, and is only still represented in that object's surroundings. That too is a reason why the feminist aesthetic keeps returning to the body. Which naturally brings with it problems of quality, because the way image and representation are understood is examined. The female aesthetic informs the creative process and the way the work's visual character comes across.

The quality of the cultural work lies in the deliberations made over this difference. So a female aesthetic is not as easily realized as we had hoped in the 1970s. It is hard to characterize because, viewed from a feminist position, one still has no idea what the image of woman really should be like because it has always been determined by man, or rather by society. If the image is rejected, then at least the rejection is presented, which relates in turn back to the image. Recognizing and working through these problems is where the claims to quality can be identified, and for that it is necessary to know the theory involved, not just the intentions or brushstrokes. Another important point that should not be forgotten is that now in the 1980s woman has freed herself from her victim status, as was still quite evident in the 1970s, above all in Body art. And as I wrote in the introduction to the catalogue for the *Kunst mit Eigen-Sinn* exhibition, women have developed an aggressive energy in response to the obliteration of people and animals, an aesthetics of resistance that liberates the social body from the traces of colonization: society is denuded and, naked, woman turns the mirror back on it. This aesthetics of resistance is the feminist aesthetic. The definition of what female aesthetics includes can already be honed by looking at a number of women artists.

SR/FR: Could you elucidate the structure of a female aesthetics by an example you see as successful?

VE: The picture on the cover of our catalogue by the Portuguese artist Helena Almeida. It is a self-portrait in which her body, clad in black cloth, blends seamlessly with the black-painted surface around her. By letting her black-covered body flow into the blackness, she shows us the non-space, the void or place of woman. Speaking about this experience in blackness, she says that she extended out into a living, indeterminable space, as if her inner self had fled to the edges of her body and, unable to remain there, left her and spread out in all directions in an undefined outsideness. One can observe in this self-staging of the body how much the question poses itself regarding female identity and having a life and mind of one's own. But she also points out that women regard their own bodies as alienated. Woman is a construct of male culture, which is why the feminist aesthetic focuses almost exclusively on decoding woman, because woman is covered in projections, codes, and images. The feminist aesthetic invokes the image of woman, because the image is the commodity. Naturally the question arises as to whether the empty space is seen as positive or negative. It is the space where ego-loss is incurred, the space in which a woman withdraws from every definition, classification, and identity. It is her space because otherwise she has none. This dilemma cannot be clearly resolved.

SR/FR: How in your work do you tackle this insight into the irresolvable entanglement of female identity between identity loss and identity refusal?

VE: In my films and photographic works I take, for instance, body parts, or sections of physical expression that are not seen as specifically female portrayals, which either are hardly noticed or very frequently used. The first example might be hands, the second legs. I assign the various body parts to different media and forms of expression, thus placing them forever in a different context. So, the first image is destroyed by the presentation of the second, the third image destroys the second, and so on, while all the time remaining with the same body. Practically speaking, this means that I employ video, slides, film in film, and projections that relate to one another. Video shots meet up with film footage, say, which may on occasion show the same thing. I employ a great variety of media and in that way

transfer content into different contexts. It is like a
narrative technique in which I constantly rearrange the
words in a sentence, swap a term around, expand it or
contract it. I call these medial anagrams, which determine the formal sequence. On the content level I try to
find topics that involve a neutral female identity that
cannot be categorized. The identity is not attributed to
the person in the film, instead their identity realizes itself split into a social identity, a female identity, an ideal
identity, and a merely possible identity that is as yet in
no way definable. That would be the level of agency.

SR/FR: Peter Gorsen has spoken of "polytechnical
dilettantism" in regard to female methods of production. That would apply to you given the way you
employ the available media and materials for your
work. But when one imputes a trace of dilettantism
to women's art, which would counter the pressure
for professionalization on the art market, one could
also see it as the reason for the low acceptance
shown towards women artists.

VE: Gorsen is correct in his description of the polytechnical method of production among women. It comes
from the women's position in art and society as Other,
from the fact that the meaning of my text can only be
conveyed and accepted by inscribing it in the text of
the Other, in the text of the other culture. The polytechnical production arises from this intertextuality, but the
designation of dilettantism is wrong. It comes solely
from the men's different system of norms and values,
from a kind of colonizing gaze, the way Europe looks at
the culture of so-called savages. In utter contrast, the
male "dilettantism" evinced by the neo-expressionists
was enthusiastically greeted under modernism. I work
in various media because I cannot stick to just one
medium for my artistic expression, and because each
of the media gives my work a different dimension.

Obviously I lay claim to professionalism in my work, but not in the manner demanded by the art market, which for me is capitalist professionalism, design, and overdressing. That was very evident at documenta 8, where everything was inflated into vast dimensions. It is clear to me that there is no art today on the art market because art is not a commodity and does not exist as art in the sense of today's art critics. All that exists in our capitalist society are commodities, even ideology becomes a commodity. That is the two-fold dilemma facing women, because what should artworks be like if they confirm both woman and art in their commodity status? Perhaps one could take the works of the American artist Barbara Kruger by way of example. For this reason topics that many women are currently exploring are not that provocative when seen in terms of feminist aesthetics. The work of the Belgian artist Marie-Jo Lafontaine at the documenta 8 was one such significant example of an aesthetic concept rooted in the male world. The work's structure was phallic, but made by a woman, which also was the reason for its enormous success.

SR/FR: As you described your way of working, it was conspicuous that you want to experiment with various levels of presentation which you can juxtapose, superimpose, and allow to mutually destroy one another. The final consequence of that would be the disintegration of identities and the creation of indifferences. But that would come very close to a postmodernist phenomenon, the deconstruction of identity, the fascination exerted by a lack of subject, the corrosion of meaning or indeed the blurring of the real and the imaginary in a play of free-floating signs that no longer have any reference. Were these features decisive for your work, or does it have an additional, critical element that transcends the desire for disintegration?

VE: The question of the female subject is of course central to my work, because its status is questionable in our culture and society. The game with woman's identity, with the images and codes of female identity created by our culture, is a central strand in feminist aesthetics in the 1970s and 1980s. As can be seen from me, Lynn Hershman, and Cindy Sherman. Which is why I am interested in postmodern theories of subverting the subject, because I want to dispel the old notions of the subject that have contributed to women's repression, and to release woman from the social norms and enforced codes, such as that of the mother. But I cannot follow Jacques Derrida, say, when he sees the mere questioning of the subject or woman as a confirmation of phallocentrism. The phenomenological attempt to overthrow Hegelian dialectics by a particular postmodernist trick strikes me as somewhat conservative, and explains my distance and critique.

SR/FR: Where do you see the difference in your work to that of conservative postmodern versions?

VE: My concept seems to operate in a similar way, but does not confirm the theoretical concept of postmodernism. The approach using media does not provide any confirmation, it simply transforms the one into the other—like in an endless chain.

SR/FR: You initially became known through your contacts with Vienna Actionism. Actionism had already reacted against the way society was pervaded by the media, insomuch as it placed importance on the uniqueness of authentic occurrences, but it was arranged so that the events could be reproduced on film or photographs. Jean Baudrillard—today the veritable artists' theorist, although he expects nothing from art—claims that under the present condition of universal simulation every occurrence has been rendered impossible, that breaking through to reality, to the immediate or even the appearance of an Other promotes precisely this simulation. Baudrillard comes from the tradition of the Situationists, who already in the 1950s criticized the "society of the spectacle," and can be bracketed together with a belief in the possibility of subversive actionism. Nowadays this kind of actionism is scarcely practiced any more: what dominates now are stagings that operate with media, but that merely theme the endless game of references, which appears to be fascinating in itself. To what do you attribute this development, which also distinguishes your present work?

VE: I have always used the media of photography, film, and video in my work because they lend themselves best to my kind of artistic expression, allowing me to create several levels of reference and presentation in an action or performance. Over and beyond social confrontation, my artistic work aims at examining the media themselves and expanding their possibilities. My questioning of the normal view of art was done via the medium, which took me along a road from the destruction of the concept of reality to exploring the zone that lies between reality and its depictions. This region has become for me the field of simulation. It has increasingly pervaded my work with the media, which are useful for that, together with video and digital art because they enable temporal and spatial aspects to be simulated. Already at the outset of my work I devised film-in-film situations and the like, which paved the way for further developments. So my path was consistent.

SR/FR: But there was an underlying criticism at the time regarding the aim of liberation. You said that your main concern was still with undoing women's prevailing images and codes, but that a counter-image is impossible today. Likewise the earlier aim of triggering a critical awareness through shocks also doesn't work anymore, does it?

VE: I still certainly lay claim to subversiveness, on the basis of my choice of topics and the way I employ media. Naturally a shock effect was sought back then in the tradition of Dada and Surrealism. But today, society has absorbed and cushioned these shocks so well that you no longer do that in the old style of Dada and Happenings. My work is subversive because it does not accord with the normal understanding of art. Which is why my works are always manifestations on the fringes of present-day art, which does not tackle feminist art and only pays very limited attention to media.

SR/FR: Speaking quite generally, where in formal terms do you think the socio-political dimension should be brought into play in art?

VE: I have made, for instance, a video that carries on in the tradition of my Body art. In it I took the body as a commodity, as an object for sale, and showed the contrast between a male and a female body. Body parts are sold or lent out from the male body, while the female body still lets itself be sold traditionally for money, via a ticket. The subversive aspect in this little story is that everyone knows that the body today is sold via, for instance, promotional items, while the rules governing posture, body definition, and physical behavior are determined by religious morality, which has now been replaced by business. Business morality determines how the body should act and define itself. That for me was a great watershed in western thought. One can even see it now in the way business infiltrates the whole art world and increasingly defines what artistic expression should be. That's what the video was about. The provocations were just small affairs, such as handing out hosts on the street bearing company logos. Those are the church's commodities. Other pieces, such as the film ten years ago, *Unsichtbare Gegner* (Invisible Adversaries), still cannot be shown everywhere, not only due to the on-screen sex but also the criticisms of Austria. In other works the subversion lies solely in the way they resist being integrated into the art business. And that's the crux of the matter: they must remain outside the art framework, as is true of large areas of critical intelligence in the 1960s, when people could still produce critical works in literature, film, and art, and then went into exile in other regions in the 1980s, such as computers. One could see from the example of Hans Haacke's piece for documenta 8 that critique today must look like the object it criticizes, the criticism of a bank like bank advertising. That is no longer subversive, that is assimilated.

SR/FR: There is a current trend in philosophy towards art. Art is perhaps an ersatz for the loss of a political philosophy or a philosophy of history, or maybe just a suitable object for a reflection that avoids plain words and wants to present itself as paradoxical, pluralistic, and open. You were saying that feminist art should likewise open itself to critical theory. What is the affinity then between artistic production and philosophical reflexion? Is there a common starting point? And which philosophical approaches at present are especially fruitful for artistic production? What in fact is the impact of enlisting philosophical reflexion for artistic work?

VE: The theories are props. As I said, a lot of theory has been generated from the loss of the socio-political dimension. Sometimes one gets the impression that theory is produced for the artworks, which are made synchronously. There's a powerful interaction. Or it's said that now theories are produced that are instantly turned into artworks by creatives. Theory is important for me so that I can handle and work with the various concepts of reality. As such I am interested in theories which, like semiotics, psychoanalysis, linguistic philosophy, or computer work, undo the old sense of reality, and I gain a great deal of information on them during my stays in the U.S. Especially important for me is the international feminist debate.

SR/FR: Do you actually use digital technologies?

VE: As far as possible, but it is almost impossible in Europe because the means of production are too expensive and one is so dependent on the technicians.

SR/FR: Does the use of digital technologies present telling differences in aesthetic representation, compared to the old techniques such as painting, prints, film, or photography, where one still has to deal with the demands posed by the materials?

VE: It leads at any rate to a different understanding of reality, because these technologies totally confirm the theories that say depictions are not reality. One may still doubt that in film, because an ear always looks like an ear. With video there was never any doubt that it gets destroyed by transmission. The image doesn't have an ear, the sign becomes invisible. An accident occurred recently in Munich when a small airplane crashed. Austrian television already produced a simulation of how it could have occurred. One can imagine that every occurrence is already simulated in the media, and what's more one can simulate a lot of situations that we don't yet know. The image of reality will be expanded by these artificial realities, although obviously no realities are natural, they are all artificial. So those would be artificially produced artificial realities.

That will also influence film and the visual arts. One can see the backlash at documenta 8.

SR/FR: One could speak here of a grand revival of the object and materials. Which could be interpreted—regardless of whether from Kiefer, Beuys, Jetelová or Serra—as art's last howl of protest before the object is eliminated in its physical presence. Similarly paintings are growing into monumental dimensions while simultaneously disappearing.

VE: The trend to gigantomania in the installations and paintings clearly shows the fear of loss, because the simulated image is coming, which is a very different kind of image. So now the leftover rubble and garbage is being arranged and blown up in scale as a result of this fear that images will go lacking.

SR/FR: Vienna Actionism focused above all on the body and sexuality, and was almost exclusively done by men. Did it in fact prompt you to try depicting the female body in a different way?

VE: Vienna Actionism already existed as I embarked on my artistic work: it was pursued solely by men, and its concern with the body anticipated a great deal that came later in Body art and performance art. Broadly speaking Vienna Actionism was a further development of Informalism, of Action Painting and Abstract Expressionism, and occupied itself with social critique, art critique, and mental issues. Also of importance was the concept of the Situationists. Drawing on this I developed my ideas for a Feminist Actionism. There were already works by Carolee Schneemann, Charlotte Moorman, and Niki de Saint Phalle in the 1960s. Certainly Vienna Actionism bolstered my ideas of using the human body as art material. In addition I found inspiration in Yves Klein and from my friendship with artists like Peter Weibel. My works did not come about, though, as a counterreaction but rather as a corrective. What influenced me was the subject matter and the provocation, indeed, the subversive mood that prevailed back then in Vienna. The shock was also related to society at large, but this was outweighed by the fact that art was being produced here that could never slake the citizen's thirst for leisure-time distractions. This led to even more aggression because the cultural asset "art" was being handled so directly. I also think that the most important new artistic currents in postwar Austria came at that time, whether in literature, film, painting, Actionism, or expanded cinema. The starting point for my works was, as we have discussed, that woman's body, and naturally woman herself, must be freed from its outside determinants, from its male-defined history. In my actions I have always used my body as a sign carrier, as a social code from our culture, because, as I have written with regard to my actions, the discourse with my body as a locus of signs of a sexual, social, emotional, and other kind is always a discussion with society—a questioning of society insofar as the information and sign functions of the body include not only the personal but also the social code.

- - - - - - - - - - - - - - - - - - - - - - - - - - - - - - - - - - - -
## WITH HELMUT DRAXLER
- - - - - - - - - - - - - - - - - - - - - - - - - - - - - - - - - - - -
### 1991
==========================================

This interview was made directly in response to two gallery exhibitions by VALIE EXPORT that are running simultaneously in Vienna (Galerie Insam and Generali-Foundation), the first in ten years and almost exclusively focused on her film work.

HELMUT DRAXLER: As I was preparing for this interview and looking at the films, I felt I was being drawn away from the fundamental questions about feminism and Actionism, about film and gallery culture, to arrive at individual details and motifs from both the films and the object-based installations, which, when compared, can rise to statements that perhaps are not yet readily encountered as global interpretations.

VALIE EXPORT: Really?

HD: These motifs included, for instance, the foam in the scene right at the beginning of the portrait of Oswald Wiener, where Wiener is soaping himself. Which is to say, on the one hand, male foam, shaving, castration, indeed the depiction of masculinity that can be shown quite directly here, and on the other these windshields in the exhibition, which either are set up as objects on the floor or have been pieced together on the wall. Both motifs can be read paradigmatically. Let's do a bit of free association.

VE: I found the shaving scene in the Oswald Wiener film pretty exciting to do because he used a cutthroat and not a safety razor, a technical device. He stood in front of the mirror and spoke a monologue. At one point I walked back and forth with the camera between him and the mirror, so that one can see that although the monologue was directed to the mirror, it was cast back out by the camera. That produced various levels, so that it wasn't even a monologue but a kind of dialogue with his own image. That's what was so exciting about it. And then the way he covered up his whole face and obscured his physiognomy, which was followed by scraping off or scraping out what had been obscured with the blade, until finally his face was revealed and with that an identity. And all the while he kept referring to his own identity, about how he arrived at ideas, and how he felt as an artist and poet. And during this his face became increasingly bare.

> HD: Isn't this way of conducting a dialogue with one's own image, the narcissistic element in it, a very particular kind of male discourse?

VE: Self-observation? Oswald Wiener calls it self-observation. When one looks through his books, from the *Verbesserung* (Improvement)[1] to the present, he does not view it as specifically masculine. On the contrary: women also perform self-observation, self-observation is common to us all, just the way of going about it may be different. The 1970s focused very strongly in feminist or female aesthetics on self-observation, although the women looked back to mythology, which was not really my thing. So it was a matter of going back down the history of self-observation and positioning oneself in it. Wiener is not concerned with going back but with working with the material at hand, or with projecting onto some future material. Perhaps women first have to tackle the past with their self-observation in order to arrive at the position which men already set out from. Even in academic discussions, as conducted, for instance, by American feminists, what in fact is most important is dismantling and deconstructing the past. The male discourse doesn't have to do as much dismantling and deconstructing because it has constructed it all itself. I'm quite happy to go along with this deconstruction, but not with that 1970s mythology business, with its goddesses, for instance. That didn't interest me one bit.

HD: I want to come back to the shaving. It's clear that shaving is always a symbolic castration, which to my mind is quite clear in the film. And if we stay with mythology and fantasize about it in a slightly perverse way, we see the foam from which Venus arose. Which is to say it harbors a very specific aspect of male discourse that says that although he is happy to castrate himself symbolically, it is only so that he can keep his phallus even safer in the real world.

VE: The connection between shaving and castration, that's right, but one can also view it differently, as change, for instance, as a civilizing thing. The beard could be the civilizing element, and the bare face simply nudity, a naked skin, which in turn is like a blank screen on which things can be projected. That would be in the exact opposite direction, because the phallus is the civilizing element, and it is that which is removed, shaved off, if you like, in order to be free from it. And then what would be left is the pure body, the naked skin, and there would be nothing more that would make one say that's now phallocratic or feminist or whatever. What I thought then was: The woman is always shown naked. In the last hundred years she has been stripped bare at a breathtaking speed, from the tips of her toes to . . .

HD: . . . under her skin . . .

VE: . . . to under her skin. Yes, it's astonishing how quickly woman has been undressed. But one can reverse that and say that for once the woman has turned the mirror round and undressed society. Look and see what happens.

HD: But the beard as something savage is classic, and civilizatory work consists in taking the beard away, erasing or razing the rank growth. In that case the naked skin would be civilizational . . .

VE: Gem? A polished gem. Yes, but one can by all means view it differently.

HD: There is one more point in this scene which in some ways is structural: Directly after he finishes shaving, Oswald Wiener says that he is fully aware of how little all the psychologisms and tales and handed-down resources can help us, because we are simply automatons, highly heteronomous subjects, and that he has in no way managed to convey this evidence or belief, to transpose it and simultaneously remain a writer. During this scene he has a very martial look, a bit like Cézanne in a lot of his portraits, and something of the pathos of failure about him. Doesn't feminism also have to say the same to itself, once in a while?

VE: It's not failure. Naturally there are some partial failures, that's obvious. But I see statements like these from Wiener and other writers as referring solely to their own lifetimes. He says okay, those were now the last thirty years, and I have still as many more to live. I no longer have the time for this matter or that, and others simply don't interest me any more. But feminism cannot be related to a lifetime. There's an up and down. If one were to say we now have postfeminism, or a post-women's-movement, that overlooks the fact that the first women's movement already achieved a great deal before the war. It all drifted apart after the war, so that people had to start again from scratch, and that is why it cannot be integrated into one brief lifetime. One can only really ascertain how productive the feminist idea has been as and when one is genuinely able to deconstruct and not controvert the major images of our century, such as Freud and Lacan. Only then could one say that feminism had retained its power to assert itself.

The women's movement has fallen apart, admittedly, but I see a difference between the women's movement and feminism. Feminism is a political and human attitude that wants not simply equal franchise or the right to decide about one's own body—my uterus is mine, and so on—but much more. It's rooted in cultural politics, how one sees civilization and culture, how they can be molded. The women's movement, on the other hand, has failed because it let itself be gobbled up. Just what shrewd and cunning opponents one must confront in society could also be seen in the left-wing movements, and women were much weaker. That can be seen quite explicitly in the new Hollywood films. The ideal woman is fifty percent a *Cosmopolitan* model, a bit Jewish, nicely settled down in her career and equipped with a certain ambition, she isn't overdemanding on her marital partner, and becomes a mother with the associated ups and downs, which is to say she's allowed to cry and then afterwards to have a laugh. In this she embodies the whole essence of the women's movement, having a career, etc. The woman should simply achieve everything, while being completely exploited, of course, which in plain terms means that these serious goals have simply been swallowed up in full.

HD: Isn't a figure like Julie Burchill reacting to exactly this situation in *Ambition*? As a yuppie strategy adopted in a feminist way, the aim is to play

along in every game and master the men without
them ever noticing. Ultimately as much benefit as
possible must be derived from the existing situation.
Do you see a prospect there?

VE: That is a cost-benefit calculation. And that to my
mind doesn't add up. By dropping the perspective of
change one ends up with idealized illusions like this,
getting the most out of a situation because such and
such won't be allowed to cream off everything. Yet
it's by no means about winning and gaining, but about
changing the attitudes held by men and women and
achieving a mutual dialogue. One cannot conduct a dialogue with one-sided reactions.

HD: Perhaps we can move on now to the *Windshields*
in the exhibition. How far can one grasp them as
dialogic in structure, or aren't they perhaps barriers? Duchamp's "Large Glass" has always struck
me as being a barrier in the Lacanian sense between
a sign and its meaning. The two realms flow, by
and large, independently of one another; although
the barrier is permeable, that is only in a very undefined and fortuitous sense. No real communication
occurs. As ever, what is decisive here is difference,
and ultimately the conflict over the phallus as super-
signifier remains irresolvable.

VE: I am not arguing against barriers or different
levels that cannot instantly be connected up. Nor am
I at all concerned with pushing something through in
a linear manner. What is interesting is that such interfaces exist. And that is also what my work aims at.
In the case of the *Windshields* one can start first of all
with the glass. It is there as material and generates
images; the images are present, but as immaterial
images on the surface. Simultaneously they are images
in space. On the other hand, the syntactic link to the car

is important as a means of transport through time and space. That corresponds in fact to the camera, but just as equally to the typical screen on which images of our times with claims to deconstruction and dismantlement are brought to life in a cinematographic language.

HD: If I understand you correctly, that means the deconstructive potential of the windscreens lies in their complex model-like nature as simultaneously object and structure. Something that is evident in every object but that one scarcely sees in any one. Quite to the contrary, as barriers wouldn't they be extreme compactions of relationships?

VE: That's right, that has been key to many of my works. But with these windshields set on the floor, which in the catalogue are titled *Empty Windshields*, yet another element is involved. I only realized that much later on, and they should in fact be titled *Aura*. I am not referring to the auratic but to Benjamin's explanation of the aura as an image that is not there yet nevertheless present.

HD: I think that's rather a dangerous concept. What is interesting about the aura is that it does not stick to specific things, it can be everywhere. It's only a question of numbers.

VE: Correct, because the concept is so complex and does not let itself be defined either by the emptiness of the objects, or by the way they stand one behind the other, or by their materiality in space, and in that way it evokes the concept of image production.

HD: The majority of your works show that your central concern is always with ways of seeing, with looking and with one's own gaze, which is decon-structed, or with fragmented gazes that alight on you. That could lead to yet another theoretical discussion, such as appeared in your Actionism documentation,[II] where Baudrillard is interviewed and tries to distance himself from Debord and Situationism. Because, as he says, the idea of the spectacle revolves solely around the spectators and the attempt to butt in subversively, while in a simulation everything has become backdrop, so no one can stand apart anymore and simply look on.

VE: For me the program of simulation is fine. But I don't think the onlooker can be silenced. Even a simulated reality still always revolves around the viewers. So the disappearance of the spectator, onlooker, or witness, as one might say, is simply hyperbole that Baudrillard concocts so as to keep exaggerating everything. That is interesting to me as an artistic program, but is not directly related to my work.

HD: My picture of Baudrillard's theory about the death of the social goes in the direction of seeing it in fact as an enormous farce from the Cold War—the consummation, as it were, of the capitalist paradigm under the shield of the nuclear threat. The topic assumes a central position in your book (*Das Reale und sein Double: DER KÖRPER*, Benteli, 1987)—as confirmation of the enormously proliferating cultural prostheses, on the one hand, and their occupation by very definite social roles on the other.

VE: That is an extremely complicated bundle of issues. Essentially, the two areas can scarcely be linked, unless, that is, one views social roles as polyphonous or polymorphic configurations. One can arrive from these polyphonies or polymorphisms at the theory that one should avoid letting oneself be tied down any more. But that is also a refusal of identity. The upshot of this is an increasingly differentiated social aspiration that could also square with the constant transformation of woman's image. When [Friedrich] Kittler says that, thanks to the binary code, there is absolutely no need any more to distinguish genders, that there would be no more masculine/feminine, it is an attempt to escape to a technology that cannot and will never add up. Genders quite assuredly exist in the social realm. The social and the technological can only be successfully married if one keeps making the crossover points visible. The two realms must be made to penetrate one another. It is not simply a matter of shattering and fragmenting; these fragments must interpenetrate. One could compare that perhaps with a stack of glass sheets. A single pane is transparent and fragile. That would be a fragment. But placed in layers they produce a weighty mass that loses all transparency. One must drive a wedge into it so as to make the penetrations visible. That would be a step forward.

HD: Kittler's arguments really are grotesque. The concern rather is with access to technologies and media, and thus of who makes them, who uses them, who consumes them, etc. If one breaks that down in social terms, the result looks . . .

VE: . . . sad, really sad.

HD: In your book you also criticize the drawings by Louise Bourgeois, who repeatedly uses the common metaphor of the woman as a house. The connection between woman and architecture also crops up in your own works.

VE: Louise Bourgeois always uses woman in a totally patriarchal sense as a walk-in house, while my work tackles not only the so-called phallic but equally the urban signs that are decoded by woman. That goes back to my works in the 1970s, the "body configurations," but nowadays the body is even more mediatized in its semantic construction.

HD: Conversely, not a little feminist criticism has been aimed at you. This was already true of the early Actionist film ...*Remote...Remote...* (1973), and your fundamentally positive view of genetic engineering as having a certain liberating potential.

VE: Women have always rejected *Remote*; not until the 1980s was it deciphered in a feminist light by a woman theorist. Men found the film easier, which is to say comprehensible in an art history perspective. For women in the women's movement it was simply too hard, too destructive. I cut into the flesh under my fingernails with a knife. That was misread as self-inflicted suffering, but it was an attack on a fetish. That had to be done with strong means. The women's attacks were rather for other reasons: because of my constant rejection of the ideology of motherhood. Motherhood has to be replaced ideologically, not necessarily biologically. I am against surrogate mothers and similar forms of exploitation. It is already impossible to predict the things genetic engineering will come up with one day. Obviously I reject genetic engineering that exploits and manipulates. But the ideology of motherhood should be abolished because it always rebounds on women. So these women said: I won't let anyone take that from me, that's a woman's own potency. But it doesn't figure that way. It's so that women keep still and silent, as if they'd been drugged.

HD: How can one construct something like a social identity, for instance as a woman artist, if one abandons these ideological bridges?

VE: The pressure to conform is at its lowest when one keeps as far as possible on the outside. Which is why at the age of thirty-two or thirty-three I had lost all

identity outside of the physical one. But one needs
a permanent attitude in order to remain productive and
subversive. Nowadays I find my identity at its most
satisfactory when I can see the subversion, at least
for myself. Which does not of course create any identity for me in social space, none at all. This is all the
more complicated in that my generation has become
far more extreme in its demands for power and in the
way it is manipulated. I am by no means saying that
the ideas of the 1960s have been repudiated—they have
long since been carried to the grave.

HD: That's easy to understand. After the father was
killed with such vehemence, people now seem to
have developed a fear of actually becoming fathers
themselves. The problem is not about abandoning
the ideas, but of swapping roles.

VE: Perhaps I must speak here for the first time as
a woman. The men have long since recognized that
ideology is a means to power, which is why it is used; it
is wielded against women as a tool, and a lot of women
are simply in the dark about that. The ideology is there
and it should be scrapped. Because the question is not
about attaining power. What I believe rather is that
what the women theorists, artists, and the whole range
of feminist inquiry achieved was the purest pioneer
work. People will only recognize that later. It is not
recognized at the moment because everything goes so
fast and immediately gets absorbed. But basically it's
like the Wild West, when the settlers arrived in their
covered wagons, trailed across the land, and finally
noticed that merely a barren layer of soil had to be removed and that if one dug long enough one could plant
potatoes.

EDITOR'S NOTES

I    Oswald Wiener, *Die Verbesserung von Mitteleuropa* (1969).
II   *Aktionskunst International*, 1989.

- - - - - - - - - - - - - - - - - - - - - - - - - - - - - - - - - - - - - - - - -
## WITH ROSWITHA MUELLER
- - - - - - - - - - - - - - - - - - - - - - - - - - - - - - - - - - - - - - - - -
### 1994
===============================================

ROSWITHA MUELLER: Since the beginning of your engagement in the arts in the mid-sixties, you have been interested in the technological media and you have especially concerned yourself with the potentials of the new electronic and digital processes. What has sustained this experimental attitude over the years?

VALIE EXPORT: The technological media allow for a new kind of image production, which is completely different from earlier image productions such as painting. I am mainly interested in the difference in materials as the condition for artistic statement. The image production in digital technology is based on the construction of models. In this case I see image production also as the production of models, which allows me to expand and continually change the process of representation, which has been important for my entire artistic production. A few years ago I began work with the computer. I confronted analogic photography with digital photography, in order to foreground the disjunction between the two media. Then I transferred the digital photography to different materials, for example, textiles, transparent materials, chemical materials, etc. I can also use digital images for holograms or for cyberspace. It is always my goal not to create a photo-realistic environment, which is how it is mostly used at this point.

RM: I am very interested in this notion of models. What puzzles me is that it seems to be such a static

and normative approach, when all your efforts are
directed toward change.

VE: Certainly, it is true that models are static, which can
be a disadvantage for the artistic process since they
evoke uniformity. In contrast, in painting, the gestures
of the hand, body, and mind can be expressed freely.
But in the nonobjective art of the classical avant-garde,
signs of a model character can already be detected.
Digital technology determines our view of the world
today and in turn this technology was informed by our
mathematical explanation of the universe. The question
is whether this is the only representation of our world.
I don't think so.

RM: Since your stated goal is *not* to create photo-
realism, do you search for specific strategies,
depending on the particular medium you are using,
to counteract its effect of realism?

VE: Every medium has its own relation to what we
call reality and can be subverted in its own specific
way to counteract this effect. What is most important
to me is to have at my disposal different languages
of expression and of meaning. I define language here
in the broader sense as a system of signs and meanings. Society restricts the plurality and differences of
languages by demanding that only one language be used
as its language, the language of socially sanctioned
ideology while discriminating against and exiling
divergent elements. My works may be following philosophical, social, cultural, sexual, psychological, or technological insights; and for each of these avenues the
medium of expression and of artistic representation is
different and can also pursue various methods. In other
words, not only the means of expression but the themes
are important to me, since I am interested in showing
aspects of the phenomenal world. Multidimensionality,

transformation, and difference are the common denominators of my work. I sometimes have termed my productions "medial anagrams."

RM: Can you describe how medial anagrams function in your work?

VE: Medial anagrams are units of representation which are transposed into different contexts and codifications. What interests me is that even minimal shifts in context will bring out differences in signification for the same unit of representation. It is a kind of language system for image production in the technological media.

RM: This technique has been likened to postmodern strategies of the deconstruction of identity and to a fascination with simulation. Does this correspond to your intent?

VE: I am interested in postmodern theories of the subversion of the subject since I would like to dissolve the traditional view of the subject, which has contributed to the oppression of women. It could also be helpful in freeing women from social norms and enforced codes like motherhood. But I do not follow the postmodern philosophers when they equate the question concerning women's subjectivity with a confirmation of phallocentrism. The phenomenological attempt to overcome Hegel's dialectics in certain postmodern theories seems rather conservative to me.

RM: An Austrian male critic took it upon himself to characterize the mode of production specific to women as "polytechnical dilettantism." How do you respond to this term and do you think we still need to be concerned about defining a feminist aesthetics?

VE: The term "polytechnical" is justified. This mode of production has its base in the position of women as Other both in the world of art and in society. It is a consequence of the necessity to inscribe my text into the text of the Other in order to make it acceptable and to communicate in the first place. But the label "dilettantism" is not appropriate. It derives from the difference in the system of values and norms established by men, which is a type of colonizing view similar to the way Europe as a whole looks at the cultures of so-called savages. The "dilettantism" of male artists, on the contrary, was enthusiastically affirmed by modernism and neo-Expressionism. I work in different media because I cannot confine myself to one single one, since each medium adds a different dimension to my work. I do claim professional status for my work but not in the manner of the art market, which is for me capitalist professionalism, design, and overproduction. The documenta 8 where everything was raised to a gigantic level demonstrated that very well. In our society things exist only in their commodity form, including ideology. That is the double dilemma for women. How should a work of art look if it must confirm the commodity woman and the commodity art? The work of some women artists *follows* aesthetic concepts that are informed by phallic structures. More often than not, these attempts are marked by immediate success.

RM: This argument would seem to support the specificity of feminist aesthetics, not just as a consequence of women's marginality to the art market but structurally as well.

VE: There definitely are structures specific to women, but they are not inherent, eternal forms; they are time-bound results of our feminist debates and feminine acculturation. I agree with Irigaray's so-called "essentialist" intervention, which to me is not so much essentialist as it is a counterstrategy at a specific historical point in time to the determination of women's bodies by male tradition.

RM: In the seventies, video technology was sometimes called a "feminine" medium. You yourself have connected video with feminism. Can you clarify this further?

VE: There is nothing feminine about video and there is nothing masculine about computer technology. Neither is art feminine or masculine. The points of departure of expression, content, and representations may be gender specific but not the medium itself. If there is male dominance it also means that women have not tried hard enough to get ahold of the media and to use it for their goals. This is hard work because women have never been granted access without a struggle. Yet, it is necessary for us to succeed in this. On the other hand, we know that video was very important for women artists in the seventies, because the medium was not yet historically coded as male among artists, nor was it hierarchically determined. At the same time, it could provide information about forms of representation which are of great significance in feminist discourse. Video allowed for new explorations of concepts like "truth," "nature," and "reality." New technologies shed new light on problems involving notions of the imaginary, the fictional, and the real.

RM: To take a concrete example, can you imagine that your video *Silent Language* could be as effectively produced in any medium other than video?

VE: It could be done in cyberspace, but the meaning of representation is totally different. Cyberspace uses imaginary bodies, which means that the interesting clash between the fictional bodies of the ancient painting and the living body of the modern woman will disappear, because the body of the modern woman will naturally be based on the model of the frozen image from history. In that sense the whole point would be lost. In other words, history cannot be represented in cyberspace in this way, because this break on the level of representation is no longer visible.

RM: How does your contention that the new media expand our description and perception of the world apply to digital technology, since that technology no longer directly reproduces images from external reality.

VE: In the analogic media like film and photography or video, the image comes from the outside into the apparatus. There is an external reality, which, in whatever way, is reproduced. For some years now I have confronted digital photography with analogic photography, the images from the outside with the images from the inside.

RM: When you say "images from the inside," you are primarily talking about images that are technically produced inside the apparatus. Do you think that this is the continuation, by means of technology, of what the classical avant-garde has tried to achieve in the first place to distance itself and break with the reproduction of reality?

VE: Naturally, it is a continuation of one of the aims of the avant-garde, to part with the reproduction of reality. But it is more complex than that. In other movements of the more recent avant-gardes, one has tried to bring reality back into art. What I consider important in all of this is the continued investigation and questioning of reality and its reproduction. Interrogating

the perception, the concept, and the representation of
reality is the crux of all of my work. And the new technologies allow further extensions of this investigation.
Human history is the history of representation. As
long as we are caught in the dualism of the real and its
representation, our thinking will be reduced to binary
oppositions, like nature and artefact, or body and
mind. I would welcome a departure from this deadlock
position.

RM: When you look at the actual uses of digital
technology, it seems to me that the opposite is happening. The technology is placed into the service
of the simulation of reality. Would that not constitute
the epitome of binary reductionism?

VE: Absolutely, and furthermore, here the representation of reality becomes the commodity of reality, *"die
wahre Ware"* (the true commodity). The most important
potential of digital technology for artists to explore is
to invent models of reality and to exercise our power of
alternative thinking.

RM: Does this imply a utopian project?

VE: I am not a utopian thinker in the traditional sense,
but models of reality can only be utopian constructions. I should add that I am interested not only in the
artistic values but also in the imaging of differences
and in the inclusion of marginal social forms and
interactions.

RM: Is it possible to claim that your work with the
body is exactly this mean and mediation between
the artistic experiment and the social investigation?
That the body is for you on the one hand material
for artistic expression and on the other the bearer of
social signification?

VE: I have, from the very beginning, considered the
human body, in particular the body of woman, as
medium in my artistic work. Society in all of its ramifications expresses itself through the body. The body
is the principle sign that allows the power of history and
history as construction to be experienced and become
visible and therefore changeable. The nexus (*Verknüp-
fung*) between body, technological science, and society is
a cultural expression of our times that my artistic work
and my theoretical investigations attempt to define. The
body as bearer of signs demonstrates a common language, which, however, can also render it exchangeable,
replaceable, and determinable. Therefore, it is of the
essence to escape from this codification.

> RM: If you advocate the escape from the codification
> of the body in order to avoid its total social deter-
> mination, do you have in mind another state for the
> body to be in, however marginal it may be?

VE: The only way to escape from social or cultural
codification is to negate, change, or destroy it. If you
negate it you have to live outside of society or dissolve
the body and the self, which is no answer. In my view
one has to constantly question and change codes and
the institutionalization of codes. Some of my deconstructive efforts were aimed in this direction, but it is
my experience that one remains caught in the textual
system, still dominated by signs. Somehow I sense that
there must be a more radical position, but I don't know
exactly what it would be.

> RM: If you had to search among the many strategies,
> formal and otherwise, of your work to find an answer
> to this question, where would you be inclined to look?

VE: All the strategies that aim at the dissolution of
the identity of the signs. It would be in my tenacious

insistence on difference, on contradictions, multi-dimensionality, and multilayered, sculptural codification, material and immaterial and ontological differences in the cultural and social process on the one hand, and the transformations of contexts on the other. What is important to me in all this is the use of different languages, such as body language or sign language. I reflect what the appropriate "language" would be for what I want to express. I am also interested in investigating the border regions of different forms (*Formensprachen*) and connecting the space of perception (*Wahrnehmungsraum*) with real space (*Realraum*). These different media- and sign languages constitute the discourse I am concerned with in my work.

RM: How do these strategies relate to what I have called the "expansive body," which I described in the *Syntagma* chapter of this book as your method of reappropriating the body especially for women?

VE: These strategies are the strategies of the "expanded body." There are two kinds of strategies of expression, those that are located in the medium itself and those that have to do with how the medium is implemented. In the first case, for example, choosing video over painting can contribute to a certain liberation because, as I said before, the medium was not yet hierarchically determined in the history of art, and the second point comprises the strategies I have enumerated above. The dialogue between technology and body leads to expansive intermedial art forms in the sixties.

RM: This decade is also the period of your most intensive production of expanded cinema.

VE: The concept and the intention of my early work in expanded cinema was to decode reality as it was manipulated in film, to transport the cinematographic apparatus into the installation of time and space in order to break out of the two-dimensionality of the flat surface. The deconstruction of dominant reality, the deconstruction and abstraction of materials, the attempt to find new forms of communication and to realize them were also in the center of my analysis. My work was concentrated on breaking with the traditional form of cinema, the commercial-conventional sequence of film production, shooting, montage, projection, and to re-place them in part with aspects of reality, as new signs of the real. Presentation, product, production, reality form a unity in expanded cinema. In the intermedial action *Cutting* (1967–68) I did not cut the celluloid but the body-screen illuminated by the lamp of the pro-jector. The sound of cutting [shaving], of breathing, and of the projector without film was the soundtrack. Lighting, development, and image were simultaneously created in the same instant. Today's expanded cinema is the digital, electronic cinema, the simulation of space and time, the simulation of reality, virtual reality, if indeed the concept is realized: not to represent the real but to question it. This concept also applies to cyberspace. In this sense some video installations and techno-body performances of the seventies are the precursors of the cyberspace of the eighties and nine-ties. The point was to open up limited patterns of per-ception and representation, limited views of the natural and artificial image and space, and a limited concept of truth and reality. Expanded cinema found its contin-uation in my medial body-material performances, into which I introduced the body as sign and code for a social and aesthetic expression.

RM: Along the same lines, the goals of expanded cinema as you describe it, with reference to "cut-ting," of mixing body experiences with elements of the technological process in the present moment or "instant time," could also be considered a precursor

274

of virtual reality, which aims at a conjunction of body and machine and of the body's experience in actual time.

VE: Potentially the goals of expanded cinema, body actions, and performances and installations could be continued and taken to another level in cyberspace. In cyberspace the spectator enters into the image space, that is, the spectator becomes the actor, as was attempted in interactive experiments and also in Happenings and Fluxus events. The difference in cyberspace is that everything is on an augmented technological level. The spectator determines the process by his/her reactions, but these reactions can be just a movement of the eye to arrange or rearrange a whole event. One of my next interactive installation pieces will be a confrontation between two eyes: a video camera reflects my eye, but I am looking back, and by a movement of my eye in a certain direction and in conjunction with the computer program, I can destroy the video eye or redesign it.

RM: This marginalization of the body immediately conjures up the postmodern obsolete body, in my mind. Isn't there also an aspect of cyberspace and virtual reality that is completely contrary to your expanded body, an implosion of the body instead of an expansion?

VE: Because of the changeability and the phantasmatic construction of the image as sign, the meaning and the identity of the sign also dissolves. In as far as the human being is a sign, a symbol, an image, the assigned meaning of the individual, which is ideologically constructed, also dissolved because of this extended notion of the image. The body in cyberspace has no referent; everything in cyberspace is a free-floating sign without necessary meaning, which also dissolves the meaning of the body. This arbitrary designation of the sign has been exemplified long before, throughout the whole history of the female body. But this is precisely the reason why I do not believe in the disappearance of the body, because it is also the site of our feelings, senses, and sensuality. My secret hope is that hidden and unknown horizons will be laid bare. It is true that cyberspace is an artificial space of perception, but the spectator communicates and acts as in reality, that is to say, s/he remains a subject. Maybe the system of cyberspace will succeed in creating dreams that free us from historical traces.

RM: Your planned project about the eyes confronting and destroying each other illustrates not just the noxious quality of the gaze as Sartre had described it; since it is your own eye, the phantom of self-destruction through minimal efforts, like pushing a button, is thematized. In other words, the whole technology debate is opened up in this experiment. It seems to me that the classical avant-garde's enthusiasm for technology is the most in need of revision.

VE: I agree. The classical avant-garde connected their technological enthusiasm either with fascist war or with socialist revolution based on the Enlightenment heritage of progress, and a belief in the ever receding barrier of nature, which the Frankfurt School had critiqued early on as an attitude of domination. This enthusiasm was almost a cult comparable to that of humanism. Now we have to ask ourselves how far nature can be destroyed and with it the basis of survival for an expanding population. Nature can no longer serve culture as it has so far for our societies. A subversive use of technology would be to break with these traditions and modes of production. Maybe it will be precisely the new technologies that will allow us to live in a re-determined social and physical reality. In any case, the delineation of the concept of "nature" is also drawn into question, and technology emerges exactly at the cutting edge between human and animal. Technology is usually pioneered by the military industrial complex. For cyberspace as well, very few of the programs were designed by artists. The challenge for artists now, and especially for women artists, is to take charge and responsibility also for the programs.

RM: The technology of reproduction has figured prominently in some of your writings, especially in "The Body and Its Double." Some women see a danger in your insistence on refusing the biological body's reproduction, seeing in it just another overevaluation of the biological functions of women. In a sense it is the obverse of the equally biologistic notion that the directness of the body's expressions is somehow more "true" or more "real" than words.

VE: First, I do understand the dangers of my recommendation to women to refuse natural reproduction. Yet, I think the whole essentialism debate has to be taken out of its abstract philosophical framework, because there one can always find yet another logical trip-up. What I am trying to call attention to is the necessity to change the whole concept of motherhood, the ideological coercion of women to become mothers and wives that is at the core of the cultural determination of our bodies. Only in this framework can what I say make any sense. Certainly, I do not propose in actuality that an individual woman should no longer give birth if she feels like it; rather, it is the coercion I am trying to counteract. And from this perspective, artificial reproduction is equally dangerous, because it can potentially increase the pressure on women if they are not in charge of their lives and if they are not involved in these debates.

RM: In your engagement with the avant-garde in technology, art, and thought you have arrived at conclusions similar to those of some postmodern theorists who have applied their knowledge of the technological media to cultural and social criticism, yet I come away with a greater sense of hope in your texts, as if the future were not necessarily headed for implosion.

VE: That is because I look at life as an endlessly moving sculpture, an extension of the body's cavity into the galactic labyrinth. It is a genetic sculpture, billions of years old, and is unfinished. The trope of this sculpture is caught in the realm between reality and potentiality.

- - - - - - - - - - - - - - - - - - - - - - - - - - - - - - - - - -

WITH ELISABETH LEBOVICI

- - - - - - - - - - - - - - - - - - - - - - - - - - - - - - - - - -

2003

========================================

ELISABETH LEBOVICI: As a starting point, what strikes me is that you didn't just produce new artworks: you had to create your own media, your own territories, and your own "definition" of where an artist can expand . . .

VALIE EXPORT: In the early years, the only thing I knew was that I wanted to be an artist, and I only knew I didn't want to be a painter. I had painted at a very young age, and painting wasn't satisfying me any longer. By that time, I had the impression that already everything had been said and done via painting before. Painting was without movement in space. Then, I got to know the works of Constructivism, and was very touched by it. I was impressed by the use of space, the use of space for art and *as* art form. After that, I discovered photography for myself. I liked photography, as one doesn't see the image, only its negative. One can see the apparatus, the photograph, but not the image itself. To receive the picture a further process is necessary. I liked for instance, slides going very fast, and their movement in speed. Then I discovered film and the film camera. During that time I had started to be interested in snakes. I had a friend at school I accompanied when he went to hunt snakes. Their fast movements fascinated me but also their peeled-off skin, the detached skin without body.

EL: Could you identify with other artists?

VE: At that time I didn't know any artist I could identify with. First, I should say that in the 1950s I didn't
know a lot about modern art. At home we had a library
with a small amount of good art books, which my
mother had hidden during the war, and displayed again
after the war, but in bookshops, there was a real lack
of art books. I was familiar with Surrealism, Constructivism, and Dadaism, but my identification was with art
itself, and not with specific persons. I was aware that
Dadaists did something in public, that wasn't called
performances yet, and I felt that I wanted to do such
things, and to be an artist in the Dadaist manner. The
main reason why I couldn't identify with an artist was
that most of them were males. I wouldn't identify with
a male artist. This was too far away from myself, too
authoritarian. I rather had feelings towards Leonora
Carrington, for example, even though I didn't get into
Surrealism. But also being young wasn't the same
feeling as it is today. It was a completely different
world, without a youth culture.

EL: Postwar Austria and Germany weren't on the
"good side" of Europe . . . How was the situation
culturally?

VE: Since we were occupied until the mid-1950s, Austria
was following the Marshall Plan. I lived in Linz, in the
American sector. I attended a Catholic school, then
a school for arts and crafts in Linz, and then—after my
divorce—went to Vienna to study at the school for
textile design. My mother was not very happy with my
decision to become an artist; nonetheless she supported
me. In the '60s, the atmosphere in Vienna was repressive, depressing, and quite conservative. Only a small
student movement existed. The galleries and museums
predominantly presented traditional conservative art,
and consequently nourished the bourgeois conception
of art. In spite of this, a change became apparent within

the new artistic movements. It was small groupings like the Wiener Gruppe, the Wiener Aktionisten (Viennese Actionists), the experimental filmmakers, etc., which were fundamentally engaged in the artistic, aesthetical, and political renewal.

EL: When did you engage in performances?

VE: Most likely, when I was 18, I wanted to act. I didn't say I wanted to make performances; I just wanted to act. At that time, I had produced a series of photographs, which unfortunately got lost, engaging my boyfriend and myself. We switched gender; we switched our looks, our outside appearances. The boy was nobody specific, but he was nice and he voluntarily agreed to do it. However, it was easier for me to "turn" into a man, than for him to "turn" into a woman.

EL: Did you use yourself as model because it was easier and cheaper or were you conscious that it was conducting some kind of new experience for you?

VE: It was engaging in new experiences. To be involved myself was a way of making experiments and of acquiring experience.

EL: Which was the first artistic act you gave a name to?

VE: It was *Abstract Film No. 1*. The *Self-Portrait* of 1966 was my first filmic piece and *Abstract Film No. 1*, in 1967, my first art piece.

Before that, I had produced the *Menstruation* piece. I knew that giving birth and menstruating were related with miscellaneous feelings of anxiety and stress amongst women. Motherhood for me was not embedded in my femininity; it anticipated my recognition of responsibility. I was more impressed by what defined me as a so-called female. For that reason I created the menstruation piece, which had a lot to do with sexuality, but with a kind of "bad girl" sexuality, not the bourgeois kind of sexuality. I produced the piece in Switzerland, at my sister's. I was sitting on a white, quite high, wall, and was pissing during menstruation, the stained piss was running down the wall, creating a kind of abstract pattern, red and liquid. My sister filmed it.

> EL: Could one say it was then that you discovered
> your space, a generic, gendered space?

VE: I had discovered my space before, but here I was experiencing an active and provocative space. From that point also *Action Pants: Genital Panic* and *Abstract Film No. 1* emerged. Eventually, I used other colors, as in Vienna at the exhibition in 1997; if I did it in red, it automatically got associated with blood. I did it always with water, sometimes oil, sometimes colors . . . what I had on hand.

> EL: Did you understand the contradictions at hand
> in performance art, as making the unrepeatable
> quality of the live act interact with the more time-
> less, repetitive features of the artwork?

VE: I repeated the action, as I considered it as Expanded Cinema. I presented it as Expanded Cinema, where I was present, where I acted myself, where I was a component of the film. In general, several copies of a film are printed; these copies can be projected, without the necessity of my presence, the film action can be done also by others. Expanded cinema, actions, and performances require a person. Back in 1967, Expanded Cinema was also intended as a strong attack on authorship: it was my idea, my thing, but it could also happen anywhere in the whole world, and anybody could make an *Abstract Film No. 1.*

EL: So how was a VALIE EXPORT Abstract Film created?

VE: The basis is the screen; in *Abstract Film No. 1* a reflecting mirror-screen is placed opposite a reflecting movie-screen. The movie-screen is also a mirroring screen, as it mirrors the patterns and signs of the celluloid. Both reflecting screens are engaged in a dialogue of images. A film projector projects its light on the mirroring space, on the mirror screen, on which I have poured different liquids—rapidly running liquids like water, viscous, slowly running liquids, and differently colored liquids. The movements of the vertically running liquids formed different patterns and signs, creating drawings that were illuminated by the film projector, and projected onto the movie-screen, where they materialized abstract patterns and images. Colored images, moving images. An abstract film developed, which was not created by the means of traditional cinema, but without celluloid and camera, like an action in front of a film projector. Each abstract film was presented in real time and in real cinema space. That way, I always created a different, new abstract film.

EL: In what context did you do your abstract cinema?

VE: I was invited to different places. I could present it in a regular movie theater, or in independent and underground places like Xscreen in Cologne, organized by Wilhelm and Birgit Hein, or at a festival, and be on the program like any other film. It was another kind of cinema; either it had the title *Abstract Film No. 1*, or *Cutting*. I preferred having an event during the film program or within the context of the film festival. In London, for instance, I was part of the First Underground Film Festival. Two years later, I attended the

Avant-garde Film Festival, and again some years later, I took part in the International Film Festival, where I won a prize. Step by step the underground was changing.

EL: Were those works actually reenacted by others?

VE: Paul McCarthy intended to re-enact it with his students, but it didn't work out. But in Latvia a group of young women exists, artists and students who study art history and call themselves "VALIE EXPORT fan club." Occasionally, they reenact some of my performances.

EL: You were traveling a lot in the 1960s: Was it as an artist? As part of a movement?

VE: In the 1960s I barely had the possibility to present my works in Vienna. But there existed an international underground movement. In 1968, when I created *TAP and TOUCH CINEMA*, there was a meeting of international independent filmmakers in Munich, where I was invited. All filmmakers met for some days; it was a big exchange. As a consequence, we all got invitations to other festivals. In 1967, I also was a member of COOP, the Austrian Filmmakers Cooperative. At that time, Peter Kubelka ran the film museum in Vienna, which wasn't open to Austrian filmmakers, only to traditional and American filmmakers. This situation led to a riot against this place and its occupation in 1968. This was a kind of historical event in Vienna.

In the mid-'60s I met Peter Weibel, and the cooperation with him during the '60s was very fruitful for both of us. In spite of this, as a female I couldn't gain real recognition, neither in the male word of artists, nor in that of filmmakers. I was always treated as co-pilot. For example in Germany, where we were invited and I was on stage, the audience asked other filmmakers about what I did, I wasn't asked at all, as if I wasn't there. Nowadays, one cannot imagine how ignorant the art world was of female artists in the 1960s. In those days you couldn't associate or compete with other women, because women, like myself, were alone within a male dominated art world. I couldn't compete with my male colleagues, because I thought I was different. I was on my own, for better or worse. It was not until the beginning of the 1970s that I could make a tour with my Expanded Cinema works to the Netherlands and Great Britain on my own, where I presented *Cutting*, *Abstract Film No. 1*, *TAP and TOUCH CINEMA*, and other works.

EL: Is the performance where you walk with Peter Weibel on a leash, a sort of revenge?

VE: No, the performance *From the Portfolio of Doggedness* has to do with the question: What changes when you behave like an animal although you are not an animal? It was a kind of context variation, and had less to do with gender, even though gender is particularly obviously represented in this performance, and obtains its own indication.

Subjectively and ostensibly, *From the Portfolio of Doggedness* had nothing to do with masochism and sadism; it was more about exchanging or changing roles, or playing with role behavior. When I was writing about it in my texts of the 1970s, I explicitly pointed out the relation between human and animal behavior, and especially from today's perspective, this reference seems to me as important as the reference to masochism, which was also mentioned then. But the performance is not to be read that simply as a statement on sadism and masochism, and I do not want to have it brought down to my own person.

The performance was about exchanging material and a change of status; we are of the same material, human, but exchanging roles, being like a dog. What does the external perception tell the internal perception? The performance is also a piece on identities and the perception of the real, the symbolic and the imaginative through aesthetical and collective perception. That's how I see it today. Where is the border between nature, culture, and civilization? Also, animals are "transverse" subjects as Freud indicates. The human being as machine would be the upshot.

Also today, I see the performance in the context of an artificial animal-world and an artificial human-world. I do not have to deal with this performance any longer, except in the context of my artistic biography or when I am asked about it, and I can answer the question out of the perspective of that time only in connection with today's perspective. If they talk for themselves, the early artistic works are to be understood in the language of the time when they were created, as well as in the language of the present time.

> EL: Exchanging roles is the cue to all the performance work you did?

VE: Yes, to bring this about in different contexts and different meanings. This is a thread that runs through my own works. It can relate them even further back to the transfer identities I did very early, without considering them as art pieces. I just did them as creative pieces for my own mind; I did a lot of self-portraits for myself with the camera.

> EL: How did you move from that specific piece to the other, from this role to that one, from this material to the other?

VE: I can't tell that definitely. I was reading, I was feeling, I was thinking, I was living, it was and is still my nerves which are talking. In case of the body performance *Eros/ion*, I could say, I used my body and explored the means to explain the body under different conditions.



EL: Why did you choose to expand yourself in the city? Is this choice of expanding from the private space of the body to the public space an early one?

VE: I chose the streets and everyday life surroundings at a very early stage. I didn't want to perform in a gallery or a museum, as they were too conservative for me, and would only give conventional responses to my experimental works. It was important for me to present my works to the public, in the public space, and not within an art-conservative space, but in the by then so-called underground. In the public space one has a different audience than in a gallery, an audience in the everyday urban run. My works also present different concepts than simply for the museum space. When I was performing my actions in public, on the streets, in the urban space, new and different forms of reception developed. In the streets I provoked new explanations. I wanted to be provocative, to provoke, but also aggression was part of my intention. I wanted to provoke, because I sought to change the people's way of seeing and thinking. Nonetheless, provocation was not the sole aim of my works, but definitely was part of it. If I hadn't been provocative, I couldn't have made visible what I wanted to show. I had to penetrate things to bring them to the exterior. I wasn't doing traditional art, I needed a different audience, and this audience was outside the museum; it was only natural for me to choose the streets, the urban public, the "underground." Anyway, there was also no interest in presenting my artistic works in the traditional art space, museums or galleries.

When I did *TAP and TOUCH CINEMA* the first time, it happened at a film festival. With *TAP and TOUCH*

*CINEMA* I introduced a statement. The next action was located on Stachus, a public place in Munich, a completely different space.

EL: One of the lead sentences of feminism is to appropriate or "reclaim the streets," which are or were a male space . . .

VE: The city is still a male space, but you really can make it sensual, and you also can adjust to it. A gallery follows historical tradition, which in some way complicates contemporary dialogue.

EL: When you made *TAP and TOUCH CINEMA*, did you encounter women? On the tape we only see men approaching you.

VE: You see, documentation wasn't that important at that time. Hence, I guess the cameraman didn't shoot more than five to six minutes, but in reality at the location there also were women and children.

EL: Was there a dialogue or were words exchanged afterwards?

VE: No. It was about going to the movies. You only watch, in this case touch, the movie, and then it's over. People of course laughed, some of them really have been spellbound, because it functioned as I had announced.

EL: How was it for you?

VE: It was exciting for me as well. It confirmed that I definitely wanted to do performances in public again, that's what I learned from it.

EL: Why did you stop?

VE: I had told what I wanted to tell. Just as I had stopped painting earlier on. You move on to do another thing. I had to move on, otherwise I would have repeated myself. There is not one reason, but a context. I went on with films and installations. Three years ago, I still did a kind of lecture performance on female mutilation, but back then, I had said what I had wanted to say.

EL: When you say you met feminism, do you mean you met with other women, were you part of an activist group?

VE: No, when I was in Sweden, approximately in 1966–67, I got it out of magazines. There I saw those magazines. With Peter Weibel I also discovered the term "expanded cinema" in a magazine. To be precise, the term we discovered was "extended art," and we changed it to a more accurate term "Expanded Cinema". I also knew that there was a feminist movement in the United States. But for myself I discovered the collectives and most of the female artists later on.

EL: Did you know of women artists that you could relate to in the '60s? Hannah Höch? Meret Oppenheim? Maria Lassnig?

VE: Of course I knew the works of Hannah Höch, and also those of Maria Lassnig, but I didn't know them personally at that time. I met Maria Lassnig in the '70s when I invited her to the exhibition *MAGNA Feminism, Art, and Creativity,* which I organized in Vienna. By then, she was living in New York. I had worked out the concept of the exhibition in 1972, and originally it should have been an international exhibition. I offered the concept to several art societies, and museums, but all of them refused: Quote: "Very interesting, but who is interested in that exhibition?" So, the exhibition only presented Austrian female artists, but was linked

to an international side program where I, for example,
presented films and videos of Carolee Schneemann
and Rebecca Horn, and introduced music of Dorothy
Iannone and Franca Sacchi. In the context of the exhibition I did an interview with Meret Oppenheim, which
was published in the exhibition catalogue, along with
a text by Meret Oppenheim.

I also received texts by Carolee Schneemann and
Lucy R. Lippard for the catalogue. Further I organized a series of lectures, where for example Karin
Thomas and Alice Schwarzer were invited, who by
then lived in Paris. I also have presented documents
of the group AUF Aktion, a grouping of the women's
movement. *MAGNA* focused on feminism in Austria
for the first time, and was the first international exhibition of female artists in Europe; in the States, I don't
know.

EL: Very early, you mentioned Gertrude Stein and
Virginia Woolf. In what sense were they important
for you?

VE: At that time, Virgina Woolf was very important
for me, as she was a pioneer in feminist thinking. For
me Virginia Woolf was, as I have written in 1973, "a
brilliant example of the link between female sensibility and creative impulse, that leads to commonly
applicable art models."[1] Gertrude Stein is the pioneer
of poetic use, of poetry applied to language. By then I
wrote: "In Gertrude Stein it is also clearly evident how
female problematics, subjective sensibility, can lead
to a common artistic model, an objective technique.
Her works, held in the tension between her phrases
'well feudal days were the days of fathers' and 'once
upon a time I met myself and ran,' between acquired
Puritanism and innate passions, searching a new form
of self-definition, of identity, that is independent from
society and culture."[2]

EL: Did you have any connection to Elfriede Jelinek?

VE: Both of us have the same social and political critique, the same approach on feminism. Both of us have a strong concentration on the body as political issue. Jelinek's concerns are expressed in her texts. We had a short co-operation in 1968, when I did a film-script after her novel *The Piano Player*.

EL: How does the experience of the body and the performances interact with the conceptual part of your art making?

VE: It's a bit naïve to say it like that, but I read a lot. I didn't make the whole work primarily out of my belly! But some of my work is intuitive. I read and I knew or felt that I had to bring my artistic work into the context of theory, because theory is the context of thinking, of life, and of other theories. The artistic work as such is not the main thing, it is related to a theory, and this theory is related to other theories, and it is linked to present times, as well as to history, past time and future. I also was very interested in concepts. My conceptual photographs emerged from the process of thinking that there is a concept in relation to this apparatus, the artificial space of the photographic apparatus: how to use the apparatus, the gaze of the apparatus, how to use my gaze, the beholder's gaze, and the gaze of the photographed object, since the object too represents a gaze; how to transform a real object into a visible object through this complex apparatus? How is the reality or how are the realities of the artificial space of the apparatus? How many communications can we have? At the time, when questions relating to the notion and function of representation, the inner image, the image in the image, presentation and representation were raised, it was important for me to investigate the origins of those transformations. In our head, we don't have a photograph, but the image of an image. We can say we don't know if this image exists, but we agree that the objects exist; it's an agreement between all of us on this planet. What we see, hear, feel and do emerges from this agreement, but then we have a number of images that we only manage for ourselves. I thought the technical apparatus of photography had a life of itself, a different gaze, and a different behavior: I can use it, but it can use me as well. The apparatus seemed to be a very important example for the explanation of the philosophical construction of subjectivity. The photographic space is an artificial space, a space that doesn't exist, but it has its own realities.

EL: Did you have any training in philosophy?

VE: Sometimes I read four or five hours every day, and I made notes. I have a lot of notebooks from that time. We spoke about it, although there were no real discussion circles, and this also had to do with the male understanding of society for females.

EL: There are many works where you find yourself inside the image, but as a "mise en abyme," as an image in the image . . .

VE: Yes. It also has to do with time. The photographic apparatus is not timeless, it exists within time and space, but this is made invisible, or less visible. I used a car as an example to bring space and time into a photographic run. I shot a series of photos sidewards out of the car, while the car was moving in space. I drew a line on the side-window of the car, consequently the line was on one hand static, but on the other hand it was moving as well. The car and the camera moved as a cinematographic apparatus.

EL: Your film *Syntagma* seems to be a synthesis of your work?

VE: Yes, it's an index. For me it resembled a sort of notebook to put everything together, which was then reassembled in moving images. It was also about re-thinking narratives: I eventually made a feature film.

EL: What about your drawings?

VE: They are called children's drawings because their naïvety resembles that of a child. They are so-called memories of childhood. I created them when I was in school, but my decision was not to go back to those years, but mimic a child, to draw in a childish manner, and to put a little bit of feminism in there as well. The Madonna is like a modern witch; a certain amount of masochism is implied in housework, etc.

EL: Can you explain your tattoo (the garter)? Is it art?

VE: It's an art piece that will live as long as I live. Art-pieces live as long as the artist, and then they are history, the tattoo emphasizes that. It's an artwork that is permanently present, it's always with me, I take it with me, it's hidden—but not always—, it's on my skin, it has to do with body work, it's a drawing, and the drawing tells something about identity and female history, about sexuality, it's also a sexual icon, it describes a fetish.

EL: Your recent shows go back to the body, in pre-senting sculptures like heads with their face cutout, within a selection of images based on torture and women's violation. Why?

VE: At that time, I was re-organizing my library, and I found a book about Surrealism, where I discovered

a series of works by Paul Eluard, in which one or two
letters were always missing, something was missing in
each word. I figured out that in each realization that I
had achieved, something was always missing, nothing
was ever finished. I also figured out that you miss something if you see a person that is not identifiable. The
identification of someone has a lot to do with his face.
There is the body, of course, but the face is an essential
aspect of identification. As the sites for speech and gaze
are located in the face, they are the sites of the exchange
of myself with others. Without the face, without the
senses of the face, you cannot see, you cannot hear, you
cannot speak and you cannot smell. In my sculptures
*Heads – Apharäse* (aphaeresis) something is missing,
the space of the face is missing; the inside of the head
is missing. The sculptures show the shells of the facial
body, the shells of the sensual body, of thinking, of
emotions, of life. Nonetheless, in my imagination these
heads laugh, and cry. Hence the sculptures represent
the cut-off, the exclusion from identity as well as from
communication of identity, although we can—if we
ignore what is missing—communicate with them very
well. The missing sign presents its own identity.

I named my piece *Heads – Apharäse*, it comes from
Apharsie, aphasia, and to me this means the inability
to project the missing, the face. It's also an approach
to anonymity. In that context I created a film on tortured human bodies, with the title *Dead people don't
cry* where the faces and the body parts were destroyed
by torture and aggression. The absence in a way is also
a kind of torture, of cry . . . I assume that this work continues my bodywork with a new working-body.


NOTES

1    VALIE EXPORT, "Feminismus und Kunst: Gertrude Stein/Virginia
Woolf," *Neues Forum*, vol. 228 (January 1973).
2    Ibid.

-------------------------------------------------

## WITH BRIGITTA BURGER-UTZER
## AND SYLVIA SZELY

-------------------------------------------------

### 2006

=================================================

SYLVIA SZELY: In the essay "Expanded Cinema as Expanded Reality"[1] that you wrote for the University of Milwaukee newsletter, you began with a kind of artistic autobiography. You said that you were particularly interested in Futurism, Cubism, and Constructivism during your student years. When and how did you come in contact with "art," and what was it about these movements that particularly interested you?

VALIE EXPORT: After the war, my parents' library was reinstalled in our apartment, and that's when I first consciously came in contact with art—whether visual art, or literature. When I was about ten or twelve, I discovered Surrealism, which I thought was highly interesting, especially the quality of the imagery. There weren't any normal pictures in Surrealism, in the sense of depictions, or that is how it seemed at the time. Later, I was particularly taken by Magritte. And then we evidently had Constructivist and Dadaist books as well in our library—or else I saw those books in other libraries. What I really liked about Constructivism was not only its stagelike quality, the feeling for space, but also its depiction of processes, which was not as stiff as the painting I knew at the time. Looking back, I would say that it was the conceptual tendencies that interested me in Constructivism . . .

BRIGITTA BURGER-UTZER: Was it a particularly large library?

VE: It was a normal library in terms of size, but it
contained a wide and interesting range of books. We
also had a box of Anker building bricks, which you
could use to reconstruct buildings block by block after
historical models, such as the Arc de Triomphe . . .
That's how I found my way to history and above all
to architectural history. And from the age of twelve I
spent a lot of time out and about, my oldest sister was
living abroad and when we visited her we often went
to museums and visited churches and historical buildings, in Venice, for instance, and Munich . . . I also
loved to draw, already during the war, but generally
there wasn't any paper so I drew on the blank pages
in books, especially at the back of them. My drawings
made me very popular in my family circle. Later I
thought about painting, but I'm done with that now. All
I want to paint has already been painted, I would only
be repeating. Apart from which, it wasn't enough for
me to simply work on the surface, two-dimensionally,
what interested me was the third and the fourth
dimension.

SZ: But then you went to the textile school in Linz.
How did that come about?

VE: I already wanted to do art back then, and my
mother always encouraged me to do what I wanted. But
art school wasn't possible for a number of reasons, so
I went to the arts and crafts school and chose textiles
because I like craftsmanship, it suits me. During that
time I took my first photographic self-portraits. Then
I went a step further with a school friend: we photographed him as a girl and me as a boy, which was like
the forerunners of the *Transfer Identities* series[2] . . .
In short, I began to think about what one can "do" with
a camera.

SZ: When did you actually go to Vienna, and why?

VE: I had married, and remained so for a year. After my divorce I wanted to get away from Linz, that was in 1960 . . . I was in a difficult situation: I was divorced and had a child, but I nevertheless wanted to continue my studies and finish my training. But that was only possible with the financial—and emotional—support of my family, and I also worked on the side. So I landed in Vienna and got my diploma in design at the Höhere Technische Lehranstalt für Textilindustrie—the college for the textile industry. But it was pretty clear to me at the time that I didn't want to become a fashion designer or a pattern designer, although I was really interested in design and I sometimes felt sorry I hadn't studied it as such. Design and architecture still interest me today . . .

BBU: . . . One can see that in some of your works, such as the Art and Architecture projects or the *Gläserner Kubus* (Glass Cube),[1] or even your installations where the architectural element plays a part.

SZ: I've read that you began weaving tapestries with Ingrid Wiener while you were still at school.

VE: We met at the textile school and started weaving rugs together: Hundertwasser tapestries, and also for Arik Brauer. But that's a dark chapter . . . *(Laughs)* We actually sold the Hundertwasser tapestry. I came up with ideas back then for things one could weave.

BBU: . . . including other things, not just fabrics and carpets?

VE: Yes, exactly. They were in fact conceptual projects. A crack in the wall, say, or banknotes for a bank, or a knife stuck in a wall, things like that. I wove my first tapestry at the applied arts school in Linz, which had this very narrow countermarch loom, so I wove a giraffe.

BBU: Then in the mid-1960s you adopted the name VALIE EXPORT. What was the significance of that for you?

VE: It was in 1967, I was confronting my identity at the time. Identity is something that comes with your name—but not only. I first had my father's name, then my ex-husband's name. But I wanted a name of my own, one that I chose myself and which I could use as an artistic concept. Valie was my nickname, you know. And I hit upon EXPORT because I was looking for a name that could serve as a trademark or as something broader. I chose EXPORT because I wanted to export my ideas, my thoughts, and also because it's easy to remember. Once I was sure that my artist's name was going to be EXPORT, I looked around for an object that visualized it nicely. That's how I hit on the package for Smart Export cigarettes, which a lot of people smoked back then. Well, I thought, it's the obvious choice. There weren't that many mass-produced items I would have wanted to use. I covered the picture of the globe on the packet with my face—the picture of the globe remained underneath—and circling this picture are the words "semper et ubique, immer und überall," always and everywhere, along with "Made in Austria," which is true, right?

BBU: You immediately know where it is from. You also proposed a self-portrait as part of a television project for women artist portraits (1987). What would that have been like?

VE: I was concerned with the question of how one can generate identity, whether identity can generate itself, and if so, how does it do that. How do I deal with my own identity, or do I even have an identity? When I say "own identity," does that mean identity is some kind of possession? Obviously I have an identity, every person has an identity, even if it is perhaps a non-identity, or they even have several of them, but what kind of shifts are involved, what kind of deliberations? It was supposed to be a brief portrait, around the concept of identity and the concept of doubling. Because I have often turned my attention to doubling in my works, such as the double canvas in *Splitscreen Solipsism* (1968), or the notion of the double in *Unsichtbare Gegner* (Invisible Adversaries, 1976), or doublings of the one and the same thing in different media, such as photography, film, or video. How can one double identity, or be the double of oneself? Does my identity have an echo? Can I see, hear, feel, recognize its echo? How polyphonic is identity? Or, as I once wrote in a poem: "my hands are my identity" . . . I have done a lot of works on the subject of hands.

BBU: Are you also addressing doubling here in the sense of reality and representation? That is one of your frequent themes: a photo and above it the "real body" . . .

VE: Yes, image and reality, or different realities, or reality in the electronic media—that of course is what interests me. I envisaged this self-portrait as like a cinematic diary: What happens when I think about myself? Although I wouldn't have been interested in people recognizing or getting to know me in some sort of way. I've always done a great many self-portraits, in drawings or film or photography. It would have been about how I see myself, but not in the sense of a self-portrait.

SZ: Back to the chronology: You were clear that you wanted to work as an artist after you had finished at school?

VE: It was clear to me that I would never put my
studies into practice, but that I didn't want to do something completely different, I wanted to work freely.
I was already moving in artistic circles, knew everyone
at Café Hawelka and from the Adebar . . .

SZ: You mean the Vienna Actionists or members of
the Vienna Group, and the like?

VE: Yes, I knew them all. But I had yet to make any art
myself.

SZ: You were still a consumer, as it were?

VE: Exactly, I had already drawn and attempted to
paint, but I hadn't shown my works. One of my first
steps was to come up with an artist's name, and the
cigarette packet was also the first object in my artistic
career.

BBU: And how did you arrive at moving images, at
Expanded Cinema?

VE: Well, obviously I was interested in the medium
of film, and had gotten to know the films of Marcel
Duchamp, Viking Eggeling, and Hans Richter—the
classics of the 1920s—fairly early on while abroad,
as well as in Vienna during the first film presentations put on by Peter Kubelka, which took place in
a room at the Technical University on Karlsplatz,
if I remember correctly. At any rate, I wanted to
make artworks that focused on motion, that weren't
purely static, like photographs, so I arrived at moving
images.

BBU: But there must have been something like
an initial action. That would probably have been
*Abstract Film No. 1*?

VE: That's right, 1968. I had the idea in 1967. I should explain that my ideas hadn't been any help to me before that, because I didn't have any opportunities for presenting myself to the public. I could scarcely have found a space for projects like that as a woman artist.

BBU: The time was only ripe for that later on?

VE: The first invitation for film screenings came in 1968. And through my travels I discovered that expanded film arts also existed elsewhere: in London, for instance, or Germany with Birgit and Wilhelm Hein. As Peter Weibel and I traveled to Sweden we read a journal on the expanded arts and it became clear to me that *Abstract Film No. 1* was Expanded Cinema. So from 1968 on I received invitations from what was called the underground scene or experimental film scene, but without them always insisting on specific works.

SZ: What exactly do you mean when you say you weren't invited with specific works?

VE: Well, some organizers couldn't imagine what something called *Abstract Film No. 1* might be about . . . all the things that Expanded Cinema can entail . . .

BBU: That must have been a great leap forward for you. You were also suddenly very active. Beginning 1968 there was an explosion, any number of Expanded Cinema actions and already by then films.

VE: Yes, the international underground scene established itself in 1968, above all in Europe—everything began much earlier in New York. You could show films and Expanded Cinema actions, invitations were extended. That of course really spurred me on.

SZ: So your early actions all took place abroad?

VE: I didn't receive any invitations in Austria at the time, but I wasn't the only one . . .

SZ: Well, the Actionists occasionally did some spectacular manifestations . . .

VE: But in quite different contexts. My Expanded Cinema actions also came a bit later and differed significantly from Actionism on a number of counts. For example, several of my works only culminated in a finished statement through the action of the audience; including the audience was really important. This inclusion already existed back then in Happenings or Fluxus events, so it was sort of in the air.

BBU: Your work had a political dimension, right from the start. It wasn't just about the inherent questions of film and the media, but also about socio-political issues.

VE: . . . and cultural-political ones.

SZ: You could also say it was about the process, the process was in fact the artwork. The conventional understanding of art was to be questioned and boundaries broken. Which, as you once wrote, also included transforming the illusion of film back into the material of film.[3]

VE: Material thinking was of course very widespread in a lot of art movements. I tried to give an overview of its history in the ORF documentary *Aktionskunst International* (Action Art International, 1989). Otto Mühl talks a lot about the material body, as does Allan Kaprow. But for me, the main point at that time was the thesis that the artwork is only finished once the audience has contributed something to it. The expanded film action *Ping Pong* (1968) is a piece that shows how the director lays down the rules, but *Ping Pong* requires the action of the audience for this to be recognized. Against that, the drawing that was made in *Auf + Ab + An + Zu* (Up + down + on + to, 1968) during the projection of the film and the action by the actor was the actual film . . .

BBU: . . . the object that is left over.

VE: The drawing was not something left over, it was the goal, the climax, as it were. And then you could take this film home with you, everyone had his or her own film at home. So does that make you a producer, or are you an author, and in this particular case: Is there any such thing as an original? In *Auf + Ab + An + Zu*, the actual product is created in interaction with what is missing on the celluloid, the passages that are painted over on the celluloid are supplemented by the drawing. Which means that anyone who dares to go up to the screen and draw has their very own, totally unique film. But the film action looks different every time, if you project the film on a large scale the result is a large drawing, and small if the film is projected that way. For some it goes too fast, so they don't manage to draw anything, while others manage a lot because they jump around like crazy . . .

SZ: Do you see a real difference in the way you involve the audience in works like *Ping Pong* and *Auf + Ab + An + Zu*, which is very playful, and then something like *TAPP und TASTKINO* (TAP and TOUCH CINEMA, 1968) or the action *Genitalpanik* (Genital Panic, 1969), where evidently it was much more difficult for the audience to respond actively?

VE: There are always different factors one must allow for. As for *Genitalpanik*,[4] there is a myth—which is by no means uninteresting—that the action took place in a blue movie theater. But it actually took place in an

303

arthouse cinema: I walked along the rows of seats and said: "What you may possibly see on the screen you can now see in reality." I addressed the audience directly, went from one person to the next—moving on as soon as it was over . . . I set a viewing limit, just as there was a touching limit of thirty-three seconds for the *TAPP und TASTKINO*. You look—and then it's gone again. These are inherent issues with film. But obviously it's also an examination of the content shown in the films, such as sexuality and eroticism.

BBU: And above all, feminist issues are brought up here, such as the voyeurism of the audience. What did the initiation trigger in you?

VE: I came in contact with feminism through my own experiences: the audience—unlike my colleagues—didn't pay a great deal of attention to me as a female artist. Questions were always directed to the film-makers. So I thought, what's this all about, hey, those are my films. I was already wondering around 1968 what kind of art one must show as a woman before one is seen and noticed. I realized that people hadn't a clue about women artists. That's why I have also occupied myself with art history, as well as with the question of how woman's role is determined in society.

SZ: So in a way you were looking for role models?

VE: That's right. And in that way I discovered that for some time a feminist examination of art had already been going on in New York. Later I also occupied my-self with the theory. In 1971–72, I began to draw up the first drafts for *MAGNA*—an exhibition solely with female participants. I contacted women artists at home and abroad and approached women's groups. But the political feminist groups were appalled by my plans, to their minds art was utterly bourgeois.

BBU: But that wasn't the case in New York, was it?

VE: Not at all, the scene was different there, a critical appraisal had already been going since the 1950s, especially through the new dance theater and dance performances, as well as people like Yvonne Rainer. At any rate, my exhibition didn't meet with much interest at first, neither nationally nor internationally, it was probably too early. I offered my concept to Galerie nächst St. Stephan, among others, which at the time was *the* address for more progressive art, but Monsignore Mauer kindly declined. It was not until Oswald Oberhuber took over the management of the gallery that *MAGNA*[5] could take place, in 1975. But for various reasons not in such a broad sweep as I had conceived. The exhibition was national, and in addition I mounted an international supporting program and curated and organized the gallery's 21st International "Art Talks" on the subject. That was the first art symposium in Europe, perhaps even in the U.S., on the subject of feminism . . .

SZ: And you invited colleagues from abroad to write for the catalogue.

VE: That's right, the catalogue for *MAGNA* was reprinted in 1997 to accompany my exhibition *Split: Reality*.[6] But to return to feminism: my thoughts revolved around how sexuality is represented in film, or how female sexuality is received. These considerations led me to works such as *TAPP und TASTKINO* and *Genitalpanik*.

BBU: One of your first performances, or actions, was *Menstruationsfilm* (Menstruation Film, 1967–68) . . .

VE: Except it wasn't done in front of an audience. At that time I tended to speak of actions, by performance I meant something else.

BBU: *Menstruationsfilm* was an action for a film;
your sister shot it. This film from 1966 is an important female statement. Did you already call it
a feminist action, not least to distinguish yourself
from the Actionists?

VE: No, I didn't distinguish myself from the Actionists
at that time, because I was doing my own work, but
I didn't call this film a feminist action, either. That distinction only came later, when I noticed that people
wanted to categorize me as part of Vienna Actionism,
but I never belonged to that group or movement, and
never emulated it. The mood of the times, the revolutionary awakening, as I perceived it, doubtless swept
me along; artistically, though, I was more aligned to
Body art. And I almost always worked in the media of
film, video, and photography.

BBU: You have always said you are interested in the
material of art, and also see the body as a material
for your artistic expression. You have channeled
some of your ideas on social change or oppression
within the family into relatively extreme body performances. How did you find the courage to do that?

VE: I've often been asked that, but it's not a matter of
courage. If the concept is right and you want to realize
the piece, you just do it.

BBU: You have mounted some of your actions more
than once. Could one say that they had the character
of a script for you, or a play?

VE: I repeated some actions two or three times. But
not like a play, because the situations were always very
different, a different audience, a completely different
setting . . . as, for instance, the performance *Eros/ion*
(1971), which I did a number of times, just like a film is

shown more than once. I also presented the *TAPP und TASTKINO* several times.

BBU: Yet sometimes you decided to use actors . . .

VE: It was always my body in the actions and performances, especially in my body works. Even in the planning phase. But in other pieces it didn't necessarily have to be me, other people could perform them. For instance, Erika Mies showed *TAPP und TASTKINO* on one occasion in Cologne, and participated in the presentation of *Cutting* in Amsterdam and elsewhere . . .

SZ: But it makes a difference whether you are standing there with the proscenium box and Peter Weibel is urging the audience to enter the cinema— or whether Erika Mies is standing there with the box and you do the talking. What was the difference between your speech, your way of speaking, and Peter Weibel's?

VE: Actually, it made no difference at all, because it was always the same cinema, and the presentation with Erika Mies as the performer and me making my statement about the *TAPP und TASTKINO* was regarded as highly provocative, because two artists, two women, were presenting an action like that in a public space. There was a charged, challenging atmosphere in Cologne, stronger than elsewhere, and the passers-by acted very aggressively. Peter Weibel's speech was very political; he said things like: "You Germans must realize that even Kissinger slept his way to the top," and so on. And among other things: VALIE EXPORT presents her *TAPP und TASTKINO* . . . It's important to note that I presented the *TAPP und TASTKINO* a number of times in different constellations:[7] On the first occasion in Vienna I read out my manifesto on it, about voyeurism and so on. Two days later, the *TAPP und TASTKINO* was presented in Munich with a speech by Peter Weibel. I also presented the *TAPP und TAST-KINO* at the Underground Explosion at Cirkus Krone (1969), which was a larger event with all manner of goings on: Films were shown by Kurt Kren, Wilhelm and Birgit Hein and others, various groups of people made music and sounds, Peter Weibel gave a speech, the two of us tossed bales of barbed wire into the audience, I whipped the audience, and finally I went into the audience with the *TAPP und TASTKINO* and invited people to visit the cinema without any accompanying speech. Wolfgang Ernst went along with me as a sort of protector, in case somebody hit me . . . (*Laughs*) Because that also happened: a presentation of the cinema at the Volkshaus in Zurich was brought to an abrupt end when someone hit me over the head with a bottle. The video you know of the *TAPP und TASTKINO* was made specially for Apropos Film.

SZ: So the *TAPP und TASTKINO* was reenacted especially for Apropos Film?

VE: It was not reenacted, it was rerun—like any other film—and an excerpt was shown in the broadcast. So, to sum up: The history of the *TAPP und TASTKINO* presentations is long and varied.

BBU: In your body actions—such as *Delta: Ein Stück* (Delta: A Piece, 1976–77) or *Asemie* (Asemia, 1973)—the ostensible biographical aspect was not important, but there was always a lot of theory at the back of it. It was about you as a projection surface for a whole range of codes and norms.

VE: Biographical or autobiographical themes in the narrower sense, or working through a problem that one sometimes has. I reject all that, that's not what art is for, it's not a therapeutic instrument. Autobiographical aspects do enter into it, of course, because it's me who's doing it, who is now serving as a projection surface for signs and norms, that's clear. But that's not the point of departure. As for getting down to the theory, that's always been important for me. Various media and materials come together in an action or performance, which prompted questions about their symbolic charge, their meanings and connotations. Or how can one change the context, and what happens then? There was already interesting literature on semantics and semiotics in the 1960s, which I could read in translation.

SZ: Starting with Claude Lévi-Strauss. I nevertheless have the impression that you picked up on this pretty early on—especially the French theorists. How did you come across these theorists?

VE: Through reading. And going to bookstores, even abroad. Language theory really interested me, and if you're interested you inevitably come across things.

SZ: Did you have partners or associates for your studies, people with whom you could discuss the things you read?

VE: Hardly anyone, in fact. I looked for the texts and read them myself. I liked Lévi-Strauss very much and read him a lot. Mostly I read the German translations, I couldn't read French, and English was usually too strenuous for me. I must add that I could always get the literature I was interested in straight away at Brigitte Herrmann's bookstore. Of course, you could also find interesting information in magazines.

BBU: Now that we've got to the subject of language theory: An interest in language was obviously very important to you. Language as a normative instrument of power or—to take this in another

309

direction—language disorders or communication disorders in general.

SZ: That already began in fact in 1969 with your project *Tonfilm* (Sound Film), where you began focusing on the organ that produces speech. And again in recent years you have turned your attention noticeably often to the throat, presumably thanks to the technical development of the laryngoscope?

VE: Yes, that method of investigation was still unavailable in the 1960s, but now at last one could get closer, penetrate the body and see what happens inside the body itself. How do individual sounds and letters arise, what physical formations produce sounds inside the body—in particular the glottis, tongue, and the teeth—and outside it, the lips and mouth, etc.?

BBU: So phonetically, physiologically?

VE: Yes, the technical apparatus. Because none of us know as yet what thinking looks like inside your head; but the way the letters originate in the technical, in the material apparatus can now be explored and rendered visible. And what if the technical apparatus is disrupted, what effect does that have and what happens in your mind? At the same time, there are a lot of sounds or letters that only occur in certain languages, yet the apparatus is the same. How can we explain that? How does the apparatus change, and how does that make things different? The glottis as a physical instrument. These were the questions that interested me. Doubtless they were shaped by a material turn of mind. And language, of course, is an artistic medium, a form of expression—so what can be done artistically on the basis of these considerations? I'm thinking of vocal images, sound images, phonetic images, etc., of the kind we know from Schwitters and the Dadaists, or Concrete Poetry . . . Speaking as a composition with the instruments of speech. So I was interested in the material of speech, in recording the speech apparatus, it fascinated me so much that I immediately used the laryngoscope for several different artworks, films, and installations.

SZ: During that period you also made the video *Vaginan* (1997), where you used a vaginal ultrasound recording and also went inside the body . . .

VE: Going inside the body, looking at what's beneath the surface, what the architecture is like inside—that idea runs like a thread through my work. It's already there in *Cutting* (1967–68), where what was important was cutting the projection surface, the paper, in order to read the word, but also in *...Remote...Remote...* (1973), as well as *Eros/ion*, where I also wrote that the cuts on the outer skin serve to show the inside of the body.

BBU: What interested you in pathological communication disorders? You've dealt quite often with the subject, in body performances such as *Asemie* and more concretely in the television documentary with Oswald and Ingrid Wiener, *Das Unsagbare Sagen* (Speaking the Unspeakable, 1992).

VE: Identity and communication—they're interrelated things. Our abilities to communicate are very strongly regulated by life in the western world. Anything that doesn't correspond to the norms is labeled compulsive and pathological. However, these pathologies are also realities and truths that are possessed by people. They cannot be denied. I wanted to know why these pathologies are pushed aside and what the fringes look like where they have been pushed to. That was also the starting point for the body performance *Asemie*. If our society with all its norms had developed differently, we might have abilities to communicate that we don't ever suspect, but which are definitely in each of us.

BBU: On the one hand, you're talking now about disorders, but on the other about a form of under-development that we owe to the fact, say, that rational speech is more important in our culture than physical expression.

VE: It wouldn't automatically mean the end of ratio-nalism if we were to communicate differently, perhaps we would have a different kind of rationality. Mind or reason are in any case there. So there is behavior that is normed as normal, and behavior normed as patholog-ical. I regard both as "normal" forms of communication.

SZ: At least equally valid forms of communication. That, after all, is the attitude that makes a film like *Das Unsagbare Sagen*, where the phenomena are simply named and described.

VE: They are all quite customary forms of expression that are used by humanity, but which are subject to certain constraints in order to regulate them. Picture this: in my project *Tonfilm*, everybody shouts when the sun shines, and whispers when it is dark, and nobody understands anyone else . . . If conditions like that were to escalate, we could no longer live "constructively" on this planet. We would have to develop other forms of behavior and communication, and the interesting ques-tion is, what would they be?

BBU: You of course are one of the few who, apart from body works, has always worked structurally, both in film and texts, and of course photography. Did these fields mutually influence each other? Where did the need come from to take the struc-tural ever further?

VE: I do think that these fields and the various media have influenced each other. In conceptual photography, for example, I was interested in introducing movement, cinematic movement, that is, into photography. As for instance in the photographic work *Schriftzug*,[8] where I labeled a railway car with the word "Schriftzug."[II] Looking at the moving train it was like a fast movie, while every railroad stop became an exhibition . . .

BBU: That's a further aspect of your work, you've not always kept to the art space, but also deliberately gone beyond. Why? Were you interested in expanding the art space? Or reaching people who don't necessarily go to an art event, but then are suddenly confronted with one?

VE: Not so much the second one, that sounds a bit like missionizing to me. I am keen on expanding the art space, but not that I want to turn everything into one . . . But I wanted to create an awareness that there are other spaces outside of the art space which art can also embrace. This of course is a very theoretical notion, inspired by the idea of extension—an idea incidentally that informs all of my work. Just as EXPORT also means extension or expansion, getting out of the port, the harbor . . . Expansion contains the possibility for change. Other parts come to join it and then it's a different, perhaps even new product. This ability to expand determines our capacity to think, which in turn makes us human beings.

SZ: Up until now I have got the impression from our conversation that your work is extremely conceptual, that you consider what you want and how the work should look very carefully. Is there any room for something like spontaneity in your work?

VE (*laughing*): . . . the gut feeling in art? Obviously
I want to express something, the starting point is kind
of impulsive and spontaneous.

SZ: So that's there in the idea.

VE: Yes, I have a great many ideas. But by the time
I start to realize them, the concept, the structure is
already there.

SZ: I'm asking this because of your *Drehbuch zu
einer neuen Interpretation des Vampirthemas*
(Screenplay for a New Interpretation of the Vampire Theme). You told me you can still remember
the exact situation in which you drew it. I have the
impression it all went very quickly . . . Can you tell
me how it was?

VE: I clearly remember the evening I drew it. I was
watching a lot of vampire movies at the time, the
Dracula movies. But I found them very unsatisfac-
tory because nothing really happened . . . you know,
opening a coffin and filming inside was not the
be-all-and-end-all for me. And then I thought, what
makes it all vampiric? The sucking! So the figure in
my drawing is sucking everything out—books and
schoolgirls and then Nobel Prize laureates, checking
everything: What's in there as regards knowledge or
whatever? And then there was a second figure, who
sucked out stuffed bell peppers from Inzersdorfer
cans, who stands for the proletariat—a commonly used
term back then. There are little fantasies like that in
there . . .

SZ: At any rate, it's a very cinematic realization,
true to the conventions of normal feature films.

VE: Yes, that was the idea.

SZ: But did you actually watch vampire films like that at the movies? Did you even go to the movies, and what did you watch?

VE: Everything from Antonioni to Westerns, everything from A–Z . . .

BBU: And what prompted you to make narrative feature films yourself?

VE: I already wanted to tell a story and put the various ideas I had accumulated, which were actionistic or performative, into a plot. I got the initial idea for *Unsichtbare Gegner* while I was walking around Vienna—that must have been in 1972—and I thought to myself, what would I do if a force was to land on this planet, in this city, an invisible force? My only hope would be to photograph it, to capture it. But if this force really was invisible, it wouldn't come out on the photos, the camera would be taking photographs of something completely different, and so on . . . And I had a second element, the name Hyksos, which is the name of an ethnic group that suddenly appeared thousands of years ago and then quickly vanished. I had learned about the Hyksos at school and I liked the story because it was also political. In *Menschenfrauen* (Human Females, 1979) I wanted to place four women in relation to one another. And in *Die Praxis der Liebe* (The Practice of Love, 1984) there was this journalistic aspect, so once again grabbing on to something, researching—especially around the subject of the arms trade, arms production, arms supply, which occupied me a lot at the time; on the other hand, Judith has two men, that's another constellation with other possibilities.

SZ: But wasn't the feature film viewed as the most conventional genre of all? Or actually frowned on?

315

VE: Peter Kubelka always spoke of the industrial film . . .

SZ: I even come across pronouncements from other corners back then that feature films are ruled out for political reasons. Did such considerations play a role?

VE: I don't really remember. But I don't think so. Ernst Schmidt Jr. also made feature films, for example, or Hans Scheugl . . .

BBU: Yes, one, and that was much later. You set up your own production company in the 1970s, shortly after state film funding was introduced. What did that mean at the time?

VE: I produced *Unsichtbare Gegner* still as a private enterprise, meaning I had to see to all the accounts myself, which was very risky and landed me with a great deal of debts at the end. At first I wanted to produce *Menschenfrauen* with Satel, but I quickly realized that I couldn't work independently in such a set-up. So I searched around and took an exam in film production at Wifi; the material was a mixture of film technique and business know-how. During the exam, I was asked among other things what a "triangle" is. The examiners said there was no way I could know what a triangle is. A triangle is when you've produced such a fantastic film you have to make three negatives right away. After the exam, I heard that I should be happy to even have scraped through because I was simply an artist. I knew it all, except for the famous triangle. Anyway, then I launched my company . . . which made me independent, but producing feature films always meant running up debts.

BBU: I think the way that your feature films convey a socio-political, feminist message is more noticeable than in your structural and performative works. Do you agree? And do you think it's to do with feature films per se, with the narration? I'm thinking, for example, of the door marked "defenseless," or Joseph's sweeping misogynistic remarks in *Die Praxis der Liebe*; or the solidarity between the two women who were pregnant by the same man in *Menschenfrauen* . . .

VE: . . . which doesn't exist.
*(Laughter)*

BBU: . . . yes, it's a bit utopian.

VE: It was also planned as utopian. But I can answer your questions with a yes, the narration helps communicate the themes and subject matter. Writing "defenseless" on the door, for instance. I could have done that as an action in public space, but that wasn't enough for me.

BBU: Your feature films all had their festival premiere or world premiere in Berlin. How were they received at the time?

VE: They were well received, often very well because they were art films. There had already been other filmmakers with feminist claims, such as Bette Gordon or Yvonne Rainer. And since Laura Mulvey's article "Visual Pleasure,"[9] there was also a feminist focus in film theory. One can see how well the films came over from the crits. They even went down well in Vienna, apart perhaps from *Menschenfrauen*, which Rudolf John[10] described as "feminist masturbation."

SZ: *Menschenfrauen* generally tended to receive poor reviews back then in the German-speaking world. One of the main objections was that the film was too clichéd.

317

VE: But that was the whole point, showing the clichés. It has fared better since then. There's one scene where the two pregnant women are standing on the flak tower, talking, and then a text fades in: "A society must be created in which it is possible to be a mother and self-reliant." That is more valid now than ever. It was just pathos then, but now it is practice . . .

SZ: It is interesting to note what a varied reception the feature films got. The reviews in Austria always picked up on you as a person, with all your "scandalous" past, with the *TAPP und TASTKINO* and similar performances. And *Unsichtbare Gegner* was itself a scandal in Austria, which led to questions in parliament.[11] There was already more distance in the rest of Europe, and also a certain astonishment: the artist VALIE EXPORT is making a feature film? Among the film critics in America— although *Unsichtbare Gegner* was first shown in the U.S. in 1978—there was, I would say, a much greater readiness to review your films independently of your person, as far as that is possible. Your films were taken seriously, in a different way, especially the feature films. Do you also see it like that?

VE: Yes, definitely. Americans could approach it without prejudice because they didn't know much about my history. Apart from which, this kind of film had already been seen long before that in America, so there was already a different context.

SZ: In 1991, you wrote in the aforementioned article "Expanded Cinema as Expanded Reality": "Today I make feature films to the extent that the situation— and by that I mean the financial situation—allows it . . ."[12] Your last feature film, *Die Praxis der Liebe*, had been in 1984 . . .

318

VE: . . . But I still thought I could continue to make feature films, or would certainly make another. But . . .

SZ: You had a whole number of projects, beginning with the screenplay *Das Handicap* (The Handicap, 1978) with Renate Czapek, which looks at a mother-daughter relationship. A gesture prompts the main character to recall a long stream of memories of her mother . . .

VE: Renate Czapek asked me if I would like to make a film with her. The book was her story. I was interested in realizing a film version of a story like that, outside the normal run of things.

SZ: Another project was *Flammen* (Flames, 1988), in which an older woman falls in love with a young girl; and then there was a variation on that theme titled *Grenzlose Liebe* (Love Unbound, 1989–90), where it turns out that the young girl is actually a young man. That's a theme we don't really know from you, which shows an interest in what today is termed gender. These scripts were written in the late 1980s, at a time when the gender discussion had only just begun . . .

VE: What interested me in fact was tackling gender, or transgender, or the transsexual—the ambivalent, you could call it. I'm sure that time and again this played a role, and still plays a role in my works in the form of not defining or of extending. The story is an extension of the gender issue and is told through extended cinematic means. But it wasn't really possible at the time to make the film the way I had envisaged it; the project was rejected. I had perhaps broached the topic too soon.

SZ: Then there was the complex around *Unica* (1987) and *Alaska* (1987), whose themes almost return to

your search for alternative role models. Your pre-
occupation with Unica Zürn brings your reflections
on linguistic philosophy, language as an instrument
of power, and language as an artistic medium, on
the one hand, very nicely together with the body,
on the other. In your text *The Real and Its Double:
The Body*[13] you describe how the problem with the
female body, as something disciplined by society and,
most of all, imposed from without, led Zürn to find
new meanings in existing linguistic material . . .

VE: Yes, Unica Zürn's anagrams . . . I first came across
them in the slender volume *Hexentexte*, published
in 1954 by Galerie Springer in Berlin. Unica Zürn was
and is a summation for me of many of my themes, as
a woman and artist, which is why I wanted to do a film
on her. In *Alaska* I was concerned with the question
of what kind of dialogue could develop between various
female characters—Danielle Sarréra, Linda Lovelace,
Ada Lovelace, and Unica Zürn. I would have acted in
it myself—as the person making the film. My concern
there was with role models: How did these women work
in their various fields? What were their destinies?

SZ: And finally there was the project with Elfriede
Jelinek, *The Piano Teacher* (1986). Interestingly,
you both wrote a screenplay, independently of one
another . . .

VE: As far as I recall, I asked Elfriede Jelinek about
the possibility of doing a film of her novel *The Piano
Teacher*. We had known each other since the 1970s.
I would have really loved to have made the film of *The
Piano Teacher*. She had already written a script, which
she gave to me. Then she, or rather her publishers
reserved me the rights for some time for a pittance,
and during that time I wrote my script. But that script
couldn't be realized . . .

SZ: It couldn't be floated financially?

VE: The program editor at ZDF said, overdramatically, that Wolfgang Lorenz of ORF said he wouldn't produce anything more that ended up languishing in the basement, like Novotny's *Staatsoperette*.[14] A production company in Bern wanted me to rewrite my screenplay, because: "We don't steer pianos around on rails in apartments." It would have demanded a lot of rewriting. Even Gerhard Schedl of the film advancement program in Austria got me to rewrite scenes. He asked me how I envisaged the scene where they're doing it in the taxi. I had to laugh. I said to him, Herr Schedl, I can write it all down: either one sees nothing, or one sees everything, or one simply sees the car bouncing up and down . . .

SZ: But what effect did that have on you when all these projects floundered? That must have been a real disappointment for you, particularly when film funding had at last been instituted in Austria? And you were extremely successful as a feature film director . . . .

VE: It certainly was frustrating. But the film funds in Austria wanted regular feature films that also brought in money, and not more festival films.

SZ: Was that one of the reasons why you subsequently went to work for ORF, where at that time you could still continue making films without such commercial pressures?

VE: No, there's no connection there. Wolfgang Lorenz invited me. At first he wanted me to do a portrait of Arnold Schwarzenegger, but nothing came of it because Schwarzenegger never had time. And then I made a series of documentaries together with Oswald and

Ingrid Wiener . . . Wolfgang Lorenz really gave us a lot of support for those documentaries.

SZ: But before that there was *Das Bewaffnete Auge* (The Armed Eye, 1984). What was the remit for that?

VE: I don't remember that too well. There was no specific remit. I suppose Wolfgang Lorenz invited me to do a piece for *Kunst-Stücke* . . . or asked me if I would like to do something about film, I really don't remember that too well . . . And then I made some concrete proposals . . .

BBU: The very first television piece, *Facing a Family* (1971), warned about the dearth of communication in the family brought about by television. The child has to keep its mouth shut while everyone's watching the box—so it started out with a critique . . .

VE: *Facing a Family* was in the series *Kontakt* (Contact), a youth program. But it was planned for the evening news, that was certain. You're sitting in front of the TV while the presenter reads out the news, when all of a sudden you see a family that represents you, and there's you looking at this family. But that wasn't possible, even then—although generally speaking more was possible back then than today . . .

SZ: What did the move to television mean for you in the 1980s? How did you approach the medium, which you also criticized—as for instance in a piece like *Facing a Family*? Was television simply another opportunity for your work?

VE: With programs like *Kontakt* and editors like Hans Preiner, the 1970s were still full of hope, as was also true of *Kunst-Stücke* in the 1980s. *Kunst-Stücke* was still doing in-house productions, and when they bought in they bought in well. They knew that a small slice of the television pie was there for art projects. It's quite different now. And the manipulative nature of the medium was much clearer back then. Now even the manipulation is so manipulated that you can't really see it any more. But it was already clear of course that we, who were making the *Kunst-Stücke,* were not the people the country bumpkins paid to see when they bought their TV sets . . .

SZ: There are two noticeable things in your television productions from the 1980s: On the one hand, you used television very much as a didactic medium. In *Das Bewaffnete Auge* you convey a high level of film history and theory, such as you probably only did as a university professor, and *Aktionskunst International* also depicts a piece of art history. On the other hand, the regular collaborations with Ingrid and Oswald Wiener, in *Tischbemerkungen* (Table Comments, 1985), *Yukon Quest* (1986), and *Das Unsagbare Sagen.* Which makes me ask: In what contexts do you find it desirable, if not necessary, to collaborate?

VE: I proposed a film portrait of Oswald Wiener to Wolfgang Lorenz, *Tischbemerkungen,* and then we made *Yukon Quest* and *Das Unsagbare Sagen* together. *Das Unsagbare Sagen* was Oswald Wiener's idea, he also wrote the script for it. And the collaboration on *Yukon Quest* came about because Ingrid and Oswald were living in Canada, Oswald also suggested that topic . . . some topics simply come from the situation. I see myself as a solitary worker, but in larger projects, such as a film, I like to work with one or more people. I also like to collaborate on the script, because I'm not that good at dialogue. I wrote the script for *Praxis der Liebe* by myself, including the dialogue, but I still think film is teamwork.

BBU: You've generally taken a strong mediatory approach, not just in your feature films and television work, and you've also published texts and constantly given interviews, curated exhibitions of feminist art, and so on. Did you hope in this way that you could influence or even change people's minds?

VE: Change is a bit of an exaggeration, but I definitely wanted to indicate that not only the forms we are used to, but also others are conceivable and also exist. Change always entails a long and complicated process. I would never have said that I was changing society . . .

SZ: And in the first raptures of 1968?

VE: The hope, the utopia that one could really achieve something was great . . .

SZ: In your early feminist texts—such as in the manifesto for *MAGNA*[15] or "Gertrude Stein/Virginia Woolf"[16]—you were forever concerned that women should become artistically active and in that way raise their awareness, because art according to you was also a form of reality . . . and that by changing art, to some extent women change reality as well.

VE: Yes, that's correct, but I was never a missionary. I hoped of course that society would change and that people themselves could join in and help change society into the picture, into the utopia we stood for. That was already the goal and still continues to be the goal somewhere or other, even if the goals are not generally as explicit these days. The 1960s thought in terms of large, powerful utopias, that was a rich substrate and without it probably nothing would have happened. But society also keeps enforcing its own constraints. Women of course are still worse off economically. Yet people now are already more aware that women must be visible and have a say in politics and the public sphere. And it wouldn't have come this far without the utopian demands and visions from 1968.

SZ: . . . and also the second women's movement in the 1970s. There again, certain areas have hardly changed, or not in a positive way. Do you also see it like that, particularly with regard to the ideas of the women's movement? There are also areas of disillusionment . . .

VE: Yes, of course, the desire for a great, visionary change is anything but fulfilled in many areas, it doesn't happen that quickly, the time frame is too short. What has worked for hundreds of years cannot be totally changed in thirty or forty years. But that mustn't be taken as an excuse, an alibi . . . At least tools have been developed that set changes in motion. And at the same time, there are other cultures where the role of women in particular is exactly the same as it used to be—I don't even want to go into that now, you can read about it every day in the newspapers. What's more, I must clearly state that while women have become very strong and far more self-determined, in some ways they have also fallen into a trap.

SZ: In what way?

VE: Society is still patriarchal and so is the legislation. Society has donned the mantle of equal opportunities, and that was the trap, in many cases women have adapted. We all know it's not true that women have every opportunity open to them: Who's the first to get laid off? What are the family structures like? A great many women are still dependent on a man—and then get a slap in the face from society for allowing it to get that far. Mistakes have been made, of course, but women get the blame.

SZ: But isn't also partly the problem that we have lost all our utopias? We've relied too much on realpolitik, in everyday life—getting child care and a little more pay, etc.—while the utopias have completely disappeared, haven't they?

VE: Visions and utopias are foreign words right now.

SZ: And not just with regard to feminist demands, it's a fundamental feature of our society.

VE: It's easier for society if it negates utopias and visions, because then it can run things better. Utopias and visions are uncertain, unstable factors. It's easier to shape a society that satisfies a few basic needs regarding realpolitik and reality, and indefinitely postpone any thoughts of utopias and visions. We are currently in a time and society that is completely lacking in vision. We have no vision of how to go on, apart from the vision of having money and a sort of prosperity. While the gap between rich and poor is getting larger and larger . . .

BBU: But that's also connected with the fact that certain problems can no longer be grasped, not least due to globalization. Turbo-capitalism has also doubtlessly stirred up a lot of fears.

VE: And I think that the fears are very strong. I tell you, neither I nor my colleagues were afraid back then. I know from students and young female artists just what a role fear plays today: Will I make it? Will I find a gallery? Will I get an exhibition? The fear is already there when they insist that it has to be the best museum. Everything is uncertain. You scarcely know for instance how museums will be run in twenty or thirty years time. By the state? Or will they be completely private, run by the VW plants? Art that reflects this fear, this uncertainty, would be good contemporary art. But that is generally regarded as too strenuous. Some artists try to make artworks that portray the VW plants exactly like a state-owned company. That's why the art market has also become so important in recent years.

SZ: There is the tradition in the avant-garde of always being interested in or even enthusiastic about new technologies and media. The role of video has been discussed several times, as a new, non-coded medium—especially, but not exclusively, for feminist artists. And digital techniques were also welcomed.

VE: Yes, right. But the digital technologies also had certain formalisms which for their part were also assignable, such as writing software . . . The whole of computer science of course has male connotations . . .

BBU: In "Expanded Cinema as Expanded Reality"[17] you wrote that the new digital cinema is the closest equivalent to expanded cinema because it is an extension of virtual space, as well as of virtual time and virtual reality. Is there hope here for perceptual and cognitive expansion?

VE: When I wrote that article, I still expected developments in cinema in which the concepts of space, time, and different realities would be fantasized into virtual realms, as it were. But that has yet to happen. At the same time, the time frame may still be too short for that. Technically speaking, we are still pretty much in the opening phase. But I genuinely believe that the virtual and digital realm, which is multifaceted and also consists of nonartistic elements and factors, has this potential for expansion. I cannot say what such extensions might look like. There definitely won't be any more pictures or photographs. The context will be different, one that I cannot establish . . . And artistic expression will rest on a different concept of art and a different aesthetic. Art as you now find on the art market will be obsolete.

> BBU: Perhaps we will be able to approach this other context through computer games. One reason they are so popular and in such demand seems to be because the players can take on other roles more or less as they choose. A next step would be to bring the game closer to the player: a chip implanted in your body so that you can hook up with the network and arrive at expanded perceptions . . .

VE: That's the direction I'd take. I put together a few ideas on that for a lecture this year at the Ars Electronica.[18] If you had chips that made you in some ways like a machine . . . although people are in any case machines. We've already been using technological enhancements for a long time now, for centuries . . . but a chip implant would be the next step toward interactivity. Then the computer would be inside us—and with that we would probably stop calling it a computer. And what would be the source, and who stores this machine? Us? Or are we stored by the machine? That brings us back to the subject of communication . . .

> SZ: . . . if we were all linked up by a circuit we could communicate telepathically . . .

VE: And communication would become even more manipulative.

> SZ: There are great dangers lurking there.

VE: Yes, but also great possibilities for expansion. Every change brings its own dangers. The first fish to come out of the sea were asphyxiated . . . But then we can live quite differently and the only thing that would dominate us is nature—a thing we don't really notice and don't like to acknowledge. However, we are also a self-constructed form of nature. It is we who would have to adapt to nature and not the other way round—something we have struggled against for thousands of years. That would be the triumph of nature over humanity. We would have technology within us and be once again nature. A new image of man would emerge, a new way of being human.

SZ: Is that a utopia? Your utopia?

VE: It's a vision. The actual models of such a utopian life, of how such a society would be, have yet to be designed . . .

NOTES

1    VALIE EXPORT, "Feminismus und Kunst: Gertrude Stein/Virginia Woolf," *Neues Forum* 228 (January 1973).
2    Ibid.
3    VALIE EXPORT, "Expanded Cinema as Expanded Reality," *JAM* [The newsletter of Media Jar, Milwaukee's media arts collective] 1, no. 4 (July 1991), 7. [Talk]
4    *TRANSFER IDENTITIES*, photo series, 1968.
5    VALIE EXPORT, "A Fragmentary History of 8mm Film in Austria," in *Exit Art: International Forum of Super 8*, exh. cat. (New York, 1988), 44.
6    The action *Genitalpanik* was followed by the poster *Aktionshose Genitalpanik* [Action Pants Genital Panic], a photographic mise-en-scène featuring the action pants and a MG (not used in the original action).
7    *MAGNA. Feminismus, Kunst und Kreativität*. An overview of the female sensibility, imagination, projection and problems, suggested by a tableau of pictures, objects, photos, talks, discussions, readings, films, videos and actions. [Press release]
8    *Split:Reality. VALIE EXPORT*, exh. cat., Museum Moderner Kunst Stiftung Ludwig Wien, 20er Haus (Vienna, 1997).

9    For the history of the presentation of the *TAPP und TASTKINO,* see the corresponding section in the chronology of moving images in the present volume, 137–139. [Referring to the original place of publication, ed.]

10    *Schriftzug,* in Heimrad Bäcker, ed., *Photo/Literatur* (Linz: Edition Neue Texte, 1974) (photographed 1973).

11    Laura Mulvey, "Visual Pleasure and Narrative Cinema," *Screen,* 16, no. 3 (Autumn 1975), 6–18.

12    Film critic at the *KURIER,* an Austrian daily newspaper.

13    Cf. the details in the chronology of moving images in this volume, 104–7. [Referring to the original place of publication, ed.]

14    VALIE EXPORT, "Expanded Cinema as Expanded Reality." English in the original.

15    VALIE EXPORT, *Das Reale und sein Double: Der Körper* (Bern: Benteli Verlag, 1987).

16    Franz Novotny & Otto M. Zykan, *Staatsoperette.* Film, Austria 1977. For the scandal surrounding the production of *Staatsoperette* by the ORF public broadcasting corporation, as alluded to in Wolfgang Lorenz's words, see Elisabeth Büttner, Christian Dewald, *Anschluss an Morgen: Die Geschichte des österreichischen Films von 1945 bis zur Gegenwart* (Salzburg, Vienna, 1997), 207–12.

17    VALIE EXPORT, "Women's Art: manifest zu der ausstellung MAGNA (arbeitstitel frauenkunst), einer ausstellung, an der nur frauen teilnehmen. Geschrieben im märz 1972," *Neues Forum* 228 (January 1973), 47.

18    VALIE EXPORT, "Gertrude Stein/Virginia Woolf: Feminismus und Kunst," *Neues Forum* 228 (January 1973), 48–50; VALIE EXPORT, "Feminismus & Kunst. II. Teil des Aufsatzes 'Gertrude Stein & Virginia Woolf,'" *Neues Forum* 230/231 (March 1973), 59–61; VALIE EXPORT, "tapp & tast kino etc. III. Teil des Aufsatzes 'Gertrude Stein & Virginia Woolf,'" *Neues Forum* 234/235 (June/July 1973), 57–58.

19    VALIE EXPORT, "Expanded Cinema as Expanded Reality."

20    VALIE EXPORT, "Combined Images Combined Media," lecture given at Ars Electronica, Linz 2006 (unpublished MS).


EDITOR'S NOTES


I    *Kubus EXPORT – der Transparente Raum,* 2011.

II    Schriftzug means logo or lettering in English, but read as a compound of two words, "Schrift" (writing) and "Zug" (train), it can be taken to mean "writing train."

- - - - - - - - - - - - - - - - - - - - - - - - - - - - - - - - -

## WITH YILMAZ DZIEWIOR

- - - - - - - - - - - - - - - - - - - - - - - - - - - - - - - - -

### 2015

=============================================

YILMAZ DZIEWIOR: Since our conversation will be published in a book which negotiates the history of photography with the help of the self-timer or shutter release, I would like to focus on this topic. At the same time, some of the earlier drawings from your childhood and youth seem to be quite important within our context, because of their very titles, in which you explicitly use the term "self-portrait." Series titles such as *Die Vorstellung eines Kindes "Gott ist ein Mann"* (A Child's Conception "God Is a Man"), which you use for your drawings, in which you appear as the author, should also be mentioned here. Why have you yourself been such a significant starting point for your activities from such an early age?

VALIE EXPORT: I started with these "childhood drawings" in the 1970s. I also included them as a category in my works. I call them "childhood drawings" because I have tried to find my own childlike drawing style, since they deal with memories, fantasies, dreams, and emotional states from my childhood. It was/is important to me to have this self-determined childlike drawing style as a form of expression, so I might express myself with it. To me, these drawings are a very important part of my artistic and emotional expression, the representation of my identity, my various identities, which have never been binding to me, but often rather obstructive to my imagination and the demands I place on the life that I live. The childhood drawings are very important to me. For me, they are sketched poems, perhaps also to represent, to jettison, my mental baggage.

I created the childhood drawing *Die Vorstellung eines Kindes "Gott ist ein Mann"* (A Child's Conception "God Is a Man") 1971 in memory of my school and Catholic boarding school days in Linz. In 1971, I could still remember clearly how I had perceived the altar, the impressive presentation of the altar; how incisive it had been to find a male identification figure in God, in Jesus. Several years later, I included this childhood drawing, these child's fantasies, in my film *Menschenfrauen* (*Human Women* [also trans. as *Human Females*], 1979), when Elisabeth takes communion, receives the host, and then builds an altar in her apartment with pictures of her father, before which she kneels and sticks out her tongue to receive the host, and says/thinks, "Father is a man," which is when the mother enters, cries, "What, you stick your tongue out to your dead father?" and slaps Elisabeth. What is also important to me in the drawing is the monstrance, which holds not only the host, but also the drawing of a young man, as part of the "Body of Christ." I incorporated the Body of Christ in the Holy Communion, and Elisabeth, as my proxy, incorporated the body of her father, who was killed in the war. I was always deeply impressed by the transformation of the host into the Body of Christ in the consecration of Mass, and I also showed a recording of the Holy Consecration by an actual priest in a video monitor next to my sculpture *Geburtenbett* (Birth Bed) at the 1980 Venice Biennale. Later, of course, I left the Catholic Church.

YD: I find it remarkable how abstract your drawn self-portraits sometimes are. Your drawing *Selbstportrait. Leben a parte post, a parte ante* (Self-Portrait. Life a parte post, a parte ante) from 1974 shows a hand where your face should be, which holds a rectangular block with the inscription "Selbstportrait," as if to throw it. What is this work about?

VE: This drawing came out of a feeling of "helpless-ness" of being unable to represent my "self-portrait," or, to put it differently, a portrait of myself, of ME, of my SELF. Each self-portrait has a different relationship to the self, and each SELF has a different expression. In my drawing *Selbstportrait. Leben a parte post, a parte ante* from 1974, the self-portrait is inscribed in letters on a lead brick that encloses a brain and at the same time shows its vulnerability, because it is exposed, without protection. The hand holding this symbolic lead brick is holding it like a mirror. It is a drawing of my own hand. There are several studies of my hands, which are very important to me as forms of self-expression.

Time and again, I have made several self-portraits, such as, for instance, the folding screen *SPUREN: ID-Gravis* (TRACES: ID-Gravis, 2000), which illustrates my genetic code on its screens.

YD: Do you remember when and in which context, or on what occasion you took a picture of yourself for the first time?

VE: I was able to borrow a camera and took a picture of myself. I did not want to create a self-portrait; I wanted to record myself, my face, instead, in the same way I was able to record my voice. Unfortunately, these pictures no longer exist. I wanted to record myself using audio tape, using a camera, and not to create a portrait of myself. To me, there is a considerable difference between self-portrait and self-recording. I created the photograph *Erste Selbstaufnahme* (First Self-Recording) in 1954 in Linz, on the Bauernberg, near the Gugl, where I always enjoyed spending time. I still have photographs from 1959 in which I pose as a "mannequin" as transfer identity.

YD: In 1967, you invented your pseudonym VALIE EXPORT as an artistic concept and logo, specifying

that it only be written in capital letters. Several
portraits are part of this empowering statement
in which you assert yourself in what at the time
was a clearly male-dominated environment. For
instance, you exchanged the round world map on
the Smart Export brand cigarette box with your own
face. Instead of the word "Smart" you used your
nickname "Valie," an abbreviation of "Waltraud."
Conversely, you did not remove the lettering for
"semper et ubique—immer und überall" ("always
and everywhere"). In another photograph, you osten-
tatiously show this modified cigarette package to
the camera, while you pose with a cigarette dangling
coolly from your mouth. What was the motivation
for this action, which led to the aforementioned
self-portraits?

VE: I had chosen my own artist name VALIE EXPORT.
Like many others, I smoked Smart Export cigarettes
at the time, and once, one might say suddenly, I had
the idea, pack in hand, to use this pack of cigarettes as
a "logo" in order to export my artist name around the
world. I then created this montage; there is only one
cigarette pack, which is in the MoMA now. The Smart
Export packaging was exactly right; I could change
a few things, as you have described, and I was particularly fond of the lettering around my portrait: "semper
et ubique—immer und überall." But also "Made in
Austria," which is also quite fitting.

YD: In some of your early films you seem to negotiate, or rather to expose, the very medium's
means of illusion as its intrinsic subject by filming
yourself. This is how one might interpret *Selbstportrait mit Kamera* (Self-Portrait with Camera)
from 1966–67, in which you film yourself, camera
in hand, in front of a mirror. *Selbstportrait mit
Kopf* (Self-Portrait with Head) is similar; it is also

a one-minute film, in which your wig-bearing head appears behind a statue's head—an action with which you negotiate questions of the representation of the human being and the object, and of the present and art history. What were your motivations for inscribing yourself into these works? How are we to understand the representation of your self-portrait here?

VE: With *Selbstportrait mit Kamera* (1966–67) I wanted to record a moving image of myself as a self-portrait. The "image" is more or less static; it shows me and the camera. But the medium of film rendered it a portrait in time. Here it is not only the location, the mirror, the mirror image that is the most important expression, but also the self-portrait, which, while located on one plane, expands in "time." Each frame features my self-portrait, so there are hundreds of self-portraits. Hence the title, or the reference, "Self-Portrait with Camera."

*Selbstportrait mit Kopf* (1966–67) was taken by my sister in Lugano. The picture is not the self-portrait, but the two heads: my head with the wig and the statue's head are the self-portrait. The image of my "living head" and the image of the head as a "frozen sculptural image" were the point of departure here. The representation is mirrored in the recording time and in the minimalist dialogue of my Self and the image of the unknown head. I think it's important to note that I also wore this wig in subsequent actions, such as the presentation of the *TAPP und TASTKINO* (TAP and TOUCH CINEMA) in 1968, but not in reference to a self-portrait, a self-representation, but in reference to the artistic representation expressed via my body, decorated and expanded with "artistic[I] elements."

YD: Many of your photographs in which you feature prominently in the form of a self-portrait document an action, or, with their status as autonomous works, are means of capturing your actions for posterity. This is especially true for performances of yours which have not been documented on film or video.

How do you judge the relationship of your rather autonomous photographs as works of art in contrast to your photographs as documents of an action?

VE: I do not claim the term "self-portrait" for all self-stagings, not even "self-representation." I discussed the documentary photographs; they are even the way I wanted them to some extent, but obviously not all of them, because the way a performance progresses is multifaceted. The artwork, the artistic idea, the artistic thought and expression of the artist, is always at its center. That is the work proper. The documentary photographs reproduce the progress of the action, of the performance. Without these photographs we would often have no impression of the event.

Many of my actions and performances have not been documented in photographs, because I didn't consider preserving something for later, for posterity. An action, a performance has always been something unique to me, even if it was subsequently performed again in different contexts. But documentary photographs show the various environments, the different stagings, and—which is also important—the social and artistic reception in different cultures and different timeframes. The artwork is autonomous, with or without documentation; it is an autonomous work, an autonomous idea, an autonomous concept of the artist's.

YD: Basically, self-portraits—whether they are painted or recorded with a camera—serve to confirm one's own identity. At the same time, they managed to be a self-marketing tool very early on in art history, and were used to underpin the artists' status—who were predominantly men until well into the twentieth century. Today, with the rise of so-called selfies—self-portraits created by the use of mobile phones—this genre is given yet another meaning. Which function has the self-portrait had in your own work, and how has its use changed throughout your career?

VE: My 2008 performance *I Turn Over the Pictures of My Voices in My Head* is also a "kind" of self-portrait. This film was made at the Arsenale during my performance *Die Stimme als Performance, Aufführung und Körper* (The Voice as Performance, Staging, and Body) at the 2007 Venice Biennale. Here, the anatomical architecture of my glottis, which is located inside my body, illustrates how individual speech sounds and consonants are expressed in my interior. This is made visible by a laryngoscope on a video monitor. It can only be a self-portrait, a self-representation, because this image, which my body is in possession of, is always something individual and is also connected to the way I speak, and, especially, to what I say. Here, the staging is the spoken language; I have transferred my written language, my text, into my spoken language. Self-portraiture, self-presentation, self-representation is also a transformational process. Self-staging as transformational process, as transfer identity. When I think of self-presentation, I think of my film *...Remote...Remote...* (1973), in the description of which I point to the visibility of my interior, my psyche, "the cut into my body is the cut to my body's interior; I gnaw away my Self from myself, my exterior shows my interior, because I move toward the inside."

I feel that in an exhibition that is entitled *Self-Timer Stories*, the camera takes center stage. The camera self-times the images; it contains a mechanism that transfers the exterior image into the camera onto celluloid or onto a chip. This mechanism of "self-timing" can be programmed and determined.

YD: Not all your self-portraits were created by yourself. Do you see a difference in this context, since
you are also responsible for the staging of the portraits that are created by others?

VE: There are different representations of self-
portraits, such as the photograph *VALIE EXPORT –
SMART EXPORT Selbstportrait* (1970). Here, the
cigarette pack is the self-portrait, and the photo with
the cigarette pack is the self-staging with the self-
portrait. This means that a self-portrait can be the
self-staging of a self-portrait, which does not have to
be recorded by me. One might say that the self-staging
is the self-portrait.

EDITOR'S NOTE

I    The German original actually says: "artificial elements."

SASKIA TREBING: VALIE EXPORT, I'm afraid we're going to have to talk about sexism once more.

VALIE EXPORT: Right, let's do it. It has to be done again and again.

ST: Have you been following the current #metoo debate?

VE: I have followed it but not yet taken active part. On the one hand it is terribly important that these matters are talked about because we know that a lot is still hidden away. On the other hand, topics are being mixed together in the debate that need to be heard in a more nuanced way. This is due to a perfidious male-dominated power structure that can express itself in a great variety of ways. It's good that more women are going public on this issue, but we shouldn't expect that it will change men. It's time for men to take a stand, but their position is as focused on power as ever.

ST: Feminism wasn't first invented in 2017, yet many of the contributions to the debate sound as if the subject was being discussed for the first time. Weren't we further at one time?

VE: I don't think so. I think it is thanks to the feminists of the 1960s and '70s that we can thrash out the issues once more. A lot of people are hearing about all this for the first time because for a long time feminism was

suppressed and too many people thought: Why? It's
all been achieved. People imagine that the state had
created enough equality and that women can achieve
enough if they simply want to. But it's not true.

ST: Was it this impression of inequality that
prompted you to place the female body at the center
of your art?

VE: The female body is a construct—and this realization has always been central for me. I wanted to know:
What does the body, not least my own, mean in society?
What is the significance of the body as a sign carrier
and symbol, what characteristics are loaded onto it
from without? It is shaped according to a male image,
and men define their power through access to the
female body. I could never accept these rules, and had
to controvert them in my art. I wanted to draw attention to these forms of repression and categorization and
liberate myself from them. Radicality was an important way for me to respond to and challenge them.

ST: In your performances such as *TAPP und TAST-
KINO* (TAP and TOUCH CINEMA) or *Aktionshose:
Genitalpanik* (Action Pants: Genital Panic) you
confronted '60s audiences with your naked body
in public space. Did you meet with aggressive
reactions?

VE: The height of aggression was when I was almost
knocked down with a beer bottle from behind; I had to
have stitches. When a woman dares to step into the
limelight she is rewarded with aggression in the form
of prejudices and contempt, then as now. The street
audience found my *TAPP und TASTKINO* fairly amusing
and interesting, which is surprising because it was
one of the first actions of this kind by a woman in Europe.
The public aggression was directed to how I dared

to step out as a woman artist. And anyone who called themselves a feminist back then could expect gross hostility. People threatened to throw acid in my face or break into my flat.

ST: The milieu of the Vienna Actionists was very male. Was that related?

VE: Yes, as the German name indicates they were male actionists, there were scarcely any woman artists who could have championed feminism. I was often censured with silence because I didn't fit in with the ideas. Not only by my male colleagues but also the press. Things are no doubt different these days.

ST: Public space has now shifted to the digital realm. How do you regard this online-activism?

VE: I think the online discussions are good and fitting, because they bring a lot to light that would otherwise remain unspoken. At the same time I regard the internet as a manipulative place. People want to be manipulated because they don't like making up their own minds, and the anonymity of the net encourages this tendency. Ultimately the sexism debate is always about concrete bodies that are dominated by male power.

ST: In Austria, as almost everywhere in the West, politics is shifting to the right. Does this shift equate with a renewed masculinization of power?

VE: You say politics is shifting to the right, I would say it has long since reached the right wing and will swing ever further to the right. One can see in Austria how an economic system is being pursued in which women will once again be kept at home so as to raise the children, even though that is no longer workable in present society. Arguments are once again being warmed about

mother and child attachment, which place restrictions
on women and generate male power. When women
receive governmental positions it is because men have
chosen them for their purposes, while leaving the
women's abilities unacknowledged.

ST: What impact do these developments have on art?

VE: It has been clearly stated in Austria that arts
funding should be pruned, but there have not yet been
any discussions as to how art and the culture scene
are supposed to manage. Up until now we've enjoyed
a good climate in Austria for experimental art, which
has also received state backing. But when one stops to
listen one gets the impression that this all will change
very quickly. The swing to the right means that some of
the freedoms that have been attained will be rescinded.
But I trust that artists will pick up on these trends and
make them visible.

ST: The current debate on sexism is accused of just
registering the symptoms. Can art do more?

VE: Yes, I've always been certain about that. A diag-
nosis would amount to showing the sick body to society.
Art cannot heal the sick body, but it can show changes
that make the sick body obsolete. Art can make a very
large contribution to sharpening our awareness and
enabling us to see the world differently from the way
it is depicted by politics or religion.

- - - - - - - - - - - - - - - - - - - - - - - - - - - - - - - - - - - - - -

## WITH OLIVER ZYBOK

- - - - - - - - - - - - - - - - - - - - - - - - - - - - - - - - - - - - - -

### 2018

========================================

Born Waltraud Lehner in Linz in 1940, VALIE EXPORT grew up in a middle-class teachers' family. Her father, an inspector in the navy, was a committed National Socialist who fell on the African Front in 1942. Her mother brought up her three daughters on her own, with the goal that they all should study and lead lives of their own. VALIE EXPORT received her education from nuns at a convent school, then attended the arts and crafts school in Linz, and at the age of eighteen married and had a daughter. She moved to Vienna in 1960 to study textile design, and came in rapid contact with the Vienna Group and the Actionists. Her career as an artist commenced. VALIE EXPORT's performances have a great immediacy to them, showing as they do social injustices, above all relating to gender issues. The search for identity and expressive means has extended throughout her entire work. Her representations of the pain of speechlessness, of the loss of physical and mental integrity, using film, performances, and photo series take the viewer to the limits of tolerability. The shock rolls back repressive behavioral patterns. With her offensive artistic strategies, she seeks a female expression of sexual self-determination.

OLIVER ZYBOK: Looking back at your beginnings as an artist, how was the situation at first? What were the basic premises for your later developments?

VALIE EXPORT: The story behind my biography concerning my creative output begins well before the birth

of my daughter when I was eighteen. I was a war baby.
Growing up in Linz, I also experienced the bombing in
Austria and the great devastation inflicted on the city.
A decisive turn of events came, however, after the end
of the war, when my father's library returned to our
premises from storage. At the age of five I was especially fascinated by looking at abstract and Constructivist pictures in the art catalogues and magazines.
A little later I came across the work of Alfred Kubin
and his manner of drawing light and shade purely by
lines. I think that was when I first started to be influenced by art. As a teenager I often visited churches
and museums in Italy, and once again I was interested
in how the artists managed to depict light and shade,
and with that, space. I come from a middle-class family
which placed a lot of importance on art and culture. Yet
as a child I took in all the things I saw in a very personal and abstract way, and began to piece together my
thoughts and impressions in poems and drawings. Some
of the drawings still exist, and are now in the VALIE
EXPORT Center in Linz. At around fifteen I experi-
mented for the first time with a camera and took my
first self-portrait. Slightly later I dressed up and got
a friend to photograph me in various poses. Some of her
photos still exist. Naturally I was much too excited and
nervous back then to pursue these experiments with
the camera in a concrete way, along with the changes
in identity they involved, but looking back they seem to
mark the start of my artistic reflections. Another early
memory relating to my art concerns the piano. When
I was about seven I took piano lessons for a while, but
I saw the instrument much more as an object. I exper-
imented with the keys and sounds, placed cloths and
paper on the opened lid so as to transpose the striking
of the strings into something visual. My mother was
less enthusiastic about these experiments, so for her
the subject of pianos quickly slipped into the background. After she died I had the piano shipped from

Linz to my flat in Vienna. It stood there for a long time but I never played it again. At some point I decided to give the piano to a kindergarten with the wish that the children should dismantle it in order to see how this resounding object is built. I delighted in the idea that children would think about how the instrument was constructed and take it apart. I still have the stool. After my school exams I attended the textile college in Linz. Following a short spell in the graphics department I changed to textiles. And whereas prints and drawing soon proved too static for me, I could really let rip with textiles and produced, for instance, a small collection of ties done in snake skin. The applied arts really left their mark on me, because they made me able to produce things by myself. At eighteen I became a mother and married. But it rapidly became clear that a life as wife and mother, in the normal, middle-class way with the traditional division of roles between man and woman, was not for me. My family gave me a lot of support, and after a year I was divorced. My sister and her family took in my daughter, my mother also took care of her, we all kept in close contact with one another. That allowed me to continue studying at the textile college in Vienna. And through my encounters with the art scene there and women friends like Ingrid Wiener, my career as a freelance artist soon took off.

OZ: You spoke in connection with your childhood experiments with the camera of a change in identity, and with that the beginnings of your artistic reflections. Could you elucidate on that?

VE: Probably like everyone around thirty, the question of my identity came to a head at that age. My conclusion was that I had no identity, because I was aspiring to a free identity, which I could not really attain due to social conventions, such as the conventions about gender that prevailed at the time. Yet even this desire for non-identity constituted an identity. Naturally I have developed an identity on the strength of my biography, one that I will never be rid of, but that is not possible without outside influences. I feel this fact to be restricting. With this in mind, as a young woman I took a long look at my childhood. My *Kinderzeichnungen* (Childhood Drawings), as they are called, from 1971–72 primarily feature negative memories of things that stirred up fears, aggression, and violent associations. These resulted in childhood wishes and imaginings which obviously would have been deemed unseemly in my surroundings if I had articulated them at the time. This led to drawings like *Die Vorstellung eines Kindes "Gott ist ein Mann"* (A Child's Conception "God Is a Man," 1971) or *Die Träume eines Kindes, Toilette* (A Child's Dreams, Toilet, 1972). The works underline how the human psyche is colored by past experiences, a lot of which we store unconsciously in our minds. The film *…Remote…Remote…* (1973) was also made in connection with this. I show myself sitting in front of a police photo depicting two children in a care home after having been abused by their parents. They are holding hands. I take a carpet knife and slice into the quicks of my fingernails, which I then dip into a bowl of milk. Apart from the strong symbolic charge to both liquids—blood from the injury, milk as vital sustenance given by the mother to a new life, for a seemingly eternal intimacy, for eternal physical warmth—the film shows that there is an unconscious, mental component to time which in my view always dominates what we concretely experience, which is to say consciously perceived time. This component consists of fears, feelings of guilt, and deformations. *…Remote…Remote…* ventures to depict this split in the body, equally in light of the relationship between past and present.

OZ: You are often called a media artist. Do you agree with this designation?

VE: In the late 1960s and early 1970s a clear distinction was made between concepts like media art and intermediality. Since I was very involved with what were termed the new media, I welcomed being called a "media artist." I was interested among other things in the position assumed by classic elements of painting and sculpture in the new media. As a traditional vehicle and conveyor of information, I inquired, for instance, into the construct of the canvas as picture carrier and how its function and possibilities had changed with the introduction of celluloid. I was looking into the various ways of depicting an image, and found it fascinating how the new media changed the way they were processed and handled. Apart from painting, I never limited myself to any one medium, and in films, as well as in performances and installations, I investigated the origins and possibilities of the image. Back then I liked being a media artist, but not anymore because the term has lost its currency regarding the artistic issues I raise. Ultimately all artistic means of expression are media, painting is a medium, as is video art, and so on. So "media art" is a very woolly term.

OZ: The themes in your work keep returning to different aspects of space. Ever since Martin Heidegger, space has been seen as a place of atmospheres, as something that is determined by people and conversely also influences them. How would you formulate your concept of space? You have created a number of works connected with it, such as *Raumsprung* (Space Leap, 1971) and *Raumsehen und Raumhören* (Space Seeing and Space Listening, 1973–74).

VE: One of my most enduring memories of space also comes from my childhood. We had fled from our apartment in Linz during a heavy air raid. As we returned, one of the detonations had left a lengthy crack in the

floor of our living room, so that we now could look
through the parquet at the street below. Apart from
that, almost nothing had changed in our apartment, and
for the first time I could experience the windows—
like the crack in the floor—no longer as views out of
the room but as an opening up of space. Fleeing into the
shelters and mine tunnels during my childhood always
led to memorable experiences of how different spaces
can be, what they offer, and how clearly they mark an
inside and an outside with different rights of access
for people of different origin or religion. There were,
for instance, tunnels for foreigners, which had no roof
to them. We often had to use them when we were too
late for the other tunnels in the hills, the so-called air
raid shelters, or when those were full up. The tunnels
for foreigners gave me a feeling of being totally unpro-
tected. For me, space is strongly linked with identity
and atmosphere. The piece *Raumsprung* is one of a
small but for me very important group of conceptual
photographic works that I like to call phase photographs. Using a space-time grid, the distorted, elided
quality of photographs is shown by photographing, for
instance, two parts of a facade from different angles
and piecing them together as an abstract whole. For
me this concept was a conquest, because fragmentation
enabled me to depict the temporality, as it were, of a
space. In *Raumsehen und Raumhören,* the focus is on
the relationship between space and body, coupled with
the fact that sounds are always bound to space. During
the six-part performance, various aspects of my body
were filmed by cameras set at various angles, which
when compiled as one whole composition and combined
with a synthesizer that grew louder and quieter, faster
and then slower, convey an ambiguous atmosphere.
It was decisive for me to show that the perceptions of
an image, such as my body in space, undergo distinct
changes as the viewer alters their position. I think
of architecture as something that I can extend and

enlarge with my body. In much the same way, the film *Syntagma* (1983) shows nested views of space, using not editing techniques but different camera angles created by the motions of two wings of a door and the wing of a window on which the cameras were variously mounted. What might seem marginal today came as an incredible discovery with the introduction of the new media in the early 1970s. Essentially the films, and above all the women filmmakers at that time, were also concerned with placing female consciousness and physical consciousness in context with questions of their origins, subject-object relationships, political resistance, and sexuality. The twin views convey both unity and difference. The cinematic, actionist, photographic representations of the 1960s and 1970s especially underline that a body can belong to a variety of representational systems.

OZ: You adopted your alias in 1967 and stipulated that it is only to be written in block capitals. You created a kind of label. Could you say something about that?

VE: I saw the name right from the outset as a stamp. Although I had no idea about marketing, I decided deliberately to turn myself into a brand. I did not want to take the name of a man, neither my father nor my husband, I wanted the right to have my own name and developed it straightaway as a sign, just as it is now. With this branding, this key idea, I could open myself up without any need to justify myself. I created a new identity that enabled me to act more independently from my actual ego, which doesn't really work of course. Contrary to the legend, the cigarette pack was not what prompted the label, I first came across it later and somewhat by chance, and used it, as it were, as a visual for my new brand. I had a packet of these cigarettes in my hands everyday, so then on a whim

I replaced the original globe with a photo of my face, encircled by the words "semper et ubique—immer und überall," always and everywhere. The name "Smart" I changed to VALIE, my nickname from my teens. I recently saw a poster with the slogan "Why do we need export? Because we use it to create jobs."—The name never loses in topicality. But above all it was a big step for me in my personal self-determination.

OZ: Often your inquiry into physicality, and with that female identity, is central to your work. Yet your range of topics is much wider; you also investigate, for instance, the relationship between language and image. You have made numerous works on this, such as *Der Riss im Wort* (The Crack in the Word, 1994) and *Die Macht der Sprache* (The Power of Language, 2002). In addition, you compose poems and have written theoretical articles on, among other things, feminism. How can all these activities be brought into your artistic work?

VE: Text is also a visual image, writing is like drawing. Apart from texts and drawings, which were done to augment my actions, feminist manifestos and text fragments used in installations and videos are a constant in my work. In addition, the titles also have a special importance through their dialogic function. With my titles I attempt to convey the message and content of the work in advance, as for instance with *Asemie – die Unfähigkeit sich durch Mienenspiel ausdrücken zu können* (Asemia—the inability to communicate through facial expression), or *Mythologische Plastik: Reise zu einem nicht-identifizierten Symbol. Bestandteil eines selbstverständlichen Dramas, von wem wozu?* (Mythological Sculpture: Journey to an unidentified symbol. Ingredient in a self-explanatory drama, by whom and why? [both 1973]). In line with concrete poetry, works like *auf und ab* (back and forth) or *zick und zack* (zig and zag) from 1973 investigate the relationship between text and image, while simultaneously pointing to language as an instrument of (male) power. I always wanted to know what language looks like as a picture. In my pieces *Die Macht der Sprache* (2002) and *glottis* (2007), I was at last able to realize what I had envisaged decades before: employing technical means to film the larynx, the organ for producing sounds, while someone is speaking, and presenting this in a video installation. Language is shown here as something fleshly, inside the body, without gestures or facial expressions, thus deconstructing the notion of a body image and role image imposed from without. I am forever interested in how an image can change its effect from one context to another. And I always arrive at the same conclusion: context determines image.

OZ: A large number of your works are milestones in recent art history, as for instance your *TAPP und TASTKINO* (TAP and TOUCH CINEMA, 1968) or *Genitalpanik* (Genital Panic, 1969). Are there any works or actions of yours that have not met with such attention, but that were an important artistic stimulus for you?

VE: The feminist pieces and the performances were always very important to me, and in connection with this, Laura Mulvey's theory of the "male gaze." But my conceptual photography, which has met with scarce attention because there are very few copies, was significant for my artistic development and way of thinking, because I could determine what I as a woman wanted to see. That included *Raumsprung*, which I mentioned a moment ago, as well as *Spiegelfenster* (Mirror Window) and *Der Blick (Grünangergasse)* (The Gaze [Grünangergasse]), both 1972. Among my key works was *Abstract Film No. 1* (1967), an experiment in expanded cinema. For this, a light source was placed

351

in a darkened cinema so it was reflected by a mirror
set at an angle, and the image in the mirror landed on
the screen. A variety of colored liquids were poured
over the mirror to produce an abstract, motile composition through the reflection onto the screen. I tried in
*Abstract Film No. 1* to assume a distance to technology,
so as to break through the boundary between art and
life. The projections on the screen, which produced
different images with each presentation, show that the
designations "original" and "copy" are not consistent—
the categories do not exist. A procedure like pouring
paint onto a mirror is performed once, that is original, but the projection onto the canvas is a result of
this action and thus not a copy of it. At the same time,
*Abstract Film No. 1* demonstrates by the simplest
means the production of a film without celluloid.

OZ: You have amassed an extensive archive across
various media with the aim of stimulating an artistic
and academic appraisal of media art and performance art, and promoting research.

VE: The VALIE EXPORT Center where the archive
resides opened in fall 2017 in Linz and is now gradually
embarking on its research activities. We have already
busied ourselves since 2011 with compiling and col-
lating photographs, films, letters, newspaper clippings,
books, catalogues, and everyday objects—all the materials I have collected and used in my art. Parts of the
archive were exhibited in the Lentos Kunstmuseum
in Linz, and recently at the Neuer Berliner Kunstverein. But I have left the arrangement of the material
totally to Sabine Folie, head of the VALIE EXPORT
Center, because only an outside gaze can tease apart
the individual topics and place them in their respective
academic contexts. This approach allows the VALIE
EXPORT Center to grant access to the public and, by
abstracting aspects of my oeuvre, to make various

perspectives and artistic currents visible. I began very early on to catalogue my works and cross-reference them. What in fact I always envisaged was using them for a website, as a work in its own right, and linking it with my theoretical texts and texts by authors who support or indeed influence my ideas.

OZ: A new generation of women artists who describe themselves as feminists and are very active on various social media platforms such as Instagram, stage fictitious stories that theme, for instance, gender roles and ideals of beauty. Even if they are preoccupied with alleged flaws such as body hair, problem skin, or unwieldy body proportions, all tearfully presented in selfies, time and again what is central to these photos are images that emphasize their femininity to the extreme and convey a strong urge for self-presentation. It is noticeable how many of these artists present their femininity in a highly sexualized manner, in a way that second wave feminists—which is to say those of their generation—descry, because they regard such self-depictions as self-abasement aimed simply at satisfying the male gaze, and as reflecting gender clichés. Indeed, this new generation of artists seems to have little interest in certain feminist norms. A lot of the posts on the social media appear to document an out-and-out search for identity.

VE: It happens time and again throughout art history that an artist's own identity is placed at the center of their creative work. This is currently being done in the digital media with hitherto unknown possibilities, above all regarding the speed of production and reception. I do indeed feel that the images that above all younger artists show of themselves are more a step backwards, adjusted to the male gaze and handed-down ways of viewing the female body. Modern woman today can apparently do everything: be beautiful, have children, live in a happy relationship, and be independent and successful. But on what conditions? As Judith Butler put it, this reveals not so much boundless emancipation as maximum exploitation and conformity to a neo-liberal patriarchy. But I nevertheless find feminist actions on the net interesting because in artistic terms, we are still on virgin soil. It is a matter of plumbing and increasingly tapping creative potential. Of top priority here should be social and political issues connected with feminism. Unfortunately, one must say that at present, feminism is no longer the right vehicle to portray a just society. Like every ism, even feminism has hit up against its limits and become doctrinaire. Every woman should have the chance to be what is right for her, but rather than offer that openness, feminism continues to set down dogmatic rules about how the sexes should behave.

> OZ: How do you regard the initiators of the #metoo debate? How nuanced do you feel the discussions are? Are they being in fact dominated by a sense of revenge? One often gets the impression in feminist discussions that they are simply about realigning the balance of power between men and women, and not so much about altering the system.

VE: You have to have power in order to achieve the goals, but this power in turn shapes the goals. If feminism categorically rejects power as a male attribute, but fails to come up with an alternative, it has failed in its objectives. If I am sexually harassed on the subway by someone in a purported position of power, I obviously don't want it to be glossed over. The #metoo debate may well have pointed out such discrepancies, but instead of suggesting ways to solve the issues and describe the problem objectively and in detail, a vic-tim-offender narrative has been set up and become entrenched. As the #metoo debate got going, I thought it would result in a large number of conferences and discussions on the broader aspects of feminism and gender, and that with the aid of modern gender research, new forms of sensitization and differentiation would become possible. But none of that has happened. It has not moved on from telling utterly appalling stories. And worse still: The #metoo debate has scarcely gone beyond the small circle of women in the film world who, despite their possible dependency, have nevertheless managed to achieve wealth and success, while women from the lower strata of society, or the rights of African, Asian and South American women have been largely or totally ignored. Nor has a differentiated analysis of gender roles really been undertaken. Apart from looking at individual fates, an appraisal of the problems has been completely missing from #metoo. It is not that simple, though; one cannot stick to individual descriptions, we must keep on casting our minds back, time and again, and relate the whole story.

- - - - - - - - - - - - - - - - - - - - - - - - - - - - - - - - - - - - - - - - - - - -

WITH MAREIKE NIEBERDING

- - - - - - - - - - - - - - - - - - - - - - - - - - - - - - - - - - - - - - - - - - - -

2020

========================================================

MAREIKE NIEBERDING: When you think about yourself, who are you thinking of: Waltraud Lehner, whose name you were born with, or VALIE EXPORT?

VALIE EXPORT: VALIE EXPORT. Waltraud Lehner is also very important to me though, because she is what I grew up from.

MN: In 1966 you wrote a poem in which you say: "I was born in a hospital that belongs to the city of Linz / I drank at the breast that belongs to my mother / I hid myself from the bombs that belonged to the country of England / . . . I wept over my father whose death belongs to the fatherland" . . .

VE: I began writing poetry in my youth. When I was thirteen I wrote: "In the beginning was the word and the word was a man." But writing poetry was too fiddly for me.

MN: I wanted to go on to the last line of the poem: "That is the life that belongs to me." Was that the beginning of your transformation into VALIE EXPORT? Your change of name followed shortly after.

VE: I left Linz in 1960, at the age of twenty, studied for four years in Vienna, and then in 1966 had my daughter, who had been raised at my sister's, there with me. I

thought at the time: Right, now something really new
is beginning. What's happening to me? All at once my
life belonged to me. My new name was an expression
of that.

   MN: How did the people around you respond to this
   wish to go by a new name?

VE: I can't say what my family thought. We never
discussed it. But a lot of my acquaintances were be-
mused. But other artists had also given themselves
new names: Andy Warhol was actually born Warhola.
Playing around with one's name was not uncommon
in those days. But I couldn't play around with mine, I
needed a different one. So I thought: EXPORT suits
me best. People will remember that, apart from
which, as an artist I export something from inside me.
VALIE comes from Waltraud, and was my nickname
as a teenager.

   MN: You insisted that the name should always be
   written in block capitals.

VE: Which is why I had such incredible difficulties with
my colleagues in Vienna: my name was always in capitals in the programs. They were angry at me for always
being so conspicuous. That of course was the point of it.

   MN: In your work, women are shown time and again
   as objects shut up in the smallest of spaces. Where
   does this confinement come from?

VE: That has doubtless to do with the traumas of war.
Being cramped together in a cellar, not really being
free. We spent the last phase of the war in the countryside, one could play there wherever one liked. But
everything in Linz was very cramped, and I didn't
understand as a child that this air raid shelter we had

to keep going to was there to protect us—even though I would then see people lying dead on the street as we went home.

MN: How can I picture this space?

VE: The landlord in Linz had a bunker built in the garden behind our house, a small room underneath down a couple of steps with wooden props, roughcast walls made of gravel or the like. I never liked going into the bunker, it had simply a trap door, one could scarcely sit down inside and it was loud. I was terribly scared, that was a real emergency bunker. There was also a mine gallery in the nearby hill, the Bauernberg, which was larger. But if you were late you couldn't get into the gallery anymore, and had to go to the so-called foreigners' gallery, that was just a kind of dugout, almost like a military trench, where you sat and had to duck down or otherwise your head stuck out. I never saw bombs raining down, but I clearly remember the fighters as they flew down to the oil depot in Upper Austria, pow, zap, they came shooting past. The fighters are the reason why even now I can't watch fireworks.

MN: You were four years old. Whose hand did you grasp in those moments? Your mother's, or were your two older sisters more important?

VE: Always Mom. On one occasion my mother had to jump from a moving train because of the fighters, and she broke her two arms. She was thickly dressed, two pullovers and a coat on top. But the nurses forced her to take off the pullovers one by one. She pleaded with them: "Please cut them off!" But you don't cut up a pullover in wartime. I wonder how people can treat immigrants so badly today. They are traumatized people and children, just like then.

MN: Your father fell in the war. What does the word father mean to you?

VE: It wasn't anything special for me during the war, the fathers had all disappeared. Later, perhaps when I was eight or ten, I missed him and thought: Everything would be different if my father were here. Mom wouldn't be so strict. I transposed it then into religious things and built altars to my father. In my film *Menschenfrauen* (Human Females) from 1980 I worked in a similar scene. The daughter had built an altar for her father and is sitting there with her tongue stuck out, ready to receive the communion wafer, when her mother comes in and gives her a clip round the ear: "Why are you poking your tongue out at your father?" My own experiences often flowed into what I showed in my films.

MN: How did it affect you that your father was a National Socialist?

VE: I only learned about that later, as an adolescent. Before the war he was a headmaster, a lot of teachers were National Socialists.

MN: You did your schooling at a boarding school in a convent. What did you learn there that prepared you for life?

VE: To keep to myself, defend my territory. I never let anyone sit on my bed and play with my dolls, they were my things. I didn't put up with anything, not from my peers, nor from the older children.

MN: In one of your *Kinderzeichnungen* (Children's Drawings, 1971–72) a child is shown playing the piano while its mother is hanging dead from a chandelier.

VE: I'm not going to say now that I wished my mom was dead, but when you're young you want to get rid of all that stands in the way, and death wasn't anything unusual for me. I knew it from the war. I dealt very harshly with my mother in this drawing. She was very strict, but she worked an enormous amount and sacrificed everything for us, so that we three daughters could study. She would walk by foot in town, regardless of the distance, so as to save the fare. But sometimes I simply felt tyrannized. I wasn't allowed, for instance, to wear nylons after the war because I wasn't old enough, so I wanted to tyrannize in return.

MN: What did you do?

VE: I sneaked snakes into the house. One evening my mother opened the drawer in her bedside table and there was a snake inside. She was horrified, and I said: "You've already been sleeping right beside it for two or three weeks."

MN: How did you come to art?

VE: I enjoyed drawing, also writing poetry, and I looked at the books in my father's library, which included journals from the 1920s with works by Moholy-Nagy, catalogues on Dada, and a book with photos that one had to look at with 3-D glasses, which was curious.

MN: How would you describe your first artistic work?

VE: I did a self-portrait at the age of fifteen, and for the first time I thought: I must photograph myself, get to know myself by means of an apparatus, not only by my mirror image, which in any case is laterally inverted. That was important. Then I did small things, but I have lost almost all the photos and negatives.

MN: What would you have liked to have kept?

VE: The photos I took with my schoolmate Lothar Blöchl. We had the same figure when we were fifteen and so we dressed up, me as a boy, that was easy. But dressing him up as a girl was quite weird. Then we got some hay from the field and stuffed it into his blouse, which was really funny.

MN: Did this game with gender identities feel risky?

VE: No, not at all. We didn't know the word identity, it was more a case of swapping with the other in ourselves.

MN: After school you went to the textile college in Linz, then met your first husband at eighteen, married, had a daughter, and divorced after a year. You arrived in Vienna as a divorced woman and mother to study fashion design. How were you received?

VE: Not a soul understood that back then. A divorcee! I was regarded as different to the others. But as a woman one was anyhow regarded differently in Vienna than in Linz, where everything was very conservative and reactionary, and I in any case stood out.

MN: How come?

VE: I was the first to wear jeans in Linz, with button-up flies. And I had a very daring pencil dress for the dance school, but I never encountered anything unpleasant on the streets. That first happened in Vienna when minis became the fashion. I had a really lovely yellow dress that was too long for my liking, so I cut it off really short and sewed the cloth back on as a stand-up collar. I was really scolded, by men and women, and had to watch out when I climbed the steps to board the tram.

MN: What was the atmosphere like in Vienna in the 1960s?

VE: Pretty aggressive and conservative. But there were also a few galleries, such as the one run by Monsignore Mauer, Galerie nächst St. Stephan, which did a lot. And of course the Vienna Group was there, Vienna Actionism, Hermann Nitsch, Günter Brus, Otto Muehl, they took quite a beating for what they did as artists. Muehl was reactionary, a macho, but one didn't dare say that back then.

MN: Where did you first meet the Vienna Actionists?

VE: People would sit around in coffee houses, in Hawelka, or evenings in the Adebar or the Griechenbeisl, and rub shoulders. But the women for the Actionists were simply there for the sexual images, the women were exploited. I rejected that. Apart from Brus, he worked very analytically. The fact that the Actionists were against something, against the rules, against the state, that convinced me. Other things amused me. There was a Nitsch action in Oswald Wiener's apartment with innards, with kidneys. After the performance, Ingrid Wiener and I fried the kidneys in a pan. They weren't holy for me. But I did keep the pan.

MN: In 1968 the Actionists together with the Sozialistischer Österreichische Studentenbund mounted the action *Art and Revolution* at the university in Vienna. They masturbated on stage to the national anthem and wounded themselves. What was the action like for you?

VE: Highly challenging. The auditorium was packed to the ceiling. People knew that with a title like that they could really expect something. The whipping of the Muehl lads was provocative, but not to us. We simply watched, joined in, and laughed along. Until Muehl's lads started shaking their beer bottles until they were full of froth and then released their thumbs from them. The beer came spurting out. That was so-so, typically male, not a great leap forward for art.

MN: In the following years, you and Peter Weibel, the current head of the Zentrum für Kunst und Medien in Karlsruhe, went on a "War Art Campaign." That sounds rather bellicose.

VE: Yeah, I also whipped people. It was the mood of the times, one was aggressive and adopted aggressive means, and that was fun. But people cowered. So even though I had a very long whip I scarcely managed to hit anyone.

MN: During that Weibel declaimed: "We're whipping citizens into shape as human beings." What were you trying to achieve?

VE: We wanted to trigger aggressions. The aim was anarchy. We realized that anarchy has a utopian streak to it, and we were living in an age of utopias in the 1960s, which has totally disappeared. You can no longer say that today, it wouldn't be the same.

MN: Did anyone hit back?

VE: One time a man came and stood behind me on the stage with a knife, but the organizer was able to grab him in time. And then someone in the audience threw a beer bottle at my head. After that we wanted to run off back stage, but the police were already standing there, arms locked. Out front, bikers were wrecking the stage with chairs. Somehow or other we got out and jumped into our car. I had to go to hospital and have stitches, I said I'd knocked myself on the car but no one believed me. They thought I was a Viennese prostitute. I still have my War Art Campaign wound.

MN: Looking back now on these actions: Do you think the aggression set anything in motion?

VE: Of course! When a lot of people share the same feelings of aggression, the same anger at the state laws, change is possible. What is termed freedom of speech didn't really exist back then, nor the so-called freedom of artistic expression. If the state didn't like it the person got busted. They received a summons, some even had to go to jail. I was taken off in a police car after one action. So it already helped when a lot of people voiced this discontent. Society is like a rubber band that can be stretched and stretched—until thwack, it flies back at you. You think you have achieved something, but you can see now that not much was achieved if the state still has the same power over you it had then. Today the Austrian state is using its power in the fight against Covid-19 to protect others, but the measures are very much on the fringes of democracy, especially the rules of conduct which are at times dictatorial.

MN: The aggression was not only directed at the state, but against oneself. When did you begin to harm yourself for your art?

VE: I believe it was for the film *...Remote...Remote...*, in 1973. But it looks worse in the film than it really was.

MN: In the film you are seen sitting in front of a photo of two institutionalized children, scraping the quicks of your nails away with a knife, before you then dip your bleeding fingers into a bowl of milk. Just looking at it is painful.

VE: A lot of my own personal state is in there. One wants to work through the pain that is there. The film was intended to show an injury because one carries injuries inside oneself. Until one reaches a borderline where one destroys one's body.

MN: You wrote: "The cuts in my skin are no longer deadly, they are openings to the intima, to the innermost skin of the vessels, to our selves." What did you find under your skin?

VE: The cut into the intima is a step toward our own self. The truth lies in the cut, not beside it, not to the right or left or above or below, but in what the cut is, in the pain.

MN: Twenty years earlier, Lucio Fontana slashed his canvases. Are those cuts in any way related?

VE: I see them as something quite different. Fontana wanted to deflower his canvases, he really raped them with that slash. That is a powerful avowal of masculinity.

MN: You have often stated in interviews and articles that you didn't feel your fellow artists took you seriously. How did that express itself?

VE: After a film screening the audience had a loud discussion with my colleagues about what I could possibly have meant, despite the fact I was standing right there on the side and they could have asked me. The art press also paid far less attention to me and my works. You always come last as a woman.

MN: Were there only machos at that time? Or were there other new, nice men?

VE: I can't actually recall now any new nice men. Back then we called the men who weren't machos softies. But I wouldn't have wanted a softy either.

MN: Why not?

VE: The softies also didn't feel comfortable in their role, or they were completely passive. I didn't pay much attention to them.

MN: So you attempted to convert the machos?

VE: On no account convert, bash them over the head, rather. The main concern in those days was emancipation, all said and done. We knew the term feminism, but spoke more of emancipation. Which quickly changed into a term of abuse: "Emanze"—women's libber. And we women's libbers were dangerous. A famous male artist said to me in the 1980s: "You lot and your feminism, it's nothing but communism." We were branded as an ideological movement.

MN: Do you think men can be feminists?

VE: Of course, but a man cannot simply say I am a feminist because I do my half of the housekeeping and go out walking with the children. A feminist must take a decisive stand on feminism, talk about it, and be able to acknowledge the negative sides of his sex, if you want to put it that way.

MN: What did you personally want to emancipate yourself from?

VE: Important for me was the sociopolitical aspect. I knew we had to change the model we live in. Not to men's disadvantage, but for the best of everyone. If a wife has to ask her husband if she is allowed to work, she cannot emancipate herself. That's what it was about back then. Other things we demanded are still demanded by feminists: If a woman does not receive the same pay, she cannot emancipate herself. If a woman doesn't have any power, she cannot emancipate herself. I wanted to advance this position artistically, in works of a feminist and emancipatory nature.

MN: In some of your artworks you literally free yourself, as in the performance *Hyperbulie* (Hyperbulia), in which you climb naked out of a tangle of wires.

VE: Every electricity cable represents a societal norm. Every norm delivers a blow, society thrashes you until you are beaten down like a tame animal. In the end I came out from the wires as a tamed person. But I don't want to be tamed.

MN: Instead you tamed Peter Weibel in 1968 in your *Mappe der Hundigkeit* (Portfolio of Doggedness). At any rate you led him around Vienna on a leash like a dog.

VE: But he wasn't a dog, he was a man. The idea was to swap the role assignments. It was interesting how easy it was. People really thought that Weibel was now like a dog. As we went into a gallery, people wanted to give him paper to eat.

MN: Was it also a demonstration of power?

VE: That was an implicit part of it all. Also, for instance, with *Aktionshose: Genitalpanik* (Action Pants: Genital Panic).

MN: Your *Aktionshose: Genitalpanik* comprised a pair of split-crotch jeans in which you marched into a cinema in 1969 and walked along the aisles. How did people react?

VE: A lot of people ran out, but the ones sitting at the very front couldn't escape. A lot of men didn't want to look at me or let me go near them. My crotch was exactly level with their faces. They were scared of my vagina. Panic gripped them because they thought they would be swallowed up. That's how it is in mythology, the vagina dentata, the vagina with teeth that gobbles people up. Which leads to genital panic.

MN: Do you think that the fear of the vagina is as great today as it was before?

VE: As a weapon of woman and being a woman, definitely. It's still mysterious, children emerge from a vagina, it can give birth, and gives sacrifice when it menstruates. Why else do people sew them up? I have done pieces on this, on female circumcision.

MN: It's about control?

VE: Yes. With female circumcision it is often the mothers who insist on their daughters remaining pure, as they put it. Which is why there was also the attempt in the women's movement in the 1960s to study the vagina oneself, and in that way resume control.

MN: With a mirror or speculum. Again, something that's been forgotten today.

VE: Well, it is not forgotten insofar as women today have surgery done on their labia. They now only see the negative sides when they look at themselves.

MN: Why have you repeatedly made your body the representative of a destructive present?

VE: Because I relate the present times to myself as a woman. Art must be loud, art must shout in order to be heard. Above all art by women.

MN: You've had to wait a long time to gain recognition. Above all in Austria. Your first retrospective there was in 1992.

VE: Yes, I had to wait a long time, until recently, in fact the retrospective—*VALIE EXPORT. Lebend oder tot* (VALIE EXPORT. Dead or Alive)—took place in 1992 at the Landesgalerie Linz am Oberösterreichischen Landesmuseum. Now there's a VALIE EXPORT Center in Linz, and that's good.

MN: Do you bear a grudge?

VE: I still feel really angry.

MN: Do you feel you've been overlooked or rejected?

VE: Rejected. I couldn't be overlooked, there were good catalogues, extensive exhibitions, above all abroad. But people didn't want to face the issues I addressed. They were afraid of me, just as they were of other women like Elfriede Jelinek, whom I have worked with. She is also an Austrian artist who Austria is afraid of.

MN: How much solitude did your art practice incur?

VE: A lot!

MN: How did you bear it?

VE: By always looking to the future. That's a banal phrase, I know. But the only way is to carry on positively.

MN: Would you sometimes have preferred to lead a simpler life?

VE: Sometimes I thought perhaps I should have studied law or economics, so that now I would have a fantastic job.

MN: Were financial worries a big issue?

VE: Money was always an issue. But I also resisted the art market for a long time. I had no desire to make salable editions. One can do it that way, but the road is harder. Things also looked up for me when I landed the teaching work and professorships.

MN: How long have you been able to live from your art?

VE: Not that long, for perhaps the past fifteen years.

MN: You are now celebrating your eightieth birthday in the times of Covid-19. Does that change how you view that day?

VE: It's a pity. I would have liked to have celebrated, I think that's not bad when you've notched up eighty years. Apart from which, events were planned where I would have spoken or had other people speak, where I also learn something about my own work. It's a shame that this joint reception has been canceled. And the confrontation with the virus and the way our attention is directed time and again to death, that's all very troubling. But I am no more afraid of death than I used to be. It's tragic, of course, that almost no one can now be there when one dies. A line just occurred to me from a poem by Nikolaus Lenau that I loved as a child: "That no one but the rain shall weep / here upon our gravestone!"

MN: That's sad.

VE: Yes.

MN: Do you miss being young?

VE: No, I actually feel young.

TEXT SOURCES
Unless explicitly noted, only the original German version has been published.

==========================================

17　[I WAS BORN . . .]
English in: *Dimension: Contemporary German Arts and Letters* 8,
no. 1 & 2, 1975, p. 85.
Translated by Elizabeth Napier

==========================================

19　[BY A MASOCHISTIC FORCE . . .]
German typescript, VALIE EXPORT WVZNr._1349_AP_1
Facsimile with English translation in: *VALIE EXPORT. Archive
Matters. To read and to show documents.* VALIE EXPORT Center
Linz Publications, Vol. 2. Edited by Sabine Folie. Cologne: Verlag der
Buchhandlung Walther und Franz König, 2021, p. 79.
Translated by VOX, Montreal

==========================================

21　[TIME RUN INTO ITSELF . . .]
English in: *Dimension: Contemporary German Arts and Letters* 8,
no. 1 & 2, 1975, p. 85.
Translated by Elizabeth Napier

==========================================

23　[A TEARLESS HAND . . .]
German typescript, VALIE EXPORT WVZNr._761_AP_1 (A)
Facsimile with English translation in: *VALIE EXPORT. ARCHIVE
MATTERS*, 2021, p. 80.
Translated by VOX, Montreal

==========================================

25　METALLIC GESTURES
German typescript, VALIE EXPORT WVZNr._760_AP_1 (A)
Facsimile with English translation in: *VALIE EXPORT. ARCHIVE
MATTERS*, 2021, p. 81.
Translated by VOX, Montreal

==========================================

27　[TODAY IS SUNDAY . . .]
German typescript, VALIE EXPORT WVZNr._1350_AP_1
Facsimile with English translation in: *VALIE EXPORT. ARCHIVE
MATTERS*, 2021, p. 85.
Translated by VOX, Montreal

==========================================

29　[I CONSIDER THE COMPUTER . . .]
German typescript, VALIE EXPORT Center Linz, bundle 60,
VEC.000.881
Facsimile with English translation in: *VALIE EXPORT. ARCHIVE
MATTERS*, 2021, p. 240.
Translated by Thomas Taborsky, edited by Helen Ferguson

==========================================

# THEORETICAL TEXTS

## IN CONVERSATION

===========================================

Born in Linz in 1940 as Waltraut Lehner, the artist has
worked since 1967 under the name VALIE EXPORT,
understood as an artistic concept and logo. In 1988,
she held a guest seminar at the F+F, Schule für expe-
rimentelle Gestaltung in Zurich. From 1989 to 1992,
she taught at the University of Wisconsin-Milwaukee,
School of Fine Arts, and from 1991 to 1995 at the
Hochschule der Künste Berlin. From 1995/1996 to 2005,
she was professor of multimedia performance at
the Academy of Media Arts in Cologne. In 1980, she
represented Austria at the Venice Biennale alongside the artist Maria Lassnig. She also participated
in documenta 6 in 1977 and documenta 12 in 2007 in
Kassel. With her feature film *The Practice of Love*,
VALIE EXPORT was nominated for the Golden Bear
at the Berlin International Film Festival in 1985.

Since 1968, her work has been shown internationally
in solo and group exhibitions, including at the Centre
Georges Pompidou, Paris; Museum of Modern Art, New
York; Institute of Contemporary Art, London; MoCA,
Los Angeles; Stedelijk Museum, Amsterdam; mumok,
Vienna; Generali Foundation, Vienna; P.S.1 Contem-
porary Art Center, New York; Shanghai Art Museum;
Palais des Beaux-Arts, Brussels; Tate Modern, London;
Metropolitan Museum of Art, Seoul; Metropolitan
Museum of Art, New York; ars electronica, Linz. She
has also been represented at numerous major inter-
national film and video festivals.

The artist has received a number of awards, in-
cluding the Gabriele Münter Prize in 1997, the Oskar
Kokoschka Prize in 2000, the Yoko Ono Lennon Courage
Award for the Arts in 2014, the Roswitha Haftmann
Prize for Lifetime Achievement in 2019, and the Golden
Nica Prix Ars Electronica in 2020.

In 2022, VALIE EXPORT was awarded the Grand Decoration of Honor in Silver with Star for Services to the Republic of Austria and the Max Beckmann Prize of the City of Frankfurt am Main.

# MUSEUM LUDWIG

Heinrich-Böll-Platz
D-50667 COLOGNE
Tel. +49 (0)221 221 26165
Fax +49 (0)221 221 24114
www.museum-ludwig.de

Edited by
Yilmaz Dziewior and
Katrin Sauerländer

Editing and Copyediting
Katrin Sauerländer

English Copyediting and
Proofreading
Anne O'Connor

Design
Mevis & van Deursen,
Amsterdam

Typesetting
Daniela Weirich

Production
DZA Druckerei zu Altenburg

© 2023 Museum Ludwig, Cologne,
VALIE EXPORT, and Verlag der
Buchhandlung Walther und Franz
König, Cologne

Cover
*VALIE EXPORT – SMART
EXPORT*, 1970
© VG Bild-Kunst, Bonn;
photo: Gertraude Wolfschwenger;
repro: S. Fuis, Cologne

With the kind support of
Galerie Thaddaeus Ropac London ·
Paris · Salzburg · Seoul
Roswitha Haftmann Stiftung
Russmedia

The research for this publication was
supported by the VALIE EXPORT
Center Linz. The center is a cooperation between the City of Linz, the
LENTOS Kunstmuseum Linz, and
the Kunstuniversität Linz.
www.valieexportcenter.at

**VALIE EXPORT**
CENTER LINZ_
Research Center for
Media and Performance Art

Thanks to
VALIE EXPORT
Sigrid Guggenberger
Dagmar Schink

Published by
Verlag der Buchhandlung
Walther und Franz König
Ehrenstraße 4
50672 Cologne
Germany

Bibliographic information published
by the Deutsche Nationalbibliothek:
the Deutsche Nationalbibliothek
lists this publication in the Deutsche
Nationalbibliografie; detailed bibliographic data are available on the
Internet at www.dnb.de

Printed in Germany


Ein Museum der

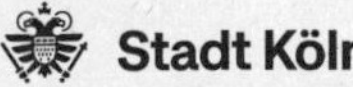

**Stadt Köln**

Distribution
Germany, Austria, Switzerland
Buchhandlung Walther König
Ehrenstr. 4
D – 50672 Köln
Fon +49 (0) 221 20 59 6 53
verlag@buchhandlung-walther-koenig.de

United States and Canada
D.A.P. / Distributed Art Publishers, Inc.
75 Broad Street, Suite 630
USA – New York, NY 10004
Fon +1 (0) 212 627 1999
orders@dapinc.com

Outside the United States
and Canada, Germany, Austria,
and Switzerland
Thames & Hudson Ltd., London
www.thamesandhudson.com

ISBN 978-3-7533-0375-8
(English edition)
ISBN 978-3-7533-0374-1
(German edition)